PRAISE FOR
My Father's ALS

"Ken Kann has taken on a gut-wrenching task: writing a memoir about how he shepherded his father through an awful death experience, the rapid onset of immobilization and strangulation by amyotrophic lateral sclerosis, known as Lou Gehrig's disease. It's a tale with many dimensions told with novelistic confidence—the conflict between a rebellious son and an overbearing father, Ken's quest to be a historian and an author, the saga of a Jewish immigrant family that began their lives in poverty in a Chicago shtetl, their migration to a comfortable middle-class life in Skokie, and an amateur's guide to ALS, a disease that brings on death without escape. Ultimately, Ken and his father, with death approaching, spent many days and hours growing together with warmth, honesty, mutual respect, and a deep love as they explored their lives, apart and together."

—**Peter Booth Wiley**, author and publisher

"A powerful and achingly honest account of a young man, alienated from his family's values during the 1960s and 1970s, watching with increasing respect his father's and mother's struggle with the relentless progression of ALS over fifteen months. In telling the stories of the family before, during, and after the struggle, Kann provides a quiet and moving account of how being needed as a son led to his becoming more fully a man."

—**Dr. Elizabeth Anderson**, physician

"Ken's experience as a historian provides him with a unique and powerful framework to understand the life and death of our father, Sam, Ken's own life, and the unimaginable effects ALS had on our family. With poignancy, pathos, and humor in the face of misery, this book will touch your heart as you travel through the fifteen-month journey of a son's deepening love and respect for his father."

—**Bob Kann**, Ken's younger brother, author

"Family dynamics are complicated, and that's before the awful diagnosis of ALS. Kenneth Kann's book *My Father's ALS: A Son's Healing Journey* is more than an account of the ravages of a devastating illness. It weaves the story of this extraordinary disease into Kann's family history in the Jewish communities of Chicago, his father's life journey as a child of immigrants, and his own baby boomer wanderings. Kann offers a complex and moving portrayal of his family's dignity in caring for their husband and father, including Kann's struggles to reconcile with his father after years of conflict. This book is a must-read as we contemplate life's meanings and the unknowns that may confront any of us.

—**Rabbi Ted Feldman**, Petaluma

"Lawyer and historian Ken Kann offers the reader a compelling treatise: *My Father's ALS: A Son's Healing Journey*. The book—as much an autobiography of the author as it is a reflection on a profound coming-of-age journey—relates his experience with his father Sam's relentless decline and demise from amyotrophic lateral sclerosis (ALS) and the care he was able to provide a father who had both nurtured him and judged him, sometimes harshly, through his younger years. Kann reflects deeply on his personal pain arising from his affectionate and sometimes fraught relationship with Sam, a proud, resourceful, disciplined, and inflexible man of an older generation. The narrative spans Kann's hedonistic and activist days in Berkeley in the 1960s to the Jewish family home in Skokie, Illinois, and his parents' sunny condominium in West Palm Beach as Sam struggles to adapt to a devastating and inexorable disease. Written with deep sensitivity and compassion in an unsentimental, honest, plainspoken, and easily flowing style, Kann's observations and emotions during this personal journey take us through periods of duress, suffering, and unimaginable sadness, lightened by moments of insight and humor. Ultimately, the book documents Kann's uplifting growth through his experience caring for Sam and supporting his mother. It is a deeply moving story of filial duty and courage through which Kann finds the resilience and wisdom that have served him throughout his life. This book is a must-read for anyone who is faced with the task of caring for and supporting a loved one with a tragic, progressive illness. There is a bounty of instruction, stoic wisdom, and comfort within its pages for the reader.

—**Nathan M. Bass**, MD, PhD

"Kenneth Kann captures the ALS experience through the story of his father's devastating illness in 1979-1980. In *My Father's ALS: A Son's Healing Journey*, Kann recounts how his family coped with his father's disease. Along with life and death battles for survival, the book conveys the humor and absurdity of losing control over your body and the bonds that develop when a loved one needs so much and such intimate help. Kann shows the utter desperation of ALS patients and families—and their grief—as they realize the disease stays one step ahead of them. Through the story of his father and himself, Kann also shows how the ALS journey can lead to deep self-discovery, transformed relationships, and stronger bonds. Though research and awareness have increased during the decades since his father's death, the book set me back with its reminder of how the experience of ALS remains the same today. This is a gripping account of one family and one son trying to cope with a father's ALS. The predicament is dire, the stories are absorbing, the characters are vivid, and the writing is beautiful."

—**Mary Ann Wittenberg**, wife of ALS patient Harry Wittenberg, who wrote about his ALS in *Out of Control: Reflections on Matters of Life and Death* before he died in 2020. She serves on the board of the ALS Network.

My Father's ALS:
A Son's Healing Journey

by Kenneth Kann

© Copyright 2024 Kenneth Kann

ISBN 979-8-88824-406-7

All rights reserved. No part of this publication may be reproduced, stored in a retrieval system, or transmitted in any form or by any means—electronic, mechanical, photocopy, recording, or any other—except for brief quotations in printed reviews, without the prior written permission of the author.

Published by

3705 Shore Drive
Virginia Beach, VA 23455
800-435-4811
www.koehlerbooks.com

My Father's ALS:
A SON'S HEALING JOURNEY

Kenneth Kann

VIRGINIA BEACH
CAPE CHARLES

For my brother, Bob, who was there.
For my daughter, Julia, who came after.

TABLE OF CONTENTS

Prologue: Dread 7

Chapter 1: Home 16

Chapter 2: The Cemetery Plots 38

Chapter 3: Falling 53

Chapter 4: The Cobra Venom Serum 80

Chapter 5: Letting Go, Holding On 102

Chapter 6: Retirement 131

Chapter 7: On My Own: Facing the Business of ALS 144

Chapter 8: "What More Could I Do?" 173

Chapter 9: With Dad to the End 203

Epilogue: After Dad 222

Acknowledgments 244

References 246

"Then come, dear father. Arms around my neck:
I'll take you on my shoulders, no great weight."

—Virgil, *The Aeneid* (Trans Robert Fitzgerald), Book II, 921

PROLOGUE
Dread

OCTOBER 1979

I thought I was flourishing in the fall of 1979.

I was writing so well that I regularly daydreamed about my acceptance speech for the Pulitzer Prize in history. I would name every friend who saw me through the struggle. I'd offer fascinating reflections on history and society.

I had hustled up two part-time teaching jobs. Commuting between UC Berkeley and UC Santa Cruz, lecturing before hundreds of students, I had an audience along with income, and I still made time for writing. Instead of following a safe academic career as a professor of ho-hum at some sleepy university, I had remained in the Bay Area with my new PhD degree and gambled on a career I would invent: freelance historian. I thought I could do anything.

I was happy. My love life could have been better. But now I was seeing a new woman. Ever hopeful, I thought she might be the one.

I had wonderful friends. These were people I had known for years, through Berkeley's radical protests of the 1960s and the disillusionment of the 1970s. I could depend on them. Friends had become a kind of substitute for family in the 1970s. I used to call them "family, without the liabilities."

And there was Chamokome, an old coastal ranch, ninety miles north of San Francisco, that I owned with a group of friends. Overcoming our socialist objections to owning land, we had glorious weekends working on our buildings and grounds, hiking the region, eating, drinking, and talking. As a member of the Chamokome collective, my life was nicely balanced between city and country, between my personal ambitions and allegiance to these comrades.

My Oakland apartment was another sign of settling down. I had lived there since 1976, three years, my longest residence in one place since 1962 when I left home for college. In Oakland, I had ended my annual migration from apartment to apartment as an undergraduate at the University of Wisconsin–Madison and a graduate student in Berkeley. Just a year ago, I had bought my own sofa, which seemed like stepping through a final rite of adulthood.

At thirty-five, I never had felt more established, more certain of my ability, more confident of my direction. It had been confirmed earlier that year when I met up with an old friend from Skokie, the Chicago suburb where I grew up. We had talked about high school friends, the predictable majority who had pursued business careers and suburban families in the Chicago vicinity, and the adventurous minority who had left Skokie for odysseys through the political and cultural upheavals of the sixties. There had been casualties among the adventurers, and I was not one of them. "You're doing okay," my friend had concluded. I thought so too.

I remain astonished by how quickly I came undone.

It began with a telephone call from my father. He called every two weeks, usually in the morning, interrupting my writing for a conversation about the weather and the family. These calls were a regular annoyance that I endured.

This morning, he launched into his strange physical ailments. It had begun with playing golf: a stiff shoulder. Now his entire body felt stiff. He was tired and run-down. He was having difficulty raising his arms above his shoulders. He had taken some spills. He insisted, "Skip, something is wrong."

He called me by my childhood nickname. This was intimate and serious.

Turned out, these problems had been developing for months, and he had told me nothing about them. He had seen his internist, an orthopedist, and a neurologist. He had taken batteries of tests with no results, and he was waiting for another neurologist's evaluation. He had arranged for a complete examination at the Mayo Clinic. He was more than scared. His voice was high and tense. Was that some hysteria?

No. Nothing is happening, I told myself. I tried to calm Dad's galloping fears.

I was dubious. At sixty-four, he was never sick. He worked full-time. He golfed and bowled. His most serious problem was falling asleep in front of the TV in the evenings. He had his share of aches, but nothing more. I thought, *This is psychosomatic.* Too many stresses somehow had gotten to him, though, when I considered it, he never had seemed stressed. But I did not give it more thought.

Two weeks later, my youngest brother Rob called with the diagnosis. Our father had amyotrophic lateral sclerosis, ALS, otherwise known as Lou Gehrig's disease.

I listened, stunned and silenced, as Rob explained what he knew. It was a neurological disorder that led to complete paralysis. No stopping it. The rate of deterioration varied, but life expectancy was around three years. My father was dying.

I immediately called home and heard Mom's shaky voice. She assured me they were all right. She told me Dad had been crying a lot since he heard the news. He didn't want to speak with me now, but he would call in a few days.

Mom added that they already had contacted a chapter of the ALS Society. There, they reached a woman who had been living with ALS for ten years. They had learned that 20 percent of the victims lived beyond five years. It was a hope.

A hope? I still could not think of Dad with a terminal disease. I could not imagine him crying. Not my father.

I called a doctor friend for an explanation of ALS. She began, "It's one of the dread diseases."

ALS began with weakness and clumsiness. The nerves that control the muscles—the motor neurons—stopped working. She likened ALS to polio, except that it continued to more complete paralysis and death. There was no loss of brain power, no loss of sensation. It was not an "immediate catastrophe," she assured me, because he would not keel over and die suddenly. He would degenerate gradually, sometimes over years and sometimes rapidly. Symptoms could be treated, but there was no known way to cure or even slow ALS.

"Dread." That word echoed in my mind over the next year as I witnessed Dad's extraordinary ailment. I learned it was the right word.

While I reeled over the diagnosis, Dad swung into action. That was the way of his Greatest Generation. They had ended the Depression, won World War II, and created the postwar prosperity and the suburban world where I grew up. Something wrong? Fix it. A problem? Solve it. Act now.

Dad was frenetic with activity. He contacted relatives and friends in Chicago and across the country, passing on the bad news and reassuring all that he was okay. He reviewed his finances and weighed his options. He sought out information on how to fight ALS and who could treat it.

I was reassured by Dad's confidence and his mobilization to fight the disease. Until I discovered he was avoiding some of the ALS literature. He said it was too frightening.

He read enough to worry about facing the impending Chicago winter in a wheelchair, descending the front stairs of their house, or simply shoveling snow. He spoke of retiring immediately, selling the Skokie house, and moving to their Florida condominium. "We have to be realistic," he told me, but this was not his usual deliberate self. He sounded desperate.

Dad had no difficulty describing hopes for resisting the disease and living with the disease. In a strong voice, he assured me he did not fear death. But his every mention of Mom and my brothers and me, my every assurance we would stand behind him, brought choked words and muffled sobs.

My father was crying to me. His life was shattered. What could I do?

Mom was outright scared. She tried to hold back the fear and sorrow. She refused to read any ALS literature. Mom insisted she would learn about the disease as it developed. She spoke about thinking positively and facing the future with dignity. Dad thought she was denying the diagnosis, denying the *frightening* disease and what would happen. But in a teary telephone conversation one afternoon, she confided her fear that Dad would die and she would be left alone.

I worried, *Will she be strong enough for what's ahead?*

My parents seemed to transform overnight. For years, I had followed their bickering through long-distance telephone calls, talking with them on separate extensions. I would be speaking about my unsettled work life—discussing a new teaching job or a publication possibility—when Mom would ask a nervous question, and they would erupt into a spat.

"Ann!" my father would yell out, "let him finish!"

"I am, Sammy! I am!"

And then they were off in their own private war.

Their bickering continued. But now, suddenly, Mom spoke of Dad's courage in facing the diagnosis. He spoke gently of protecting her from longtime fears of disease. Rob, who began visiting with them most weekends, described things I had never seen: affectionate exchanges, hand-holding, and caresses. They were, as Mom put it, "like one."

Even as I tried to absorb this surprising response to the diagnosis, I was distressed by the prospect of Dad selling their house in Skokie. I imagined my parents, aged and broken and homeless, Dad helpless in a wheelchair, cast adrift from their hard-won comfort and security by this catastrophic disease.

And it was my home, too, that would be gone. Of course, I had left Skokie for college seventeen years before. Northern California was where I lived. However, in my innermost thoughts, which now floated up inescapably, that house in Skokie still stood as my own permanent refuge. I would never have admitted it aloud, but I always had felt reassured knowing that anytime, for as long as I wanted, I could go home again. Now, suddenly, home might not be there anymore.

I was just as scared that I would have to go home permanently to help Mom and Dad cope with this disaster. I foresaw my bleak future. Rob lived nearby in Wisconsin, but at twenty-five, he seemed too young to shoulder this load. Mark, the middle son, had his own family and a secure teaching position in Los Angeles. I would be the one to return, and just the thought of it made me angry at Dad.

It was my worst fear come true. Not so long ago, I had confided to a therapist my terror at the thought of my father becoming dependent on me. Now it could actually happen, confirming my suspicion that whatever you fear most in life is bound to occur, an irrepressible destiny.

I had left the Midwest for graduate study in Berkeley in 1966, placing 2,200 miles between myself and Dad. I had fled Skokie for one of the great centers of the sixties revolt. Anchored in graduate school, I had hurled myself into radical politics and the counterculture. When the rebellion ended, I joined the retreat into the introspection of the 1970s, first simple country living in a little town eighty miles north of San Francisco and then psychotherapy, sorting out who I was.

At thirty-five, I felt entirely unprepared for my father's illness. I was the oldest son, but I had no wife and children, no house of my own. An aspiring writer, I had no published books. A college history teacher with a PhD, I had no secure tenured position. I had no financial reserves to fall back on for myself, let alone to buttress my parents at this time of need. On learning of Dad's ALS diagnosis, my life suddenly seemed built on sand.

I compared myself to Dad. When he was thirty-five, in 1950, he was married with two kids. He watched over aging immigrant parents and was a respected figure in a large extended family. He had a profession—a chemist—and a stable job that paid well. He and my mother had savings and a plan to buy a house in the suburbs.

Through the months after the diagnosis, I awoke in the night, anxious over what Dad's illness would mean for me: *How could I take care of him when, in truth, I still thought of him taking care of me? How could he be dying? I was not ready.*

I recognized the disease was already spreading into my life, just as surely as it was consuming my father's body. I thought, *Things will never be the same again.*

Like me, my new woman friend could not begin to understand my troubles. I stopped calling her after two conversations about the diagnosis.

Friends did not ease my feelings of crisis. When I told one elderly comrade that my father had been diagnosed with ALS, I was astonished to hear her chuckle with satisfaction that she was older than my father and still had good health. I was repeatedly startled by how Dad's diagnosis launched people into ruminations on their own fears of disease, dependency, and death. ALS seemed to trigger everyone's nightmare scenario.

Suddenly, ALS was everywhere. I would turn on the television, and there was Reggie Jackson invoking the memory of Lou Gehrig as he solicited contributions for ALS research. I would pick up the morning newspaper, and there was Senator Jacob Javits diagnosed with ALS. I started an Eric Ambler mystery set far away in central Europe, followed a character developing mysterious symptoms, and found the plot thickened with ALS. It seemed like I had been living in a cocoon, insulated from this devastating neurological disease—until Dad's diagnosis.

I resolved to change all that. I would launch my own investigation into ALS. I was determined to master the disease through research. As a trained historian, I thought I had the skills to help my father.

My confidence evaporated with my first foray into the main book catalog of the general library on the Berkeley campus. I discovered that books on ALS were in a separate biology library that I had never heard of until then. It was housed in the Natural Sciences Building, a huge and daunting structure that I had never entered over my many years on the Berkeley campus. Walking into that biology library with its strange catalogs and reference books, I felt like a trespasser. I thought that at any moment, I would be exposed as an impostor biologist and tossed out.

I borrowed two books on ALS. Reading the introductions, I confirmed that the cause and cure for the disease were unknown. But I could not decipher elementary terms like "motor neuron disease," "corticospinal tracts," "anterior horn cells," or "bulbar palsy." I could not see more than random collections of dots, lines, and shapes in the diagrams, charts, and pictures.

I took those books home, placed them on my newly cleared ALS bookshelf, and never opened them again. Every time I glanced at those two unfathomable tomes, I cursed myself for not having become a medical doctor when that road was open to me in college. I recognized that even research scientists had not solved the mysteries of ALS. But I felt that if I was a doctor, I could understand the disease and prepare for it.

Instead, I could not even grasp the most elementary realities of the disease. From a local ALS organization, I obtained several pamphlets in plain English on ALS. The articles described various stages, from mild first signs to an incredible end when the patient could be completely paralyzed, bedridden, and voiceless. The articles offered bewildering solutions for unimaginable problems of moving, breathing, eating, and communicating: exercise, diet, clothes, chairs, beds, toilets, braces, canes, crutches, wheelchairs, lifts, communications devices, suction machines, respirators, drugs, and surgeries. It was unreal.

One of the pamphlets concluded with a section entitled "Psychologic Aspects of Care" that left me stupefied:

> In most patients, intellectual functioning is not impaired; they remain painfully aware of the progression of their symptoms. Considering the circumstances and prognosis, suicide is surprisingly rare. The low suicide rate may be related to the

fact that in the early stages of the disease the patient either denies or does not fully comprehend the devastating physical deterioration that he must face. Once the reality of the disease is apparent, the patient may be too weak to commit suicide (Delisa 1979, 142).

Suicide? How could physical deterioration be so devastating that Dad might want to commit suicide? And be too weak to do it? It was beyond my imagination.

I must have reviewed those pamphlets once a week for the duration of Dad's illness in a futile attempt to figure out what was happening, what would come next, and what we should be doing. Everything I read and everything I heard from doctors confirmed that nothing would happen suddenly and the disease would develop gradually, allowing time to adjust to changes. And so it was. Yet each new symptom and each new problem would come as a surprise to me, and it always would be magnitudes worse than anything I had read. At no time would I be certain of what to do.

Only looking back can I see that nothing would have changed if I had understood this disease. My moment of testing had arrived, but understanding medical literature would solve nothing.

The mystery before me was my relationship with my father. Ready or not, I would have to help Dad in his coming struggle to live and die with ALS. Ready or not, I had to go home.

CHAPTER 1

Home

DECEMBER 1979

During my holiday break from teaching in December 1979, I went home.

For as long as I could remember, every time I had flown into Chicago, Dad was waiting at the landing gate. No matter how bad the weather or how late the flight, he would be there. Tie loosened after the day at work, face eager with anticipation, he was a reassuring sight in the tumult of the O'Hare terminals.

One of my father's enthusiasms was meeting family and friends at the airport. He liked helping weary travelers on the final leg of a journey. He would steer his grateful charges through the maze of corridors and escalators, confidently retrieve evasive luggage, and calmly navigate puzzling parking lots and exit roads. When I saw Dad at an airport gate, I could relax, certain he would get me home.

In recent years, Dad had confided to Mom his regret that our family did not hug at airports like others he saw. "We are not a hugging family," Mom said, but she passed on his wishes to me. After, we had a stiff hug each time we met at an airport gate.

For this trip, too, Dad schemed of ways to overcome his weakened condition and pick me up at O'Hare Field. He was at it for weeks before my flight, proposing one plan after another, until I reluctantly insisted he not come. Landing at a friendless airport, disappointed that Dad really was not there, I caught the bus to Skokie.

Everything seemed the same. The sturdy brick suburban house was safe and snug in the winter cold. Candy on the living room table, the spotless bathroom, and the kitchen full of shiny appliances all promised middle-class prosperity, cleanliness, and order. In the kitchen, eating a late dinner and talking with Mom and Dad around the table, I began the visit as I had begun dozens of previous visits.

"Don't worry," Mom assured me. "Nothing has changed."

But our conversation immediately gravitated to ALS, and there it remained. The mysterious origins of the disease, the bizarre symptoms, the doctors, the tests, and the possible treatments consumed our attention.

"It's such a crazy disease," Dad insisted. "You might not notice it."

Soon, the symptoms became clear. Most unusual were the fasciculations, the weird twitches of flesh along his arms and legs, as if his muscles had a will of their own. More worrisome, he had difficulty raising his arms above his shoulders. He walked with a limp, his left leg, carefully to avoid falling. He was tired after walking for fifteen minutes, and he stopped to rest on longer walks.

And yet, Dad would not remain still either. Every half hour, he rose, stretched, and walked about the house. He would "tighten up," he explained, and a brief walk loosened his muscles. These exercise jaunts, with accompanying oohs and aahs on rising, were a source of family amusement, and he laughed too. But in the mornings, after a stationary night in bed, he really "stiffened up" and needed Mom's help maneuvering a shirt onto his body and buttoning it.

Dad still looked like a vigorous older man. At five and a half feet tall, he had a slender, compact frame that still suggested power and speed. His face was unlined, almost untroubled, with a ready broad smile. He had a youthful look with a full head of hair, still wavy, black on top, and distinguished gray at the sides. He felt no pain. His appetite was good. He appeared healthy as ever.

Mom could dismiss Dad's symptoms as some new eccentricity. She insisted there was no disease in our family. "Everyone is healthy in this house!" she'd blurt out as if that would settle this ALS business once and for all.

At the same time, Mom was vigilant that no one else ate off Dad's plate, drank from his glass, or used his towel. The doctors and the medical literature had assured her that ALS was not contagious, but Mom's fear of germs and disease told her otherwise.

I laughed at her precautions, but I followed her orders. I had worried about contracting the evil disease from the moment I heard the diagnosis, when Mom assured me that ALS was not hereditary. There were familial forms of the disease, I learned, but Dad's apparently was not one of them. Even so, one theory had it that ALS was caused by a dormant virus, and I saw no reason why this possible virus could not be communicated from one person to another. I worried about treating Dad like a leper, but my skin crawled at the thought of contracting ALS myself. As Mom insisted, I kept my distance.

Dad did not keep his diagnosis a secret. "You don't go to the Mayo Clinic for a cold," he would proudly inform visitors. He had been to a premier medical institution with a premier neurological disease. With pride in the immensity of his ailment, he showed everyone the odd fasciculations of his arm muscles, and he narrated the saga of his medical journey from symptoms to diagnosis.

The visitors came. Since the diagnosis, crowds of relatives and friends had passed through our house to be there for Mom and Dad. Their ties to my parents dated back to the prewar Jewish neighborhoods of West Side Chicago. Others were longtime Skokie neighbors who, like Mom and Dad, had left the urban world of their immigrant parents for the suburbs after the war. I had not seen most of these people for years, and I was surprised to find them mixing in our house with a familiarity I no longer felt.

Evening after evening, Dad held court in our living room, at the center of a circle of his people. Mom would bring out coffee and cake, like any other social occasion, while Dad spoke about his ALS.

I admired Dad's public disclosure of his illness. I admired his frank talk about the disease. He was brave. He showed no self-pity. I wondered, *Could I do that?*

But his bravado at these gatherings also made me uncomfortable. I winced at his repetitive stories and jokes about the disease. I squirmed every time he read the evaluation letter from his Mayo Clinic neurologist, who praised Dad as "a remarkably realistic person" facing a three-year life expectancy with a disease that could not be stopped. Dad would read further: the neurologist had advised him to make "preparations for the care of his family." No evasion. No sugarcoating. Dad was telling us this disease is terminal.

I wondered if Dad was bluffing. Behind his brave talk, I saw an uncharacteristic public display of fear and a craving for reassurance. But friends and relatives listened intently, with no sign of embarrassment, and they joined the conversation about ALS.

Dad privately cursed those who stayed away as unfeeling cowards. Loyalty to family and friends meant everything to Dad. It was a remnant, I thought, of the struggles of immigrant families and communities to get by and get ahead in Depression-era America; they needed help from each other for places to live, business ventures, and health problems. He remembered those no-shows so precisely that my brothers and I joked about his "enemies list." Humor, gallows humor, would carry a large load in our family's future.

I was surprised by this flood of sympathy. From my vantage point in Berkeley, I had long dismissed my parents' suburban world as vapid. But now, at this time of trouble, these visitors reminded me of my family's roots in history and community that extended to their parents and grandparents back to the Jewish Old World in Ukraine and Poland, across Chicago's prewar West Side immigrant neighborhoods, and then the postwar migration to the northern Chicago suburbs. I saw my father anew as a loved and respected figure in this sprawling social network with a deep history over generations.

Despite Dad's public confidence, his private miseries had begun. Most humiliating, he no longer could drive. My father was among the first generation of American men who grew up with automobiles. He had been driving since 1927, age twelve. After his immigrant father crashed yet another car, Dad began running auto errands across the city for the family's grocery store. He was proud of his driving skills developed over decades at the steering wheel. All my life, Dad had occupied an unquestioned place at the helm of our family car.

It ended with a mortifying reversal a few weeks before I arrived. He had become too weak to hold up his arms on the wheel. Now Mom drove when they went out. She even had to buckle him into his seat belt because his arms and fingers could not do the reaching and snapping. Dad was reduced to barking out route instructions and making ill-tempered corrections to her driving.

I thought he'd be relieved to have me, his oldest son, driving him about, but it didn't go well with me either. I ran into problems with the car keys, one for the doors and one for the ignition, which I always managed to reverse on the first try. Dad had become sensitive to cold with the disease, and my every delay in opening the car door provoked a surly outburst. It made me all the more fumbling and bumbling as I helped him in and out of the car.

I considered my father the worst possible candidate for physical disability. Perhaps it was all the men of his generation. But he was inflexible, unable to tolerate his wife or children assuming his paternal responsibilities. His very identity seemed bound up with things like driving the family car. If the gradual paralysis of ALS was not Dad's greatest fear come true, it certainly was a colossal irony, for he was a man who needed to be in control.

My first run-in with him, the first I can recall, happened when I was five. I was sitting in the front seat of our car, Dad driving and Mom a passenger. At a stoplight, I could not resist the temptation. I reached over, turned the ignition key, and shut off the car. Was it curiosity about what would happen? Mischief? Or did I want to join him in driving the car? I don't know. He whacked my hand. But what I recall is his rage that I had interfered with him driving the car: red-faced, yelling, ready to hit again. He was furious as I cowered in my mother's arms. I never again did anything like that in the car.

Now, at thirty-five, my resentments covered more than cars. I had not yet forgiven him for rejecting my childhood efforts to collaborate on home improvement projects. My memory of those episodes would not fade. He never had been able to bend, even to make room for his oldest son.

Manual labor always had been Dad's province, a territory where I ventured at my own risk. There had been a summer day in my twelfth year when I entered the workshop he had built in a corner of the basement. The room was monumental chaos, to my eye, and I devoted the day to cleaning and ordering the workbench and shelves.

When I proudly showed him my contribution at day's end, he was outraged at my trespass. He stormed around the house cursing that he could not find his tools and projects.

"Sammy," Mom had pleaded, "he was just trying to help."

Aiming only to please him and expecting praise, I was shocked by his reaction. Hot, humiliating tears spilled out, and I even apologized. Dad apologized, too, later. But by then, I had made a bitter vow never again to enter his workshop.

I remembered that incident as the supreme example of Dad's refusal to allow me onto his turf. As a kid, my every attempt to help him lay a patio, build a shed, or paint a room came to an unhappy conclusion through my clumsiness and his impatience. By high school, I no longer participated in his home improvement projects.

Years later, in my early thirties, I had returned to manual labor as a member of a northern California rural collective. I was thrilled to discover I could repair a toilet, sheetrock a wall, and split wood. Dad once tried a peace offering with a solo trip to visit me in California, and I reciprocated by inviting him for a few days to work at my ranch. Dad not only enjoyed us working together with my ranch partners, but he surprised me with an admission: "Skip, I have one regret," he blurted out as we were packing to leave. "I'm sorry I never taught you boys to work with your hands."

There it was: the apology, sort of, twenty years later, with my childhood nickname for something personal and important. But that wasn't enough.

"Why didn't you teach me?" I couldn't let it go.

When he could not explain, I remained silent. I thought he really didn't know why, but I was not ready to forgive.

Even now, under the cloud of ALS, this war continued with its own mad momentum. I arrived home to discover that Dad could no longer do manual labor, but he was ready to direct my good hands and legs. At the first task, when I slowly examined a broken light fixture, Dad barked out instructions, and I became even more determined to puzzle it out myself. At one point, Dad made a futile effort to climb the ladder and do it himself. He finally retreated, exasperated with the fixture, me, and his maddening new physical limitations. I repaired it without him.

He reemerged for the second task, grouting loose wall tiles in the bathroom. It was deceptively easy. Just as I sat down with relief at a job successfully completed, he insisted that I wash the grout off my hands. That kind of categorical order prompted me to ignore him. A half hour and several orders later, he explained that the grout was toxic. Red-faced, I washed my hands. We didn't speak to each other for several hours until Mom humored us back into conversation.

There were also moments when our family seemed happier than ever. One evening, when Rob was home, we all gravitated to the den, a former bedroom that Dad had remodeled. Pictures of the three sons hung on wood-paneled walls, knickknacks from Israel and European travels decorated the bookshelves, and a comfortable leather couch beckoned. It was Dad's room, the place where he retired after dinner to watch television, read, and snooze. It also was a cozy family room, the center of any evening's activity when we were together.

That evening, Mom, Rob, and I sprawled on the carpet, engrossed in a game of Scrabble. Dad relaxed on the couch, watched television, and read. The only unusual things were Dad's book on holistic medicine and his exercise jaunts every half hour to loosen up. Mom made popcorn, we began a second Scrabble game, and the television droned on.

I looked up and surveyed the scene, satisfied with this normal moment. I caught Dad's eye. He winked, content and knowing.

I wondered if, somehow, he had contracted the disease as the only way he could bring me back home for this kind of warm family evening. Perhaps he had sensed my years of silent smoldering rage over his refusal to let me clean his basement workshop, his dissatisfaction with my high school grades, his skepticism about my college studies in liberal arts, his puzzlement over my life in Berkeley, his apparent dissatisfaction with everything I did.

I knew Dad could be kind to others. A high school friend once told me the story of his fender bender accident, at which Dad stopped his passing car to help my friend. The other motorist, an adult man, was irate at my friend for causing the crash. Dad intervened. "He's said it was his fault. He's given you his insurance information. He's apologized. What else do you want?" With nothing left to do, the motorist stormed off. My friend was forever grateful to Dad.

But not me. I don't remember his kindnesses to me, or his protection, or even his generosity. I do recall the summer I was seventeen, when a new Pontiac LeMans convertible appeared in our driveway, sparkling white with black leather seats, largely for my use as the only son who could drive. I remember that idyllic summer with my gang of friends, my high school girlfriend, and the LeMans convertible with the top down. I was riding high. But even that LeMans convertible never weighed heavily on my memory scales, not against the weight of Dad's disapproval.

My clashes with Dad became worse in the 1960s and 1970s when I set out on my own path. Leaving for college in 1962, my plan was to become a tax attorney and certified public accountant, known as a "good combination." But this was the sixties. At the University of Wisconsin–Madison, I wandered into one of the birthplaces of the student movement. By the time I graduated in 1966, with the LeMans convertible long forgotten, I had decided to become a historian, a historian of radical European social movements.

Dad supported me, like my two younger brothers, through undergraduate degrees in Madison. And then he helped each of us through PhD programs, uncomplaining. But that was expected. I gave him no special credit for it.

I had left my family and joined world events. In California, at UC Berkeley, I enrolled in the history PhD program. Eleven years later, graduating with a PhD degree, I decided to skip the professor career and become a freelance historian. I planned to create this imagined career by writing a popular history of a community of left-wing Jewish chicken ranchers. Then, I started a second book on the life of one of the community's Communist trade union organizers.

By then, I had taught at a Black university in North Carolina for two years in the late sixties. Back on the UC Berkeley campus in the early seventies, a tourist had taken a picture of me and my scruffy beard in torn jeans with a girlfriend in a flowing white dress—genuine hippies. I had tried rural life for two years, writing my PhD dissertation in a little town where the Russian River met the ocean. I had joined a nearby collective with land in the hills of Sonoma County.

As a freelance historian, I had no boss, salary, work hours, or dress code. Actually, it was no recognizable job and virtually no income, along with no wife, kids, or house. I wore shabby and shabbier clothes. I lived in funky and funkier places. I hustled for writing grants and temporary university teaching gigs. This was no work, no lifestyle, that Dad had seen in the Depression, the war, or the postwar boom.

Over the sixties and seventies, across the space of 2,200 miles, the tensions between Dad and me simmered, a stew of emotions that never changed flavor. As recently as June 1979, four months before the ALS diagnosis, my previous visit to Skokie had concluded with a furious dispute that could have just as easily taken place when I left in 1966 for California.

It broke out over my decrepit old plastic suitcase, which Mom and Dad had given to me years ago in college. The night before departure, I had packed it to the breaking point, the zipper long broken, bulging with clothes and books and Mom's mandelbrot, precariously secured with twine wrapped around the outside.

Dad took one look at that contraption. "How can you travel that way?" he railed, with a tone of disgust that said I was incompetent.

It was an inspired insult that made me feel like a thirty-five-year-old kid. I raged to myself over his insufferable bourgeois propriety. Who the heck cared if my suitcase was flimsy? I refused his offer of one of their suitcases. We passed the evening in inflamed silence.

Now, six months later, thirteen years after I had left home for Berkeley, I had returned again, not for a dutiful visit, but by need, his and mine. Now, in the family den, he winked at me, content with my presence in the family circle. I felt a vague sense of child's guilt—that my anger had caused his disease—and a child's pleasure in pleasing my father with my presence.

Dad's need for family, for me, never had been so clear. Again and again, in a living room packed with family and friends, he expressed his surprise that his sons Skip, Mark, and Rob cared so much. He had learned of our worried telephone calls about his ALS and enjoyed our sudden travels home. Dad told the visitors that our entire family would stand together against the disease, my exact assurances over the telephone.

Hearing Dad say those words made me uneasy, as if he was publicly holding me to a casual offer, just talk. But I knew I had said those things. From the day I heard the diagnosis, I had felt compelled to return home and stand with Dad and Mom and the family.

I was amazed to see how the disease had drawn Mom and Dad together. They always had seemed inseparable, my parents, Ann and Sam, bound together by battling as much as by affection. Since Rob had left for college in 1971, they had been squabbling more bitterly than ever, no longer able to contain grievances that had festered over decades of marriage. The issues always were trivial, but the argument was the same: he was overbearing, and she ignored him. I had wondered if their resentments might actually snap their bonds of years together, children, family, friends, and property. But I could not imagine them living apart.

They did not stop quarreling after receiving the ALS diagnosis. This madcap normality continued, but their conflicts no longer seemed significant. One moment, they were bickering over a trifle; another, they were holding hands and laughing. Dad spoke warmly of protecting Mom from her fear of disease. She'd once had a cancer scare, a misdiagnosis, that had been traumatic. Mom spoke with unabashed admiration for Dad's courage in facing the future, their future, with ALS.

Now, at this moment with ALS, I saw something big and brave in how they turned to each other in this greatest crisis. To me, they were heroic, as I wanted.

Mom's birthday came a week after I arrived, and Dad wanted to give her a special gift. She tearfully explained, "He wants me to have something to remember him."

One Saturday morning, I drove them to a fashionable north suburban jewelry store. With girlish excitement I never had seen, Mom tried on one piece of jewelry after another. She lingered over an elegant diamond pendant, hesitating at the cost. Dad insisted on buying it, with the pride and abandonment of a man no longer concerned about money.

Outside, sobbing, Mom vowed she would always wear it. She did.

Dad wanted to fight ALS. As a scientist, a self-described "problem-solver," he had an ingrained faith that problems could be overcome through rational thought and resolute action. He had seen it done throughout his lifetime: an end to the Depression, a cure for polio, the trip to the moon. He had done it in his own work at his laboratory and home workshop. Now he faced a supreme test of this creed of his Greatest Generation.

I was not so different. Although I professed greater skepticism toward science and rationality, I was part of a baby boomer generation that believed anything and everything was possible, whether it was free love, liberation through drugs, stopping the Vietnam War, or smashing capitalism. I had never recognized any limits set by nature, history, or society. Sure, we could fight ALS.

Dad knew early on that conventional medicine wrote him off as terminal. His internist had given him a death sentence for the ALS diagnosis over the telephone, a cowardly act that infuriated Mom and me. At the Mayo Clinic, where the ALS diagnosis had been confirmed, a neurologist had counseled Dad to accept the disease, place himself under the care of his internist, and prepare for the end of his life.

Fortunately, Dad had continued seeking medical help. He learned of a Muscular Dystrophy Association clinic at nearby Evanston Hospital that took ALS patients. Once a month, a team of specialists would monitor his disease and treat the problems of gradual muscle loss and paralysis. We felt assured that the mainstream medical system was on his case but with no cure and no stopping the disease.

Dad had no way to resist ALS: no surgeries, no treatments, not even a pill or heaps of broccoli. It was eerie. This sinister disease was claiming his body, yet the neurologist at the MDA clinic would only recommend light exercises to ease muscle cramps rather than to maintain muscle function.

Dad did the exercises irregularly, without conviction that they made a difference. I did not approve. *If I had ALS*, I thought, *I would do every possible exercise right on schedule.*

When I reminded Dad about doing his exercises, he replied, "Don't forget about what happened to Lou Gehrig."

"Lou Gehrig?"

"Yes, Lou Gehrig. He overexercised, trying to strengthen his muscles against ALS. He actually killed himself with exercise."

No arguing with that. And, later, reading about Lou Gehrig, who was nicknamed "the Iron Horse" for his extraordinary durability and capacity to play baseball with injuries, I learned it probably was so: too much exercise for ALS. Lou Gehrig, with all his fight, couldn't beat it.

Dad surprised me with his interest in other kinds of treatment for ALS. By temperament, occupation, and generation, he seemed the least likely candidate for unconventional medicine. He once told me that something was true, scientifically, when the identical outcome could be reached one hundred times consecutively in laboratory tests. But everything had changed with the diagnosis.

He had immediately contacted Nathan Pritikin, who he had once worked for, with the hope that the famous Pritikin diet would stop this ALS thing. Pritikin had claimed his low-fat diet retarded heart disease and other life-threatening illnesses, and I was certain that if he had advanced similar claims for ALS, Dad would have been on the next airplane to the nearest Pritikin health spa. Pritikin did examine Dad's Mayo Clinic test results but simply suggested that Dad go on the Pritikin diet to bring down high blood pressure.

That disappointment did not deter him. By the time I was reading about the Pritikin diet, Dad was already considering the more radical regime of Paalo Airola, who proposed a macrobiotic diet of nuts, grains, and seeds in *Are You Confused?* (Airola 1971, 72-82).

Nuts, grains, and seeds? For my chemist father in Skokie? Airola also recommended periodic fasts and enemas, along with dry brush massages to aid body cleansing and cell regeneration. Thankfully, when I arrived in Skokie, enemas and massages had become a joke, a kind of touchstone of what they would not do to fight ALS.

Food preparation was something Mom could do. By my arrival, they were making an overnight switch to the Pritikin diet. They did so largely out of Mom's need to do *something*. After cooking meat, potato, and vegetable dinners for a lifetime, she suddenly resolved to prepare delicious, balanced, meatless, nonfat meals. In the house where I had grown up on baloney and white bread sandwiches for school lunches, I now found yogurt, wheat germ, and natural peanut butter.

Food became an endless topic of discussion. At first, I was

embarrassed by how we inflicted it on our hapless visitors, but they relished the subject and merrily offered their own dietary cures for ALS. Everyone wanted to help, and each knew a way through food.

Mom felt pressured from one meal to the next with this odd new cuisine. We spent hours discussing recipes, shopping, and approaching meals. Dad feared he would not receive sufficient protein without meat, and I could not convince him there were other sources. He complained that Mom's new Pritikin diet was weakening him. After several days of bilateral discussions with Mom and Dad, we reached a compromise diet with fish, some fowl, a little beef, more grains, and a lot of fresh vegetables.

The New Age had reached my home in Skokie. Vitamins were another preoccupation in the search for how to resist ALS. Dad already had begun taking vitamin C to ward off colds, a perilous problem in the later stages of ALS, as we would discover. Other more dazzling possibilities beckoned. We considered megadoses of vitamin B12 and vitamin E, which we heard had been used in ALS experiments to resist muscle deterioration. However, Dad was more interested in something called lecithin.

Where had he heard of this stuff? I learned that Dad already had plugged into the grapevine of hard information, half-truths, and fantastical rumors about cures for terminal illnesses. A friend of a friend had passed on a health foods magazine article claiming that lecithin had a retarding effect on ALS. Somebody's nephew in Minneapolis, who was some kind of nutritionist, also believed in the healing effects of lecithin in degenerative nerve disease. So off I went in search of lecithin.

I was amazed to discover that I need not leave Skokie to purchase lecithin. Skokie, that fortress of middle-class Jewish good sense, where I thought the citizenry ate nothing more exotic than brisket and tzimmes, now had not one but three health foods stores.

From one of those stores, I brought home lecithin, a tempting creamy yellow powder. Dad was apprehensive. We held a lengthy, completely uninformed discussion of its potential benefits and dangers, and we concluded he should begin with a teaspoon a day. By the end of the second day, when he decided lecithin was giving him new strength, we could not keep him away from the stuff. He doubled his dosage and doubled it again, and I suspect he took more on the sly. Then came a day when he felt weak, and another, and the next day, he lost interest in lecithin.

Back in California, I had also investigated the possibilities of holistic medicine. In Berkeley bookstores, where I had browsed for years in the history, sociology, and literature sections, I found myself in unfamiliar corners reading about self-healing, meditation, homeopathy, and diet. Friends and strangers seized upon me with suggestions of therapies.

At the Berkeley Holistic Health Center, where I inquired about alternative approaches to treating Dad, an MD recommended that my father undertake psychotherapy and biofeedback to alleviate the stress behind his ALS.

I had always considered holistic medicine to be countercultural quackery. To me, it was the medicine of laid-back, good karma, get-me-centered, and give-me-space California. It was the spiritual healing of the 1970s that followed the collapsed political uprising of the 1960s, offering personal salvation rather than social justice. But mainstream medicine offered nothing for ALS, and there I was in Berkeley, the former nerve center of radicalism, now a spiritual navel of holistic healing. I shopped for a cure.

At that time, I was reading Susan Sontag's assault on holistic medicine, her book, *Illness as Metaphor*, published a year before Dad's ALS diagnosis. Sontag explained how modern diseases, tuberculosis and then cancer, had become associated with personal psychological traits: tuberculosis as a disease of lack of passion, cancer as a disease of repressed emotions. Unexpressed character and feelings, wrapped in metaphors, she argued, were now being associated as cause for disease. These metaphors, particularly the military ones, stigmatized certain diseases and were a call to fight them as lethal insidious enemies. But these metaphors also implicitly held patients responsible for their diseases caused by character and feelings (Sontag 1978, 5-9).

I agreed with Sontag's critique of these ideas underlying holistic medicine, where victims are held responsible for their disease. However, actually facing Dad's ALS, I thought he needed a way to resist the disease. With no mainstream medicine avenue of resistance, that led me to holistic medicine.

I could not believe that holistic medicine, with its prescription for good health through positive feelings and a virtuous lifestyle, would affect something as big and deep as ALS. I would not have believed it if I had ALS. But I wanted Dad to fight. The disease seemed inexorable in its workings, inevitable in its conclusion. Although Dad was searching for a cure, he sometimes spoke with humility about his fate, a resignation that both moved me and made me want to shake him and say, "Don't give up *so soon*."

I had brought with me from California Dr. O. Carl Simonton's strange book *Getting Well Again: A Step-by-Step Guide to Overcoming Cancer for Patients and Their Families* (Simonton 1978). It was a prime example of counterculture blame-filled psychotherapy, exactly what Sontag criticized. I was relieved that Dad read it with skepticism. I didn't want to launch him on some crackpot scheme for holistic healing. I didn't want him to blame himself for ALS. But he needed a way to resist the disease. That was the promise of holistic medicine.

Dad did not see how Simonton's explanation of stress as a cause of serious disease might apply to him and ALS. Dad considered himself mentally healthy, so he dismissed Simonton's prescription that terminally ill people get in touch with their hidden inner feelings, especially anger and resentment, and express those feelings in more positive ways. Dad had long believed that all introspection was a form of second-guessing, a kind of armchair quarterbacking, and he assured me he was not about to change now.

However, he was interested in the visualization techniques Simonton's terminally ill cancer patients used against cancer. They imagined pitched battles in which swarming armies of white blood cells, in the form of ruthless toothy piranhas, devoured weak and disorganized little gray cancer cells.

Dad was intrigued. Here was a practical do-it-yourself method of direct attack on disease. The problem was how to visualize ALS. What to destroy? What to encourage? No metaphors for my scientist father. He wanted to see the real things.

Here was my call to action. I consulted my traveling ALS library and located illustrations of the disease. Over several evenings, we scrutinized weird illustrations of the spinal cord, nerves, and muscles in yet another attempt to grasp what was wrong with his body. We fixed on motor neurons, those mysterious cells of the brain and spinal cord that seemed to control muscle movement and growth. As best we could determine, his motor neurons, the nerves that sent signals from his brain to his muscles, were dying. This led to muscle weakness and atrophy. Something had gone haywire in his energy lines.

These discussions were less than authoritative, so I was surprised a few days later when Dad announced he had been imagining cells in his nervous system—his motor neurons—and ordering them to send energy to his atrophying muscles. He thought he felt stronger! But he needed more graphic, three-dimensional images of motor neurons and the nervous system. He proposed a journey to Chicago's famed Museum of Science and Industry.

I thought this was desperation, but I also knew we had to try. The next Sunday, we set off for the museum—Mom, Dad, Rob, and me. The sun was bright, and the air was crisp. It was a fine day for an expedition across the city. We took the scenic route along Lake Shore Drive. The handsome brick and stone buildings gleamed under the icy winter sun. Lake Michigan was a forbidding deep purple. We coasted along, drinking in the urban scene, anticipating the healing images of healthy motor neurons ahead.

Dad sat in the back seat with Mom, uncharacteristically content to be a passenger in his own car. As Chicago passed by, he reminisced about his life in the city.

It reminded me of a tour he once gave me and my brothers of the old West Side, showing where he had grown up, telling tales of the old Chicago Jewish community. Dad's encyclopedic knowledge of Chicago streets was commonplace in our home, an ever-present danger that if you asked him street directions, you would receive twice what you wanted. Yet he always delighted me when he attached stories to the streets and buildings, transforming them into neighborhoods and communities, giving the city a living history that was his and mine too.

On that tour, he had taken us to the neighborhoods where his parents once had little grocery stores. He showed us Independence Boulevard, with its broad parkway where families would sleep outside on sweltering summer nights. We passed by the once fine home of a friend's father, a judge, where Dad's gang hung out, teenage boys and girls, forty or fifty of them on summer evenings. We saw former synagogues with Stars of David in the stone facades, now Black Pentecostal churches.

My favorite on Dad's tour had been the Douglas Boulevard basement apartments that had been rented by social clubs of young people. His own club was named the Delphrags, their joke that referred to "Garfield Park," almost spelled backward, where they played baseball. The Delphrags had organized sports teams, sponsored political and literary lectures, played cards, and held dances. They went out in groups to nightclubs, concerts, and prize fights. These were children of East European Jewish immigrants, leaving behind the Yiddish-speaking homes and ghetto neighborhoods of their parents, coming hard and fast into Chicago's American life. Their group stayed together for years until some of the fellas were drafted for the war.

Meyer Levin, the realistic novelist who lived in Chicago in the 1930s, later depicted their world in his novel *The Old Bunch* (1937). It portrayed a group of Jewish teenagers growing up in Jewish immigrant families and neighborhoods in Chicago's West Side of the 1920s and 1930s. For me, it is like reading about Dad and his pals, just a few years younger than Levin's "old bunch," seeking careers and girls, encountering the big city, and mixing in the popular culture of their time as they searched out their paths to become American adults in Depression-era Chicago.

Dad's West Side tour had taken us through the old neighborhoods, once filled with *shtetl*-like Jewish communities where everyone knew everyone's business. In one of those neighborhoods, around Franklin Park, he met my mother. He had relatives in that neighborhood, his sister and her family, and his school pal Nate and Nate's family also lived nearby on Kolin Avenue. My mother, Ann, was Nate's younger sister. Dad was often in their apartment, a regular at Klebansky (later the children Americanized the name to "Klee") family seders led by Nate's father, a locally esteemed Torah scholar who made a living peddling old clothes from a pushcart and passed most of his days studying in *shul*. Dad helped Nate carry chairs to the family apartment for my mother's sweet sixteen party, ten years before they married.

Dad was dashing in those days. One picture shows him in his early twenties, wearing a stylish double-breasted navy sports jacket, buttoned, with a dapper folded handkerchief in his breast pocket, set against contrasting slim white pants. He had a full head of thick wavy black hair, neatly combed, parted straight back almost at the middle. His early letters to Mom, which my brother Rob found decades later, show he was an ardent young man who could also tease and flirt. And always that straight frank gaze at the camera, with a cigarette dangling between two fingers.

Dad's every adventure had included a car, some old Hudson or Packard. Since 1934, he always had a car that carried them in the eternal quest for girls. On that West Side tour, he told my favorite story, the Saturday evening he and four pals, on a Labor Day weekend impulse, drove nonstop down to Turkey Run State Park in Indiana and then right back up to Michigan City, shifting drivers at high speed by rotating the fellas around the running boards and over the front hood, all in futile pursuit of girls they never met at a dance they never found. No matter. On the return trip, in an Indiana farm pasture, a barnstorming pilot was offering airplane rides, fifty cents for five minutes, and they took their first flights aloft.

Dad had told me another driving story on that tour, about a clash with another driver two decades ago on a West Side street we passed. Some right-of-way issue. He and the other motorist, another young man, both stopped their cars and stormed out. My father went to his trunk, pulled out a baseball bat, and headed for the other motorist, who turned back and sped away. I didn't know my father as a fighter, but he was stubborn and scrappy, and I knew his explosive temper. He didn't back down.

That day of the museum expedition, as we sailed along north Lake Shore Drive, curved into downtown Chicago, through Grant Park, and along the Outer Drive to the South Side, Dad told new stories about the passing cityscape. This was the first I had heard about the old downtown Midland Hotel, where my parents arranged their own wedding on a Saturday evening in 1942. They sent out invitations to one hundred guests for the ceremony, a sit-down dinner, and a party. It all was after dark so the Orthodox people, Mom's family, could ride the El downtown.

As Dad described their wedding on that drive across Chicago to the museum, I could imagine it from the wedding photos in Mom's family albums. They were a striking couple: Mom in a floor-length white gown with a veil and an elegant strand of pearls, Dad in a white tuxedo and white tie, with that thick wavy hair and a rakish mustache, both with happy smiles.

I remembered a honeymoon photo of Mom and Dad. They are in bathing suits, sitting next to each other on a rowboat, each holding an oar, shoulders brushing against each other. They are young, fit, and beautiful, with trim bodies. Both look straight at the camera, with content smiles, fearless, about to pull those oars. They know that ahead is a lifetime together.

I did not realize it that day as we coasted along Lake Shore Drive and Dad told stories of his young life in Chicago, but this was my father's final journey across his lifelong city. Perhaps he wanted to visit the museum for the drive across the city.

The Museum of Science and Industry was one of the joys of my childhood. It was cause for an annual family outing that ranked with our trips to Brookfield Zoo, Wrigley Field, and the seedy old amusement park Riverview. The museum building, a colossal neoclassical white elephant in the city that spawned modern architecture, promised wondrous possibilities within.

By the time we reached the biology section in the corner of the second floor, Dad was tired from the day's exertions. We wandered about in search of an exhibit that would graphically illuminate the dark mystery of ALS. We found a transparent human body, but, from our perspective, the accompanying recording was insanely upbeat in its explanation of the human organism. There was a giant replica of the heart that you could walk through, but no giant spinal cord. There was an exhibit on the human fetus, but we were searching out the other end of the life curve.

We finally discovered a small display of the human nervous system, a three-dimensional human body with a maze of spidery red lines. We hovered there for a long time, first staring intently, then gazing blankly. What, I suddenly wondered, were we looking for?

While Dad rested on a bench near the nervous system, I scouted through a multi-room exhibit on cancer. *Why couldn't Dad have a normal disease like cancer?* I thought. *With a normal arsenal of tools to fight it: chemotherapy, radiation, surgery, even healthy food. Why this bizarre ALS?*

I found a video that showed the workings of the immune system. Since one theory proposed that ALS began with a breakdown of the immune system, I thought this film might offer some useful images, and I tried to lure Dad over there.

No. He fretted about the effect it would have on Mom. Her previous cancer scare had a profound impact on her. This was a childhood mystery I had never understood. Dad considered her terrified of disease, particularly cancer, and he would not investigate that exhibit.

Our mission was a failure. There were no healing images of healthy motor neurons bringing energy to his muscles, no magical holistic healing through positive images.

Downstairs, while Mom and Rob went for the car, Dad rested on a bench. As we looked out on the tumult of the main lobby, I watched a squirming two-year-old in front of us. I thought how extraordinary it was that this toddler could move with such mindless ease while my father, a former member of the Delphrags who climbed over the hood of a speeding car to switch drivers, now sat exhausted after a brief walk.

Dad watched the same child, apparently with the same thoughts. He turned and said, "Why me?"

CHAPTER 2

The Cemetery Plots

DECEMBER 1979

After each failure to resist ALS, Dad became more pessimistic about his prospects. He considered this realistic. He was proud of facing ALS with no illusions.

He wanted to get his affairs in order, as the Mayo Clinic neurologist had advised. On that December 1979 visit, I felt I had to help him. If I could not find a cure, at least I could relieve his worries outside of ALS.

Most painful was the problem of Grandma, Dad's mother, who lived in Chicago's Jewish Home for the Aged. I had always taken for granted the tragedy of a parent living to witness the death of a child, but I had never considered the anguish of a dying son who might leave behind an aged mother. Who would take care of her?

Grandma had been the cause for my bitter condemnation of Dad. I had been irate eight years earlier when Dad and his sister Min had exiled her to the Jewish Home for the Aged. At eighty-three, still healthy and clear-minded, Grandma had wanted to live with one of her children. But she had lived for many years with Min, who refused to continue that arrangement, one of those messy adult problems I ignored. But after Grandma lived with my parents for a year, Mom wouldn't have her, an irrepressible busybody who meddled in everyone's business. Denying his home to his mother was awful for Dad. But at the time, I regarded it as a typical ploy of American-born children, guiltily disposing of an aging immigrant parent in some American old-age institution.

I had blamed Dad for Grandma's deterioration into senility. Her plight had inspired my vow that I never would allow him to make decisions for my care.

I had avoided visiting Grandma since she became senile. I preferred to remember her doting on me, stuffing me with boiled chicken, puzzling over why in the world I would leave Chicago for California. She had been a truly impossible old-world Jewish matriarch—preoccupied with her family, never recognizing her children as adults, demanding constant attention, and nosing into other people's business. And I had loved her for it, as only a favorite grandson could. I had no desire to see her fall.

But now, with Dad's ALS diagnosis, I couldn't leave him alone in his problem with Grandma. I joined him and Mom in their weekly visit to the home.

I was stunned by what I saw. The plump grandma of my memory, now ninety-one, was shriveled to some seventy-five pounds. She was bony and emaciated, a crumbled mass of sagging, wrinkled skin. Where she once was alive with grandmotherly warmth and peasant shrewdness, here she was lying in bed in a fetal position, mumbling and dozing, as she did all day, every day. Her caretakers at the home spoke of her like a holy woman for her will to live on. I had never seen anything like it.

Dad spoke to Grandma and held her hand, his futile weekly attempt to gain recognition. As he limped out of the home, he ruefully remarked that her grip was stronger than his. He suffered over the possibility that she would outlive him, that he might not be there to protect her and bury her. He wept after that visit.

For the first time, I felt sympathy for Dad's long ordeal with Grandma. Now, facing my own fearsome responsibilities for my parents, I was impressed by how he had cared for her over the years. That evening, Mom and I both urged him to stop visiting his mother, for there was nothing more he could do for her. Mom and Min could look after Grandma. He agreed without protest. He never returned.

I wanted to relieve Dad of his worries over unfinished financial business. He was preoccupied with his looming disability, when to retire, and decisions about health insurance, life insurance, investments, health care, Medicare, and Social Security. He was not only willing to talk with me; he actually asked my views. In our discussions, one topic slid into another, everything seemed knotted together, and he could not unravel it.

This was unnerving. I had arrived back in Skokie with apprehensions about future medical expenses, for I thought that ALS treatment could be enormously expensive. Rather than ease my fears, as Mom and Dad always had done about money, they frightened me with their uncertainty. With ALS, they were in new territory without a roadmap.

I finally plunged in myself. With Dad's permission, with his relief, I thought, I reached up on the high shelf in the back bedroom closet for the metal strongbox with their business papers. This was my first journey into the mysterious world of our family finances.

Here was another realm of Dad's domain where I never had ventured. Since leaving home for California at twenty-two, I had lived hand to mouth, certain I could rely on my parents for help in a pinch. I had been content to believe there were family resources for necessities and luxuries, even to share with a rebel son. But now, the ALS diagnosis forced me to question my childhood faith in our financial security.

I found myself awash in a sea of deeds, mortgages, wills, income tax returns, stock programs, investment certificates, bank accounts, insurance policies, job benefits, and retirement programs. It was my first encounter with the language of property. Reading every scrap of paper, particularly the explanations of Dad's benefits and retirement programs, I found a labyrinth of options, some compounded by the condition of disability.

My only conclusion was that I should have stuck with my original goal to become a lawyer and certified public accountant, that sensible high school career plan I had quickly discarded for radical politics as a college freshman. Now, trying to decipher these documents and lacking any reliable income or savings of my own, I felt like I was paying for my 1960s sins of irresponsibility.

I could not begin to assess our future financial problems around Dad's ALS. They seemed like huge black clouds approaching fast. I told myself that I could research and analyze these issues, much as I would prepare a lecture on the American Revolution. But I was worried. Family finances were something I would have to take on during another longer visit.

Most puzzling to me, Dad's worry over unfinished business focused on the Skokie house, to which he turned every discussion. He wanted to sell it, their home of twenty-five years, before he became disabled. He worried about who would maintain the furnace, install the winter storm windows and summer screens, clean the gutters, shovel the snow, and mow the lawn. How could he get in and out with a wheelchair? How would Mom alone sell the place? He would acknowledge my assurances that we could hire out work on the house and install a wheelchair ramp and that I could help Mom sell the house. And then he would repeat the same preoccupations in our next conversation.

"We have to look ahead," he told me with humility about his fate. He brought me back to the depth of this disaster.

I didn't accept it. I wanted to shout back, "Don't give up so soon."

I wished he had more confidence in me, even as I worried whether I could handle the house. But I decided that his urge to sell the house was a compulsion to tie up one huge loose string and set his financial affairs in order. I also wondered if it was an assertion that without him, our family could not continue our familiar life at home.

Our discussions about selling the house always gravitated to the basement, which was filled with a fantastic accumulation of stuff. Dad was plagued by the example of his dear friend Maysh, a Skokie neighbor and pal from the West Side, who had suddenly died of a heart attack one year previous, leaving behind a cluttered basement. Dad did not want to be caught unprepared like that.

Finally, there was something I could do to help now: clear out the basement, starting with several thousand books. I checked with Dad, Mom, and my brothers about their old books, boxed all of them, and arranged for the Salvation Army to take them.

The day after the pickup of books, Dad realized I had given away an out-of-print chemistry manual with material he needed for a metallurgical plating handbook he wanted to write in retirement. For several years, Dad had been considering what he might do when he stopped working. The ALS diagnosis, nine months before Dad's planned retirement at his sixty-fifth birthday, forced the issue. This plating handbook was his one idea, and for that, he needed the old chemistry manual I had donated to the Salvation Army. I was confident I could get a copy of any book through the university library when I returned to Berkeley, but Dad wanted his own book now.

There was something else I could do. I called the Salvation Army and learned where our books had gone. On a blustery Saturday morning, I set off for a Salvation Army warehouse in search of the old chemistry manual. Over my objections, Dad came along to identify the book, promising he would let me do the actual hunting.

An hour later, damp and chilled from pouring rain, we found ourselves in a gloomy cavernous warehouse teeming with recent donations to the Salvation Army. An incredulous superintendent led us past rooms with gigantic piles of furniture, appliances, toys, and tools. It was a veritable department store of used goods.

We trailed behind, Dad limping, to the book department in a massive back room. I saw before us mountains of books, thousands and thousands of books that had been donated from North Side Chicago in recent days. We were directed to the sorting bins, where the workers guessed we might find Friday's shipment. I dug in.

After fifteen minutes, I thought I had struck pay dirt, finding one of our books. Dad could no longer sit still, and to my exasperation, he tried to join the hunt. For the next hour, I alternately searched through books and corralled him back to a chair. I worked my way through the sorting bins, shelves, boxes, stacks, and heaps of books. I found our donated books scattered everywhere, but not the book we wanted.

Just as it seemed hopeless, Dad called me from behind. I turned and saw him grinning proudly, manual in hand. He had found it rummaging through a pile on a sorting table.

We straggled out, both exhausted but exhilarated. We celebrated our triumph the entire day, telling and retelling the story.

So far as I know, Dad never looked at that chemistry manual again.

My strangest project during the visit was to purchase cemetery plots for my parents. For weeks preceding my arrival, my brothers had told me that Dad wanted to buy cemetery plots. Within an hour of my arrival, when Mom was out of the room, he told me in a hushed whisper.

He wanted adjoining plots for them at Westlawn Cemetery, near where his father was buried and his mother would be buried. He already had spoken with the cemetery director, but he did not want to go to the cemetery. He did not want Mom to know about it. And he certainly did not want to discuss it.

At thirty-five, I had never considered cemetery plots, and suddenly, they became my primary care. My first thoughts about the grim task of purchase were crowded out by a puzzle: why did he refuse to tell Mom?

I wondered if she might oppose buying cemetery plots near his parents rather than her parents. Or perhaps he worried that she would fall apart in this preparation for death. I did not know, and I did not like evading Mom, but he had to have those cemetery plots. I said I would make the arrangements.

The next day, I asked him for directions to the cemetery. To my astonishment, he took out the telephone book to look up the cemetery address after dinner, right in front of Mom as she set out dessert. He knew full well how to get there. This public display had to be aimed at capturing her attention.

I watched, horrified! *What the heck is he doing?* This was no way to let Mom know something he thought she would fear or oppose! But she left the room before he could reveal his secret.

Later that evening, I asked if he wanted her to know about the cemetery plots. He did, but he was afraid to tell her. The subject was so charged that I did not ask why. I said I would take care of it.

I thought about it all night. How should I break it to her? What would I set off? How did I get into this mess?

When Mom returned from work the next afternoon, I asked her to sit down for a talk. I saw her tense. My strained nonchalance, coming after the successive shocks of recent months, immediately placed her on guard.

I told her about Dad's wish to buy cemetery plots. With feeble reassurance, I added that I thought it best to do so now, long before they were needed.

She began weeping. Between sobs, she said she was hurt he had not approached her directly. She was not opposed to a plot for Dad at Westlawn Cemetery. It was just that, well, she wanted to be cremated rather than buried. "I know this sounds silly," she explained, "but it seems cleaner to me."

I was surprised, relieved. There was no furious argument, no nervous breakdown, just cremation—an unexpected new variation on Mom's war with dirt. I was giddy, and I laughed.

I suggested we buy two cemetery plots side by side, as Dad wanted. When her time came, I would honor her wishes for cremation. I hesitated as I said it, imagining the weirdness of visiting Dad's gravesite while Mom's ashes would be scattered in Lake Michigan. But that was too far away for consideration. Dad now. Mom another day.

Mom agreed to my suggestion. Then she surprised me again, adding, "I know how I want his funeral. I've thought about it." She explained that it would be small and simple, with only the immediate family and a brief religious service.

I never asked Mom or Dad what they said to each other about the cemetery plots. Dad had to have those cemetery plots to know where his body would go when he died. But I thought he had staged the drama to tell Mom again that he was dying and make her acknowledge it through these final arrangements. After my conversation with Mom, no matter how much she denied Dad was sick, no matter how much she labored to keep up their hopes, I knew that she knew he was dying.

Several days later, driving to Westlawn Cemetery, I recalled my previous visit there. A few years before, on a balmy summer Sunday morning, I had accompanied Dad to his father's grave.

I had enjoyed that morning's conversation about his father, Grandpa, Shokhne, Sol, who had emigrated to Chicago from the Ukraine. Turned out, Grandpa was a draft dodger who fled from Kyiv to dodge conscription for the 1905 Russo-Japanese War. He'd become a tailor, a clothing cutter. He met my grandmother, Sarah, from Minsk, a seamstress in a cap factory, at a socialist Workman's Circle strike meeting, and in 1907, they married. My aunt Minah, Minnie, was born in 1910, and in 1915, my father, Shlome, Sammy. For high school, Min Americanized our family name, from Khaiken to Kann, my own last name.

Both Grandma and Grandpa were members of sprawling immigrant families who made their way to Chicago in the early twentieth century. I grew up on the West Side with countless uncles, aunts, and cousins who were part of our lives. I lost contact with this extended family and my Chicago immigrant history after 1966 when I moved to California. Even after I started a book on a California immigrant Jewish community, I remained ignorant of my Chicago immigrant family and my own history.

I have an old photo of Grandma and Grandpa, 1907, in their twenties, engaged. They are not the ancient Yiddish grandparents I remember. They are handsomely dressed, Grandma in a stylish fitted dress and Grandpa in a fine coat and tie with a mustache that gives him gravitas. Their faces are smooth, serious, and confident. They are young immigrants who have established themselves in their new American homeland.

That morning at the cemetery, I soaked in Dad's stories about the little stores Grandpa and Grandma had operated on the West Side of Chicago, one on Paulina Street, the next on Drexel Boulevard, and another on Erie Street, the neighborhoods where my father grew up. First, it was a delicatessen, then a candy store, and then a succession of little neighborhood grocery stories. They stocked whatever they could sell to their Jewish, Italian, Polish, German, and Irish neighbors: groceries, candies, soda pop, cigarettes, school supplies, magazines, comic books, fireworks on Fourth of July, and toys at Christmas. Yiddish was Grandpa and Grandma's native language, along with Russian and Ukrainian, but they spoke Yiddishized English well enough to do business on the West Side. They became neighborhood fixtures in their final grocery store on California Avenue for almost twenty years. It was a mythic place in my childhood imagination because of its soda fountain, where my father made his own ice cream treats after school. The family lived in the back rooms. The stores were open from 6 a.m. to midnight, getting the first and last customers every day of the year except closing for the High Holy Days Rosh Hashanah and Yom Kippur.

These family stores had long seemed exotic and remote to me. Over two generations, I had traveled far from my Chicago immigrant roots, several thousand miles to California, and an even greater cultural distance to a Berkeley PhD. But my past interviews of California immigrant families told me that my father's parents' stores, like my mother's father's pushcart, were common work for new Jewish immigrant families in early twentieth-century America. There was nothing unusual about this family history, not even my third-generation assimilation and separation from it.

I had my own glimpse of Grandpa and Grandma's Chicago when Dad once took me shopping at age nine in the older West Side of his own childhood: Maxwell Street, "Jew Town." Once the commercial heart of Chicago's old Eastern European Jewish community, just west of downtown, here was my grandparents' disappearing world. That Sunday morning, the once famous street was still lined with shops and peddler carts, packed with people doing business in the stores and on the street. I watched my father bargain with a brassy storeowner, in Yiddish, over a new leather jacket for me.

I recalled Grandpa as a short, gentle man with a thick Yiddish accent, sitting in a regal, overstuffed chair, holding open the mysterious Yiddish newspaper, *the Forward*, which he read backward, right to left. I remembered his last store, this one with my aunt Minnie's husband Dave, a costume jewelry store. It had a dazzling front window display, packed with sparkling watches and bracelets and rings and necklaces, with women's handbags and luggage too, on bustling Madison Avenue in a West Side Black neighborhood. I remembered Grandpa's funeral in my sixteenth year, when I had burst out crying as his casket was lowered into the ground, the only intrusion of death into my life.

On the visit with Dad to Grandpa's grave, I had been transported to another time and place. Although Westlawn Cemetery was just a forty-minute ride to the southwest of Skokie, the region had spacious open fields and forest preserves, the nearby houses were older and spread apart, and the sky seemed larger. Passing through the cemetery gates, we entered a serene world of manicured lawns, placid lagoons, stately trees, and gently curving lanes. At closer inspection, looking for Grandpa's grave, I had been fascinated by the variety of gravesites, tombstones, and epitaphs.

When we arrived at Grandpa's grave, Dad immediately whipped out a pair of clippers, trimmed the grass, and pulled the weeds. Then he picked up a nearby twig and placed it on the grave. It was his personal Americanized version of the old-world Jewish superstition that visitors leave pebbles on the grave as a precaution that the body should not rise after the soul departed. We had not paused for silent reflection. We had not spoken of Grandpa. Dad's private form of commemoration had been all action and no reflection. It had been so typical of him and, at the same time, touching to me. He was there, remembering his father in his own way.

At the time of that visit to Westlawn Cemetery with Dad in

the mid-1970s, I had begun my own circular route that returned to my Chicago Jewish history. I was starting an oral history of an immigrant Jewish community thirty miles north of San Francisco—through interviews with these East European immigrant settlers, their American-born children, and their grandchildren, my own baby boomer generation. I thought the community's history could tell the story of Jewish American immigration and assimilation over three generations in twentieth-century America. It was my way of exploring my own family's American story.

A few years after that first visit to Westlawn with Dad, I arrived again at the cemetery, now with the drumbeat of ALS and the mission to purchase Dad's gravesite. The cemetery director, who had already spoken with Dad, was a well-tailored businessman, warm and affable. He escorted me into a handsome wood-paneled office, had coffee sent in, and inquired about Mom and Dad's health. I just could not talk about ALS. It was the reason for my visit to Westlawn, but it was too big, too unpredictable except for one will-be-needed gravesite. I wanted to protect Dad from this casual nosy inquiry—and protect myself too. I didn't want to break out crying. I wanted this to be a business transaction, but Dad's illness was not normal business. I heard myself lie, saying they were healthy as could be.

The cemetery director began a polished explanation of the cemetery plots Dad had selected, the burial regulations, the price, and the contract. I found it bizarre, like we were dealing in real estate, not death. I became distraught, unable to follow. The cemetery director seemed evermore determined to oil the gears of purchase.

For Dad's and my own peace of mind, I insisted on seeing that these plots were near Grandpa and Grandma's plots. The director and I tramped across the deserted cemetery out to the Westlake section. His chatty monologue receded as I slowly absorbed the grim world around me. A slate-gray winter sky and a bleak thin layer of snow cast a somber spell over the grounds. The cemetery had lost its charm for me on this visit.

The director consulted his maps and went hunting for the plots. I stood there alone in a sea of graves and tombstones, wondering why I had come out there.

The director reappeared and beckoned me over to Grandpa's grave. Then, he steered me nearby to the plots I was buying for my parents.

I stared at that cold ground in dumb disbelief. Dad would soon be there, and that was why I was here. I tried to imagine him underground, a mound of earth above, a tombstone with his name and dates. I let that chilling vision sink in. Then, I fled back to the warm office and completed my business.

My Skokie visit concluded with a final stop at Dad's workplace, en route to the airport and my flight back to California. Dad would not hear of me taking the airport bus from Skokie.

He could no longer drive, so coworkers took him to and from work. But he still would not accept my taking an airport bus.

He had a plan. In the morning, I would ride with him to the plant, which was near O'Hare Field, and his assistant would drive me to the airport in the afternoon.

I resisted until I realized that Dad wanted to show me his job. My father's work had long been a mystery to me. TRW Cinch had employed him for the past nineteen years, over ten years in this west suburban factory. He left home in a sports coat and tie fresh in the mornings and returned tired in the evenings, shirt collar unbuttoned and tie askew. His business card said, "senior scientist," a title I knew he had created, but I did not know what he did. Now, with ALS looming, I wanted to find out.

My view of his job was based on years of his complaints about incompetent colleagues and self-serving bosses who did not grasp his ideas and the company's failure to reward his achievements. All of Dad's passion for his work had seemed to feed his frustrations.

A few years earlier, in an unusually frank conversation, I had warned him about complaining too much at work. I said he might have difficulty, in his late fifties, finding a comparable job. He surprised me by listening. He nodded in agreement.

I wanted to see how he managed now in his weakened condition. I wondered how he had continued working after the ALS diagnosis. Knowing he was a dying man, how did he face his colleagues?

When he received the ALS diagnosis in October 1979, he had not disclosed it to anyone at work while he investigated retirement options. I thought the company would try to get rid of him once it learned his condition. I had dark suspicions of large corporations from the sixties student upheaval, confirmed by my own studies of capitalist exploitation of workers in early industrialization. From California, I had investigated the legal rights of the disabled in Illinois workplaces, preparing to fight for his job.

I'd been surprised when Dad called to describe the conversation he finally had with Dick Sostek, the president of TRW Cinch. Dad had disclosed his disease and said he wanted to continue working. Mr. Sostek had assured my father he could work as long as he wanted and take paid sick leave as he wished. Whenever he was ready, the company would assist with retirement. I could not have been more wrong about my fears of his company.

By my December 1979 visit, Dad already needed help. Along with the rides to and from work each day, coworkers assisted him with opening doors, handling laboratory equipment, and setting out his lunch.

He had given almost a third of his life to this company: the years, the brainpower, the commitment to solving its metal plating problems. Now, in this time of need, Dad was treated with loyalty, decency, and friendship. He had earned it. But I already had learned you do not always get what you earn. I felt profoundly grateful to his company and coworkers.

My visit to TRW Cinch began with a revelation. Dad's large laboratory was impossibly cluttered, every counter groaning with chemicals, test tubes, metal pieces, supplies, equipment, and stuff. I recognized the disorder of his home basement workshop, where he could build or repair anything, where I once had infuriated him with my surprise gift of reorganizing it. This laboratory was my father's sovereign realm, a place where he was undomesticated. He not only created disorder there, but that morning, I saw him swear with colleagues and smoke cigarettes. Here, Dad was a different person, authoritative and bossy.

I still smarted at the memory of that run-in with Dad over twenty years ago when I had given him my gift of an orderly basement workshop. But now, with ALS threatening, I liked seeing him on the job in his laboratory, his own chaotic and productive place with work pals.

Dad gave me a tour of the plant. Pointing at huge complex machines in the production areas, holding odd manufactured products off assembly lines, he explained his projects to reduce metal plating costs for the tens of millions of electrical connectors TRW Cinch made for telephones. This work required his deep metallurgy experience and eclectic knowledge of chemistry, mechanics, and electronics.

"The job is good," he explained. He chose his projects. He was respected by colleagues. He traveled for national meetings. The company appreciated him. And, most important, he was independent: "No one bothers me."

I was relieved. I did not want to think of my father as exploited and unrecognized, disgruntled with the job, his years of work wasted. Where did I get those ideas? The sixties again?

Dad introduced me—his son Skip from California—to colleagues. One responded, "Oh yeah, the professor from Berkeley." A few actually knew about the books I was writing about a labor organizer and a California community of Jewish chicken ranchers. I thought he had never made sense of my history work. But here was evidence: he'd been bragging about me.

Dad was exhausted by the end of the tour. Back in his laboratory, he assured me he'd regain strength after a rest, and he did. Despite his growing difficulty with a full work week, he said he was more interested than ever in his work, and then he explained the innovative electroplating machinery they were creating in a special new building. His colleagues treated him as usual. When they asked about his weakened condition, Dad said he had a problem with nerves, which struck me as an accurate description of ALS.

His single regret was that he became tired at work by midafternoon. This ailing man, my father, simply wished he had somewhere to lay and close his eyes for half an hour. I asked if he could stretch out on a cot in the laboratory, and I daydreamed for a moment about bringing in that cot, but I knew the answer: impossible. But even the impossible could happen. Twenty-five years later, when I was in top management at a California public agency, I would receive a request that we provide a quiet room with a couch where employees in my division could rest during the workday. I would approve it.

Dad worked at his desk for the remainder of the morning. We had lunch together in the cafeteria. And then, it was time for my ride to the airport.

I couldn't resist some final advice. "You should stop smoking. ALS could attack your respiratory system." I'd been reading fearsome literature on compromised breathing with ALS.

How right I was about that attack, four months ahead—swallowing and choking problems, gasping for air, an unimaginable nightmare.

How wrong I was that a few cigarettes would make any difference with this profound brain disorder. But my father nodded in solemn agreement.

There was nothing more to say. We clutched each other goodbye, a real hug.

CHAPTER 3

Falling

MARCH 1980

Three months later, leaving the airplane in West Palm Beach, Florida, I was surprised to find Mom waiting alone at the gate. She said Dad was in the lobby.

"Don't worry about the bruises on his face," she assured me. "He fell yesterday. But he's all right."

I was stunned when I saw him, but not by the bruises. Huddled alone on a big bench in that busy lobby, weeping as I approached, he looked so small and frail. His thinning gray hair was disheveled. He hadn't shaved. His bony legs protruded out from Bermuda shorts. He looked like a shrunken old man.

With airport passengers rushing around us, I was swept by a wave of tenderness. I bent over and gently hugged him.

He was so weak. He needed help from Mom just to stand up. Then, he tottered toward the door, with her gripping him under a shoulder. He still took charge, issuing orders on how to retrieve my luggage and where to find the car, directing who should do what and when. But now he had to focus on every slow, small step. Dad's days of helping people at airports were over.

Over the past months, I had heard reports of his deteriorating condition. His legs had weakened, so he could not walk farther than a block. The index finger on his left hand had already atrophied, and the other fingers on that hand were faltering. He raised his right arm only, with difficulty, and his left arm was useless.

Mom had been helping him more and more. In the mornings, she maneuvered him out of bed. She put on his shirt, pulled up his pants, laced his shoes, shaved his face, and combed his hair. At meals, she cut up the food on his plate. When he defecated, she wiped his behind. In the evenings, she put on his pajamas and helped him into bed.

His decline had not been steady. He had felt limber and energetic during a February visit to their Florida condo. I had heard high-spirited reports of warm weather and easy living. Every day, they had walked to the ocean, two blocks from the condo, with Dad resting along the way on a fold-out chair Mom carried. I had imagined them as another plucky aging couple on a Florida beach.

But on returning to Chicago, Dad felt stiffer and less mobile in the ruthless Midwestern cold. He had resumed working, only with great difficulty. Each day seemed to require new adjustments as his legs and arms weakened. When he became discouraged, it bothered Mom. But he worked every day, and Mom too. She had assured me, "Really, we're okay."

Then, he had a terrible fall. Entering a bathroom at the plant, he did not raise the front of his foot high enough to clear a floor sill, known in the ALS literature as "dropped foot." Weakened muscles at the ankle joint caused a pulling down on the foot as he stepped. When his foot grazed the floor sill, he pitched forward. His arms were too weak for protection. His head crashed into a porcelain sink, and he bounced onto the floor, dazed.

Miraculously, he was not hurt, except for an ugly gash on his forehead. To the amazement of colleagues, he showed up the next day. He was determined to continue his job. But he was shaken by that fall. He had no protection. "I could have killed myself," he repeated for weeks as if suddenly realizing his own mortality.

They returned to Florida for my visit in late March, hoping that the warm weather and congenial atmosphere would restore the strength Dad had felt during the February visit. Mom planned the journey in meticulous detail, overriding Dad by arranging for wheelchairs to haul him in the airports. The journey was remarkably smooth, from Skokie to O'Hare Field to West Palm Beach Airport to the parking lot of their condominium. Then, fate mocked their best efforts when Dad tried to climb out of the rental car himself. He lost balance, toppled over, smashed his head on the car door, and crumbled to the asphalt. Neighbors had to haul him into the condominium.

The next day, when I arrived, he would not take a step alone. He insisted that someone hold him for balance whenever he walked. He continued those odd exercise jaunts, back and forth across the apartment every half hour to loosen his muscles, but he refused to venture outside for a longer walk. He was subdued.

I hated seeing him so fearful and cautious. I vowed that Dad would not fall while I was there. *Not on my watch,* I told myself. I could not imagine him tumbling over because I did not think of my father as someone who fell on his face. Not Dad. But it was happening, and I was determined to stop it. I intended to reverse his recent decline and cheer him up.

I thought my attitude toward the disease had changed. *I no longer fear Dad's ALS,* I told myself. My December visit to Skokie confirmed that we faced a crisis. However, after purchasing my parents' burial plots, I left convinced that I could handle whatever would happen.

Dad's disease had strengthened my resolve in my own life in California. Upon returning from Skokie, I began to eat better, exercise more, and live healthier. I suddenly wanted a stable teaching position, a real job. I daydreamed about buying a house.

I felt buoyant when I reached Florida in late March. I strode off the airplane wearing a new sports coat, toting handsome leather luggage. That new luggage, my response to last year's dispute with Dad over my shoddy suitcase, was an immediate self-improvement. Healthy, prosperous, and self-assured, I would give Dad new strength.

Their condominium was in Boca Raton, forty-five miles up the ocean coast from Miami. Mom and Dad had purchased it the year before, at a time when friends and family were doing the same. It was the final migration of the Chicago Jewish community: Eastern Europe to America, New York to Chicago, westward across Chicago, then to northern suburbs like Skokie, and now south Florida.

I thought my parents would never leave Skokie. It was their good life. Dad had grown up in Chicago's West Side neighborhoods, where their family lived in the ramshackle back rooms of little neighborhood stores. They once lived next door to a stable where Dad heard horses—used to deliver ice and coal—stamp their feet all night. Mom grew up in a large, poor family in West Side tenements, living hand to mouth; her father made a living selling old clothes, usually described to me as "rags," from a pushcart. Chicago, for them, was Depression-era immigrant poverty. Skokie was their promised land, reached.

After marrying in 1942, Mom and Dad left their parents' apartments and moved into their own West Side one-room flat. Expecting me in 1944, they rented another place, a spacious four-room apartment that eventually became cramped with the arrival of my brothers. The kids shared the bedroom, and my parents slept on the Murphy Bed that I still remember coming down each evening from a living room wall.

My parents rode the wave of postwar prosperity and growth. With Dad's earnings as a chemist and a loan from his brother-in-law, in 1955, they bought a new house in a north Chicago suburb. Skokie was the site of a postwar land boom that attracted Chicago's second-generation East European Jewish community. To me, everyone in Skokie was Jewish, though Jews were only half. It was all new single-family brick houses, with newly seeded lawns and young trees. Now ubiquitous family automobiles allowed easy travel to work in the city. The many empty lots filled fast with more new houses and new migrants from the West Side. The Skokie population quadrupled to almost 60,000 in the 1950s. It was a suburban boom town for the Jewish Greatest Generation parents and their baby boomer children.

Skokie was a happy place from the time we arrived there when I was eleven. I grew up with the abundance of suburban life: new schools, new cars, new bikes, corned beef sandwiches at Sam and Hy's deli and burgers with fries at the new McDonald's drive-in, Hebrew School lessons and bar mitzvah parties, high school sports and dating, and, taken for granted, college. I was in a middle-class Jewish community bubble, surrounded by a remote gentile world, and I never experienced anti-Semitism or exclusion or anyone who said I couldn't aspire to anything. Everything seemed possible in Skokie.

Our Skokie house was an ongoing interior design project for Mom, including a living room with plastic covers protecting the sofa that was always new, used only for special occasions. The house was a perpetual improvement project for Dad, beginning with planting grass lawns and trees and then building a backyard patio for entertaining weekend visitors. He was always working on something: installing summer screens and winter storm windows, constructing a shed, painting a room, or building another bedroom in the basement.

As the only members of our extended family with a house, my parents always had family visitors on weekends, with Dad barbequing and Mom cooking the rest. Old friends from the West Side were scattered nearby, and my parents made new friendships with neighbors. With "a whole bunch of the fellas," other fathers, Dad helped start the little league, where I was a ferocious competitor. Mom was active with the PTA. Our family joined the new congregation, B'nai Emunah, where we attended services on Friday nights and during the High Holidays.

My parents sent all three boys to Hebrew School for years, culminating in bar mitzvahs. They hosted a bar mitzvah party for each son in a banquet room at a North Side Chicago restaurant. At the time, I thought our bar mitzvahs were modest events, mere afternoon luncheons rather than elegant evening affairs I attended for some classmates. But now I realize that each of our bar mitzvah parties included all the relatives and friends at a sit-down meal, with an emcee, band, dancing, speeches and toasts, and cake and all the trimmings, including, for mine, souvenir matchboxes with the front cover saying, "Kenneth's Bar Mitzvah." These were important public celebrations in the life of our family.

There is a photo of Mom and Dad at my 1957 bar mitzvah party. Dad, in coat and tie, is lean and handsome, with wavy black hair, smiling and proud. Mom is stunning, a mature woman with a radiant full smile, slender, in a beautiful dress with a bare neckline and an elegant single strand of pearls. Dad is forty-two, Mom thirty-eight, at the height of their powers, with three fine boys, family, and friends, enjoying the celebration they are hosting and the comfortable life they have established.

Despite our happy years in Skokie, it was a one-generation place. The parents stayed on as the kids left for college, moved out to farther, newer suburbs, or back into Chicago, and some, like me, left for distant places. The parents remained in a Skokie that lost its rawness as homes became settled and trees matured, a lovely place with no further home improvements needed. Why leave such comfort and convenience?

Mom and Dad had surprised me as their friends and family began buying second homes, condos, in Florida. For years, my parents disparaged any mention of Florida retirement, insisting they would not join the ranks of decrepit old people decaying under a tropical sun. Then, suddenly, they sent me a brochure describing their purchase into "a waterfront condominium paradise" along Florida's "fabulous Gold Coast."

They bought the condo the day they first saw it. On the next trip, they arrived in the middle of a hurricane, but it did not slow their shopping spree. The condo was a big new interior decorating project for Mom and a big new improvement project for Dad. They were starting a second home, a new life in the tropics.

I understood their excitement when I first walked into the condo on this trip. It was bright and sunny, spacious and comfortable, fully equipped with appliances and conveniences. On entering, I was immediately drawn through the living room and onto the terrace, where I heard playful shouts from the building's swimming pool. In the distance, I could hear the hum of boats on the Intracoastal Waterway. Those passing boats sent ripples our way, gently rocking the boats docked along our inlet. Our terrace was a standing invitation to join the sport outside.

The entire Florida scene delighted me, beginning with Miami International Airport, a seedy, muggy introduction to the tropics. Aboard my connecting flight to West Palm Beach, I gazed down on an inviting turquoise Atlantic Ocean. On the ground, I saw exotic flowers, lush foliage, palm trees, and fruit trees. Drizzly Northern California, like icy Chicago, was long gone in this lotus land of sweet mornings, steamy afternoons, and balmy evenings.

Mom and Dad had bought their condo amid a land boom along the South Florida Atlantic coast. Hucksters, investors, retirees, and pleasure seekers from across the Western world were flooding onto that narrow coastal plain. Huge new condominium developments with thousands of apartments selling for astronomical prices were sprouting up along nearby beaches. Across the street, we could see a large subdivision of luxury homes ascending from a muddy field. Inland, there were endless new developments—condos, golf courses, and shopping centers.

The garish opulence of this emerging world contrasted with the majestic ocean-side estates and the dignified country clubs that persisted from a more gracious bygone era, or perhaps an older land boom. But old or new, there was wealth and leisure fun wherever I turned. And in their own modest way, with their charming little condo near the ocean, Sam and Ann Kann were part of it.

Their enthusiasm was contagious. As they toured me about, proudly displaying their sunny, booming new homeland, I imagined future visits when I would swelter in the summer heat and stand against raging hurricanes. I would see Miami, tour the Everglades and the Keys, and explore the interior and the Gulf Coast. But now, on this visit, my task was to help Dad and Mom determine if this Gold Coast paradise was the right place to cope with ALS.

During that March visit, I still thought ALS could be coped with and that we could manage it with sound decisions.

The disease had transformed Dad's view of Florida. He was soothed in the warm embrace of the Florida sun, but Florida also presented a cruel reminder of his predicament. After a lifetime of hard work and miserable weather in Chicago, he had finally reached this tropical leisure world. With retirement a few months ahead at sixty-five, he might have ambled through Florida days with morning swims and golf games, rambling afternoon shopping expeditions, and dressy evening cocktail parties. But instead of joining the fun, Dad was becoming one of those decrepit old people decaying in the sun.

It was tantalizing and agonizing for him. Everywhere Dad looked, he saw vigorous, natty, white-haired people enjoying themselves. In a restaurant one day, after struggling for an hour to move food from his plate to his mouth with a fork, he said with sad longing, "Look at these seventy-year-olds around us. They're all healthy. I would trade places with any of them."

Despite his fear of falling again, Dad insisted on giving me a genuine Florida vacation and showing off their new homeland. Most mornings, we walked at a snail's pace to the building's swimming pool, where Dad sunned on the patio while Mom and I swam. Sometimes, we drove two blocks to the beach parking lot, negotiated a jittery, slow crossing of the busy coastal highway, and cautiously maneuvered on treacherous sands to a spot where we could enjoy a couple of hours at the ocean. In the afternoons, we did driving tours of the region, always stopping every half hour so Dad could stretch his tightened muscles.

The easiest activities had become difficult. One afternoon, we went to a movie. We carefully parked near the theater and laboriously made our way to the ticket office, only to discover that the matinee was sold out, with retired people taking their afternoon entertainment. *So unfair*, I thought. But Dad, rising to the occasion of my visit, simply said we'll return earlier the next day, and we did.

Each venture beyond the condo forced me to see the world anew, through the lenses of disability. I was grateful for the elevator in our building, for without it, we could not have left the second floor. Now I understand those special parking places for the disabled, close to your destination. I recognized the amenity of public benches that afforded Dad resting points on these journeys. I was grateful when strangers in a crowd, noticing Dad's difficulty walking, made space or offered a seat.

I was fiercely protective of Dad on these public excursions. As he teetered and tottered along, I kept a firm grip under his shoulder, ready to fend for him in a crowd, ready for the jostle that might send him tumbling. If people stared, I glared back, but mainly, the world buzzed by, oblivious to our struggles.

On the first days of the visit, I made good on my vow that Dad would not fall again. There was no danger so long as he insisted that Mom or I hold him for balance whenever he walked. But as he felt more confident, he would venture a few cautious steps on his own. I relaxed my vigilance. And that's when he fell.

It happened one evening after Mom had gone to bed. Dad and I stayed up late to watch a basketball game. Basketball had been a passion for each of us in high school, and we were still transported by a championship game. This luxurious evening, we ignored ALS for the excitement of underdog UCLA challenging mighty Louisville.

Tired and sagging, Dad hung on till the final buzzer, a small triumph of his own. I escorted him to a stop in the hallway bathroom. Then, he emerged and slowly navigated alone into the bedroom.

I watched with indecision. I wanted to help him, but I didn't want to invade the privacy of my parents' bedroom. It was dark and tranquil, and I heard the soft hum of my mother sleeping—not a place for me to trespass.

Dad crept in. I meandered over to the door, not in, just to watch over him.

Before my horrified gaze, he took a slight misstep—dropped foot again—and lost balance. He toppled like a straw scarecrow blown over in the wind.

It was a deadfall. He was helpless. He did not have the strength to raise his arms fast enough, and those wasted arms could not protect him even if raised.

Somehow, he pivoted and fell on his shoulder rather than his face. He landed on the carpet with a thud, cried out, and then cursed. Mom bolted up in bed, shrieked, and wept.

It happened in a fantastic few seconds. I rushed over to Dad, saw that he was unharmed, and propped him against the wall. Then, I went to comfort Mom against this latest reminder that her world no longer was safe and predictable.

Dad sat there on the floor, face grimacing in disgust, cursing his body's betrayal. I invited him back into the living room to relax with a sip of wine. He abruptly refused, as if the suggestion was absurd. I could only help him into bed and leave him muttering in frustration.

That night, I replayed the scene in my mind: my hesitation, Dad's helpless fall, Mom's anguished groans, and my frozen horror at the unfolding disaster. A perfect evening had ended in this nightmare because I had foolishly let him walk alone.

For no good reason but my own frustration, I fumed at Dad. How could he inflict this misery on us? It was awful to witness his physical deterioration. It was terrible to see him fall like that. It was terrible to witness the impact on Mom. How could I always be there to hold him up?

His helpless rage angered me. His frustration and fury were impossible for those around him. I wanted him to laugh it off and bounce up, ready to face ALS again. I wanted him to show heroic resistance, or at least accept his new limitations with grace. But his angry cursing reaction cut off my sympathy and admiration. I could not stop him from falling, nor even comfort him after he fell.

It was a chilling lesson in what I could not do for Dad. He was too proud to accept his weakening body. I thought it violated his conception of himself as a man responsible for his wife and children, a man who took charge to help relatives and friends, and a man who solved problems on the job. He hated his growing dependence on Mom, me, or anyone else. Disabled, he would be miserable, and he would make life miserable for everyone around him. I saw it coming.

I imagined how I would face this catastrophe. *My generation is less bound by these codes of manhood*, I told myself. My identity did not depend on directing people through airports or repairing a house. Faced with ALS, I thought, I would resist where it was sensible and gently yield to the inevitable. If I could not fade out with grand heroism, at peace with myself, I would commit suicide. Anything but Dad's disgust.

I tried another way to please Dad. I read him my first book. If I could not prevent him from falling, I certainly could comfort him about my life, if not his. I wanted him to understand what I had accomplished with my writing.

Dad's ALS diagnosis in October shocked me to the realization that after years of work on two books, both were advanced, but neither was completed. At thirty-five, I had nothing to show for my labors. With Dad's ALS diagnosis, I was determined to get one into print.

For a few hours every day, I stopped worrying about ALS and worked on my book. I had almost completed it by spring teaching break when I went to Florida. My publisher was ready for production, so I brought along the project. Mom and Dad were amused and impressed to find me lugging a typewriter and suitcase filled with manuscript materials cross-country. Their son, the writer, had arrived.

That book grew out of my search into history for a tradition that I had never found in my own family or Skokie. It told the life story of Joe Rapoport, an old-time Communist trade union organizer whom I had met in 1975, a member of the Jewish chicken ranching community I was writing about. Joe was a Jewish immigrant of my grandparents' generation.

I had been attracted to Joe through his stories of life on the big canvas of twentieth-century world history in the United States, Russia, and Europe. Through lifetime participation in movements for social change, including the Russian Revolution and the American labor movement, he maintained continuity in socialist convictions and comrades that dated back to the Ukraine and the Lower East Side of New York. He could summon the teachings of the Prophets, along with Marx and Lenin, as yardsticks to measure American social justice. He had been an effective working-class organizer in the New York needle trades of the 1920s and 1930s. He had a half-century marriage, a sturdy Petaluma bungalow purchased through his hard-earned success as a postwar chicken rancher, and local respect as a long-standing community activist who built alliances across the political spectrum. I had adopted Joe and his Jewish immigrant radical working-class tradition as my own.

When I began working on Joe's life, I once challenged Dad by reading him a story from Joe's defiant youth. It was the tale of Joe's bar mitzvah when he did not learn his haftorah, his reading from the Old Testament. That day, Joe had humiliated his father before their *shtetl* with his rejection of their religious tradition. Joe's father had responded by virtually disowning Joe, saying he did not believe Joe would say the Kaddish, the Jewish prayer of mourning and remembrance, after he died.

Looking back now, I recall telling Dad this story as a needling reminder that I, too, was a son who had rejected his father's tradition. I was disavowing Dad, his generation of assimilated middle-class Jews, and their banal homogenized suburbs. Telling Joe's Kaddish story, I was denying my obligation to recognize and honor Dad's continuity through me. I had dared him to challenge me.

Dad hadn't responded to that story. Perhaps my challenge had been too obscure. I no longer cared. Now, with Dad sick, I wanted to assure him that I would say Kaddish for him one day. I was his son, and I would mourn his death and remember him.

But how could I start a discussion about my future reaction to his future death? How could I promise to honor his legacy to me when I still did not know what it was? I could not bridge the chasm between us simply because I suddenly hungered for continuity.

Instead, I offered to read to Dad from my manuscript. All I could do was show him my search for a historical tradition, for my roots and his too, in this book on the Jewish immigrant generation.

I read to him out on the terrace. We sat in our shorts, looking out to a postcard Florida scene, the yachts gently rocking in the water. It was an unlikely setting for these tales of pogroms and revolution in Ukraine, trade union struggles, and Yiddish culture in America.

Dad followed closely as my voice swung along with the familiar rhythms of the prose. I edited my reading selections, omitting stories of conflict between father and son. Dad was a liberal democrat, but not very political, and I do not think he understood Joe's life devoted to the establishment of socialism. I didn't try to explain how I identified with the story. It was enough that Dad liked the book's old-world Jewish flavor and its passionate tales of New World struggles for trade unions and social justice.

Dad surprised me when he reciprocated by showing a paper he was writing on new methods to save gold in electrical plating. It was a scientific paper, but it was also an amusing essay that poked fun at the narrow prejudices and noxious substances of his own chemistry profession. I think he intended it as a final iconoclastic message to his colleagues.

He surprised me again with a request for my opinion of his writing. He wanted editorial advice, which I could give him. We reviewed the paper together, line by line, paragraph by paragraph. Our discussion lasted several days, with my determination to help far exceeding his attention span. By the time I typed up a crisp new draft, he had lost enthusiasm for our collaboration. But I was satisfied. This one time, I really helped him.

Dad's continued dedication to his work showed a grittiness I had not expected. I was amazed he had worked five full days the previous week in Chicago. I could not imagine those early mornings when he had activated sluggish muscles in laborious preparation for the 7 a.m. ride to the plant. How had he endured exhausting, long hours in his laboratory? Had he been embarrassed suffering this terrible physical decline before the daily gaze of his colleagues? How did he ask his assistant for help walking to the bathroom? I wondered if I was tough enough to tolerate this kind of decline and disability in public.

After his recent falls, Dad questioned his ability to do even the minimal walking necessary to continue working. He also suspected the company no longer wanted him because he was not receiving enough new assignments to remain busy. That hurt his pride, and it made me wince.

He was so uncertain about retirement that he asked my opinion. He was ashamed of the temptation to stop working—as if some character weakness was seducing him toward the easy path.

I wondered how he could continue his job much longer. I thought it unfair that he should struggle so greatly to work, and I argued he had every reason to retire whenever he wanted. I was pained by the prospect of his workplace becoming his daycare center, with a loss of respect from colleagues.

But I could not imagine him home every day. Mom was away at her job. What would he do alone? What if he fell? We knew he would not stay away from his basement workshop. I imagined him tumbling down the basement stairs, sprawled out on the basement floor, hurt and helpless.

Impossible. I suggested that he continue working but with shorter days and more vacations. And back to my idea of a cot in his laboratory so he could rest during the day. I recalled the advice in the letter from the Mayo Clinic neurologist: "He should continue to work as long as possible." Intuition told me Dad should do everything possible to maintain his place in the public world, resisting ALS and the pull to stay home.

I was exasperated by Dad's refusal to accept what I thought he most needed: a walking aid. The Muscular Dystrophy Association clinic had already fitted him for a special pair of shoes designed to avoid falls from dropped foot by bracing his feet and ankles like a super hiking boot. The clinic had constructed those shoes at a mind-boggling cost of $750.

"That clinic does not know Sam Kann," Mom explained. "I could have told the occupational therapist what would happen."

Dad had tried them on once, pronounced them a failure, and never wore them again. Those special shoes now occupied a place in their Skokie basement, along with the clinic's braces, splints, and other ingenious supports to compensate for weakened muscles.

I could not resist tackling the problem. I suggested Dad try a cane, one of those sturdy three-pronged canes for balance, but he insisted his arms were too weak. I also proposed hiking sticks, a crutch, two crutches, a walker, and, finally, a wheelchair, with no success. It all was out of the question. He would not tolerate any apparatus for the disabled.

It was not just pride. Part of him wanted to concede to the disease. He ached to give up the struggle and sink into the comforting Florida warmth. When I watched Dad sitting on the terrace, reading, dozing, or sometimes just gazing out, I could imagine him passing his final days in that peaceful spot.

The view was serene. The still water, the docked boats, and the lush green lawns were frozen under a relentless Florida sun. On those timeless hot afternoons, there was not a sound, not a movement. It was a place to nod off into eternal sleep.

But not yet. The terrace was also the site of our worried discussions over whether they should live in Florida or Skokie when he retired. We went back and forth, round and round, over weather, living space, wheelchair accessibility, medical services, and proximity to family and friends. The more we tried to compare the two places for coping with ALS, the less we seemed capable of preparing for the future.

I was frightened. I thought ALS might become awful ahead. I felt we had to prepare for it. The disease was like a behemoth boulder rolling down a hill in slow motion, with Dad fighting an impossible battle to halt it, Mom at his side urging him on. I could see him weakening. I could see his life strength ebbing away. Yet the future seemed hazy; the options were imponderable, and any changes were fraught with peril. I did not know what to do.

The most practical problems became charged with momentous significance. For the first time, Dad worried about how he would pass his time if he retired. He could not stretch his imagination beyond house repairs, golf, metalwork, and all those wonderful activities that required strength, dexterity, and mobility. "What will I do?" he finally cried out to me. "I won't watch soap operas all day."

I urged Dad to gather the materials for his metal plating handbook, the project that brought us to that Salvation Army warehouse in December. He didn't see how he could write or publish it. I countered with a vast scheme in which he and I would collaborate. Then, we would publish, promote, and distribute it ourselves. I would have that metal plating handbook next to the romance novels on the supermarket book racks.

I tried to reassure him—and me—that he would find things to do. In truth, I feared that with retirement, he would further loosen his weakening grip on life.

I saw troubling signs in Florida when Dad resisted tasks like shaving, washing, and changing into appropriate clothes for outside expeditions. This was a complete reversal for someone who had always been fastidious about his appearance.

My reaction surprised me. I hated to see him disheveled and unkempt, even though I had walked around with raggedy clothes and wild hair through my twenties. However, Dad was not defying social convention so much as collapsing before it. Now, like Mom, I insisted that he make himself presentable every day by his own high standards.

If I was acting like a parent, at times, Dad seemed like a child. One evening, after a long, difficult day, he went to sleep early. Then, Mom and I met on the terrace to discuss the current situation, as if we could speak frankly now that the kid was asleep. And sure enough, within five minutes, he called out from the bedroom like a kid, asking where Mom was.

In fact, they occasionally joked about him being the family baby. That banter made me squirm. It was not how I wanted to think of my father. But that was how they tried to defuse the tensions over his growing dependence on her.

The tensions smoldered with the accumulation of simple necessities Dad could no longer do himself. He disliked Mom's physical handling when she helped him in and out of cars, chairs, and beds because she did not have the strength or confidence to do it securely. He could not abide my assistance with putting on and taking off undershirts, because I could not master their system for the shifts of cloth and limbs. When he walked with helping hands from Mom or me, he regularly chided us for pushing him off balance instead of ensuring that he remained on balance. Like Mom, I had difficulty staying focused on simply helping him walk.

Dad was most particular about his personal hygiene and grooming. He wanted no assistance from me when it came to wiping his behind; with relief, I left that to Mom. She, on the other hand, could not shave him to his satisfaction, and she gratefully turned that job over to me.

Shaving was tricky. You had to do it quickly because he did not like being shaved, and you had to do it carefully because he did not like a sloppy job. Wanting him to look his best, I was thorough, and I would try to distract him with nervous chatter as I worked on his face. He regularly lost patience as I dawdled over his upper lip and below his chin. "Come on," he'd complain, as if I was inept. "Let's get this over with."

I seethed when he criticized my assistance. His disgusted dissatisfaction inevitably summoned up my old catalog of childhood rejections: his criticism of my work at some house project, his disgust and anger, and my feelings of ineptness and failure. Those ghosts refused to disappear; I never had pleased him, he never had tolerated me, and I never would forget.

I was even more distressed by something new. Now Dad offered meek thanks each time I helped him, even after he had complained. This unprecedented gesture of dependence by my father, this reversal of roles, was frightening beyond my comprehension. I didn't want him deferring to me.

I felt like I was peeking into parts of his character best kept hidden. His alternating anger and humility seemed so exaggerated, so extreme. It made him seem defenseless and vulnerable. Even as he angered me, I wanted to protect him, from the world and from his own unbridled emotions.

But not at meals, when he was maddening. He insisted upon eating himself, but he hardly could use his arms. He wanted his plate at a certain spot on the table, elevated to a certain height, perfectly placed for what his right arm could do. Sometimes, he asked that food be arranged at more accessible parts of the plate. Sometimes, he needed help getting food onto his utensils. We fiddled around with these arrangements during every Florida meal, never satisfactorily. It was difficult for me to admire his determination to continue his independence when he was so difficult to help. Somehow, Dad managed to eat by his own efforts, occasionally with blessed humor over his dilemma, usually with ill-tempered frustration.

Following one of those meals, Mom confided, "At least I don't have to feed him." She tried to keep that hopeful view of Dad and ALS. I looked at her, puzzled, wondering what in the world she was thinking because it was clear to me that she would be doing precisely that in a month or two.

Mom was saintly in her willingness to help Dad. She had already altered his clothes to foster his autonomy: pants with elastic waist grips instead of belts, loops of string attached to his zippers, and Velcro instead of buttons. If he needed a handkerchief, if he wanted a snack, she would bring it immediately without complaint. When he itched in a no longer accessible spot, he would sheepishly request help, and she would immediately scratch him.

Dad's growing dependence on Mom was difficult for both of

them. But they found some unexpected satisfaction in their joint problem-solving.

Pride outstripped modesty, and Dad insisted that I witness their finest collaboration: Dad's shower. One morning, the three of us crowded into the bathroom for the show. Dad provided a running commentary as Mom helped him execute a series of hazardous movements into the bathtub, onto a stool, and around the stool to expose his entire body to the water stream. And then out of the wet bathtub. They had discussed and elaborated every move over weeks of showers, with ever-new variations to compensate for his growing limitations. It was a bravado performance.

I was grateful to see my parents at their best. Dad choreographed these cooperative movements with a sure sense of how to maneuver his recalcitrant body, with irrepressible pride in their solutions to these tricky problems. I could see the strong, limber athlete he had been in high school and the precise scientist he had become. Mom followed his directions, pleased with his feeling of mastery and eager to help sustain his normal life. These were my courageous parents, overcoming adversity through their affection, ingenuity, and determination.

However, now that Dad was reluctant to walk alone, his need for assistance assumed disturbing new proportions. Every few minutes, he seemed to make some reasonable little request for help. Mom began to feel trapped.

"What will I do when you're gone?" she asked me late one evening after Dad was asleep. "I can't wait on him hand and foot."

And then, to my astonishment, she added, "He's cramping my style." This was the first I had heard of her "style."

Mom pressed Dad to remain as independent as possible. After careful planning for the trip, she was shaken by his fall in the condo parking lot just when she thought they had succeeded. But she would not concede that he needed a helping hand for every step. "Try it yourself and be careful," she would say as if the problem was his carelessness, not weakness.

ALS was transforming their lives, rendering him evermore dependent on her. Mom did not want her life changed like this. She made concessions to the disease only with the greatest reluctance. One moment, she would confide with a hush that she knew he had been weakening in recent weeks. The next, she would insist that he could still walk two blocks to the ocean like he had done the month before if only he had made a greater effort.

I thought Mom did not understand the fundamental truth of Dad's disease, the truth that I was beginning to grasp. Today's surprise new weakness and disability, regardless of whether Dad fought it, was tomorrow's way of life. Perhaps she could not afford to understand it, because she had to keep Dad going every day. She had to maintain her own hopes.

"Am I too tough on him?" she asked. "Tell me. You can see."

I didn't know. She pushed Dad much harder than me, demanding more independence from him, but by his own admission, he needed it. He had already confessed to me that he had continued working mainly because Mom had coaxed and cajoled him in the mornings. I was not ready to interfere with how they coped with ALS and kept peace with each other. I ducked the question.

But I couldn't entirely stay out of it. I had one furious clash with Mom over her reluctance to bend before the disease. When I heard her travel arrangements for their return to Skokie, I yelled, "That's the craziest plan I've ever heard."

She had them arriving at Chicago's O'Hare Field at midnight because they could not rush fast enough for a morning flight, and she wanted to avoid the afternoon rush hour crowds in Chicago. They would be fending for themselves at night in the airport. Dad would be exhausted, helpless, and irascible. Mom could not cope with him and that huge, pitiless airport.

Even if they somehow maneuvered through O'Hare, I knew she would try to get home on the airport bus. Thirty-dollar taxi rides were outside her world view, shaped in the Depression-era immigrant West

Side of Chicago. They would struggle into their cold, dark home in the middle of the night if they could get up the front steps without a disaster.

Mom was surprised by my reaction but undaunted. "Don't worry yourself," she replied. "The airport doesn't scare me."

I wouldn't stand for this nutty scheme. I demanded that they take an afternoon flight and that she arrange for someone to meet them at the airport. I could hear my voice breaking into a strange, excited pitch.

When she persisted, I dug deeper. "You're going to cause a fall." I imagined him sprawled out on an airport floor or tumbling down the front stairs to their house.

That was unfair, but I continued, "If you don't change the plan, I'm going to ask Rob to drive in from Madison to meet you at O'Hare."

That was playing my ace.

"Don't you dare! I don't want to disrupt Rob's life."

"I will!"

Her lips curved into a sly, knowing smile I had never seen. She played her ace. "Maybe you want to meet us at the airport."

That was a jolt. She knew I could not help them from California. I could only consider my own guilty feelings about Dad's falls, my absence, and my inability to make everything right.

I shut up. The next day, she arranged an afternoon flight, with a friend to pick them up at the airport. We did not discuss it again.

I worried least about Mom's good judgment and more about the chasm that was emerging between her and Dad. Despite their extraordinary cooperation, the love that had sustained them through the past half-year with ALS wasn't enough. An ominous crack had opened between them.

Mom stood on one side, eager to live and ready to do anything to make their life good, whatever Dad's disabilities, if only he would think positively and remain optimistic. On the other side stood Dad, preoccupied with his body's decline, raging against his limitations, subdued after falls, uncertain what to do, despairing that he could do nothing.

I worried, *How can they hold up together against this ALS onslaught?*

Dad no longer spoke about finding a cure for ALS. He had given up hope of rolling back the disease and recovering into his former good health. He had given this subject much thought. "Once I lose a muscle," he explained, "the muscle is gone forever. I can't get it back."

"We've got to stop this thing soon," he continued, "while I can still get around and lead a normal life. It's not too bad yet. I could be happy with my present condition."

I had avoided reading the psychological literature on dying, but I knew this was classic behavior. First denial, then anger, and now bargaining. He would concede past losses in exchange for future stability. Yes, he was ready for a reasonable compromise.

Dad had lost all faith in mainstream medicine. He dutifully went once a month for checkups at the MDA clinic. They gave him some light exercises to strengthen his "good muscles." But with each visit, he felt weaker and could do less, and the doctors always said they saw no significant change in his condition.

Nor would the doctors provide an estimate of how much time he had left. Dad already had learned to stop asking the doctors that nagging question, but he did ask me, knowing that I had read a lot about ALS.

It was a frightening question for me. I had already concluded he would not be among the lucky 20 percent who survived beyond five years with ALS. In fact, I had read an article citing an average two-year survival rate for men diagnosed in their sixties, but I could not assume he would be statistically average. I thought that a doctor experienced with ALS could determine how fast he was declining. Today, online, I can find functionality measures for speech, salivation, swallowing, movement of extremities, and breathing that calculate the progress of a patient's ALS. But at the time, over forty years ago, I could not answer the question with any confidence. With an awful feeling of deception,

I retreated to vagueness like Dad's doctors.

ALS required living with uncertainty. How fast were his muscles wasting away? What body functions are the next to go? How much suffering? When does he die? And with that uncertainty came fear . . . fear of what was next . . . fear that nothing could be done to stop this affliction and return us to normal. None of us had adapted to the uncertainty or fear.

Since my December visit to Skokie, Mom and Dad had embarked on a new possibility for resistance with holistic medicine. They had learned of a homeopath who had some success with ALS patients. Dad had been skeptical. Mom had been hopeful. She prevailed, and they went.

Dad's attempt to suspend disbelief collapsed when he saw how the homeopath prescribed vitamin supplements. He hooked Dad up to some machine, shook bottles of vitamin pills near Dad, watched a meter, and prescribed supplements for mineral deficiencies. "He didn't even touch my skin with the pills," Dad told me, shaking his head over this bogus science.

He believed he was in the clutches of a witch doctor. Mom wanted them to do the homeopath's diet recommendation. It was close to the modified Pritikin diet they had been following, but with the addition of periodic three-day fasts to cleanse Dad's body of impurities.

Mom wanted to try a fast while I was visiting. It sounded big and dramatic, just the thing to drive those ALS bugs from his body. Dad was reluctant, but he hesitated to forgo even this remote possibility of help.

I thought a three-day fast was too extreme for someone in his condition. It also seemed like cruel therapy since food was one of Dad's few remaining bodily pleasures. His relish for food had increased even as the disease atrophied his muscles and wasted his body. He was reduced by over ten pounds in recent months, from lost muscle mass, but his stomach had a satisfied plump curve.

We agreed on a one-day fast for the three of us. The homeopath allowed citrus fruit drinks, so the day before the big fast, Mom and I went on an expedition to roadside stands. We returned with bags full of oranges, grapefruits, and tangelos. That fruit had a bright, healthy, curative look.

The next day, Dad and I acceded to Mom's citrus juice breakfast with much cheerful complaining. Then, a citrus juice lunch and a citrus fruit dinner. The day stretched on, bland and blurred, without our periodic gatherings for food. I felt bad for Dad, first with this pernicious disease, and now we couldn't eat. It was kind of sad, as if we were doing penance for sins.

Dad went to bed uncomplaining that evening. I admired his resolution, but I could think of nothing but food. I was fixated on the hunk of lamb in the refrigerator, leftover from yesterday's pre-fast feast. *That succulent lamb*, I thought, *had already violated any variation of the Pritikin diet, so why not have some more?* I retained a shred of honor by waiting until one minute after midnight, the official end of the fast, and then I raided the refrigerator.

Despite my transgression, I found the fast strangely satisfying. At least we had done something to fight the disease. Something was better than nothing. But there was no sign it had the slightest effect on Dad.

Before the end of my Florida visit, I managed to establish contact with someone Dad did believe in for treatment of ALS. A half-year earlier, in the weeks following the diagnosis, they had heard of Dr. Murray Sanders and his ALS treatment with a controversial cobra venom serum. By sheer coincidence, Dr. Sanders was located in Boca Raton, a few miles from the condo. During the past half-year, they had called several times, but a secretary always told them that Dr. Sanders was not accepting new patients.

I called again during my visit, determined to reach Dr. Sanders. Representing myself as Dr. Kann, I talked my way through to him. I described Dad's circumstances and stressed our proximity. To my surprise, I convinced Dr. Sanders to see Dad. It was a triumph. We were excited.

The Sanders Foundation was located in a small office building on the edge of downtown Boca Raton. On entering, it looked respectable, with a receptionist and a well-appointed waiting room. Dr. Sanders came out to meet us. An elderly gentleman in a sports coat and tie, he was friendly and soft-spoken.

Dr. Sanders escorted us back to his office, explaining that his main research laboratory was in another building. I imagined an antiseptic glass and steel structure, with serious young scientists in white lab coats pouring over microscopes. Perhaps it was close to a swamp, near the snakes that provided the serum.

My attention was drawn to a large chart on an easel showing statistics on patients, medication, and longevity. It promised life, as did the small vials on a nearby shelf, which I presumed to be the famed cobra venom serum.

Dr. Sanders directed the first question to me, and I nodded to Dad, who took over. He represented himself as a chemist with a responsible position at a large manufacturing concern. It was a fine self-description, substantial without being pompous. I liked the sound of Dad in this office.

Dad narrated his case history clearly and concisely, from the first symptoms to the present. He was entirely factual without a trace of self-pity. I was already glad we came if only to hear this ten-minute presentation. He was the most self-assured, confident, and reasonably forceful I had seen him through my entire visit. Here was my real Dad. I remembered that this was how he presented himself to colleagues at my December visit to his workplace. It told me again that he must continue his life outside the home, in the world, where he would be truly himself. He must continue working.

Dr. Sanders explained his success in treating ALS patients. He didn't claim a cure, but he was convinced that those who used his cobra venom serum had significantly greater longevity than the average ALS patient. Pointing to that large, reassuring chart for proof, he told Dad that a few of his patients actually had recovered the use of muscles once atrophied.

However, the Food and Drug Administration had recently ruled that there was not evidence to support Dr. Sanders, and he could not take new patients for the snake venom serum. Dr. Sanders thought there might be a reversal based on new data he had submitted to the FDA. In any event, he was considering continuing the program outside the US, perhaps on a Caribbean island.

Dr. Sanders had a reassuring presence. When we entered the office, he showed concern for Dad by directing him away from a chair near the chill of the air conditioner. He listened carefully to Dad's story and expressed great concern for the danger of falls. When he complimented Dad's perseverance in continuing to work, Dad broke down in tears.

Tears again! Where did they come from? I had never seen him cry before ALS.

Dr. Sanders was like a grandfatherly family doctor, the kind who would make warm and reassuring home visits and say, "Now, now, everything will be fine." He seemed to take a personal interest in Dad as a human being, not just as another ALS statistic. I thought Dad might be better off under Dr. Sanders's kind care, cobra venom serum or not. This man was a healer.

Dr. Sanders said he liked Dad and wanted to help if possible. He was especially interested because Dad was still in "good condition," an assessment at once comforting that Dad was not degenerating quickly, yet chilling in its sinister implication that if we did not act soon, there would be a "bad condition." Dr. Sanders suggested that Dad call him in a week, before returning to Chicago.

Outside, I was exhilarated. I had found our first real possibility for treatment since the diagnosis six months before.

Before I could celebrate, Dad broke down in rage and despair. Crying, with his face twisted in agonized helplessness, he cursed the Washington bureaucrats who had prevented him from getting that cobra venom serum.

I was startled. Dr. Sanders had made me hopeful, but beyond his assurances, we knew nothing about the serum or the controversy around it. We had not even thought to ask about the cost, let alone consider the logistics of living in Florida for treatment. And here Dad was, ready to shoot that cobra serum in his arm at the first opportunity . . . today. What happened to his realism? His skepticism? His science? This was my first recognition of his utter desperation.

I promised Dad I would research Dr. Sanders when I returned to California. A week later, the day I first found an article on the cobra venom serum controversy, Mom called from Skokie. "Dr. Sanders will take Dad as a patient in two weeks."

I was swept with apprehension. I was scared for Mom and Dad. What had I gotten us into? Cobra venom serum! The danger, the cost, and the move to Florida. What had I gotten us into?

I wanted to stop Dad from falling. I couldn't.

I wanted Dad to be strong and brave. He was, often, but not as often as I wished.

I wanted a way to resist ALS. I found one.

CHAPTER 4

The Cobra Venom Serum

SPRING 1980

The week after they returned home was a nightmare. Dad caught a cold. He could not blow his nose himself. Mom could not help, not how he wanted. It became a crisis.

Mom tried to explain their turmoil. Dad could not clear his nose of mucus because he could not lift either hand to his nostrils. Mom tried everything. She held his hand with a handkerchief up to his nostrils, held the handkerchief up to his nostrils, and dug the handkerchief into his nostrils to clear them. She could not satisfy him.

Dad was exasperated. He was furious. He became frantic as he could not blow his nose. Mom reacted. They had some terrible fights. She told me it was "unreal," that she never had experienced anything like it.

Mom asked me to speak to Dad about his preoccupation with the cold. I assured him the cold would pass and urged him to persevere, but problems with the telephone interfered. With weakened hands and arms, he could not hold the receiver to his ear, and Mom could not place it as he wanted.

I heard him shout, "*Ann*. Hold it *up!*"

"I'm *trying*, Sammy."

"Aaach." Then he snarled. "This is impossible." They hung up. The dependence on Mom. His wounded pride. His temper again.

I had a bad thought: *I will never be able to keep up with ALS.*

I had left Florida confident that I understood the current situation, particularly Dad's falling. I was certain their most pressing problems would be solved when Dad found a walking aid. Suddenly, this new set of strange problems exploded.

The ALS literature warned about the dangers of colds for the ALS patient's compromised respiratory system. But nothing had prepared me for this bizarre combination of his stuffed nose, weakened arms, and emotional clashes. Like the first reports of Dad falling, I could not picture the problem, not even on the telephone with them while it occurred, let alone solve it. The moment I left them in Florida, events passed me by.

I was puzzled by Dad's frenzy over a stuffed nose, but I was more distressed by Mom's disarray. During my Florida visit, she already felt chained to him as he requested help with every step. Then, this cold brought a suffocating dependence on her every few minutes, day and night.

Mom was also unsettled by the prospect of returning to Florida in a few weeks for the cobra venom serum treatments. Another cross-country journey filled her with apprehension. She feared several months "cooped up" with Dad in the condo, trapped, while Dr. Sanders would determine the correct dosage of his serum.

She was squeamish about her coming duty: inject the cobra venom serum. Dr. Sanders allowed his patients to return home after a six-week initiation period in Boca Raton. He would mail the serum, and the patient was responsible for injections. That would be Mom's job. Despite her lifelong fears of disease, she faced the prospect of becoming Dad's nurse, complete with sticking needles in his body.

If she had to do it, she insisted, she would. Mom was game.

But it was too much. Dad's cold crisis precipitated a collapse of her own. She caught the cold. Then, she developed a turbulent stomach and was unable to hold down food. She became exhausted. On the telephone one evening, she confided her fear that she had cancer. Beset by her worst devils, she admitted, "I'm not sure I can handle this."

Mom's illness frightened me. If she became sick, if she could not cope, who would care for him? They would still not consider calling on me or my brothers for help, interrupting our lives. That was crucial. That was their way. Never bother the boys. Instead, they began talking about sinking together.

What did "sinking" mean? I didn't know. But for one, they considered placing Dad in a nursing facility.

That upset me. Until then, I had offered steady reassurance that Dad's cold would pass, and Mom was healthy. Now I insisted, or perhaps I yelled, that no one would sink, and Dad would not go into a nursing facility. I threatened to fly home.

The next day, Rob came to Skokie for a chance visit. No one had told him about the cold. He relieved Mom of nursing responsibilities. He told me the three days at home had left him exhausted. He had never seen Mom and Dad so low, so bitterly at odds, so scared. But he gave them the support and rest they needed. Suddenly, Mom was on the phone warning me against flying to Chicago and chiding me for feeling guilty about my distance from home.

Looking back, I wonder if the problem was not just a stuffed nose but his lungs filling with mucus. He might have needed much more strenuous pushing on his abdomen or even a cough assist machine to loosen the mucus by pushing air into his abdomen.

That cold gave us a terrifying glimpse into our future with ALS. All the ingredients were there: Dad's frightening new ALS problem and frantic reaction, Mom's tentative assistance and boiling anxieties, and the possibility that everything would spin out of their control. From California, I followed that cold—worried and helpless.

The crisis passed the next week as antibiotics smothered their infections, and they adapted to the new ALS problems with colds. They both resumed working—back to normal, or as much as they could resume their normal lives. I thought, *So brave.*

In the aftermath, Mark located nursing services that could provide relief for Mom. I began thinking that in the near future, they might need a son around all the time. As I reflected on their living arrangements in Skokie and Boca Raton, I suggested they also consider moving to Oakland, where the weather was mild and I could help them.

Yes, I could offer my own California refuge. I didn't consider how that would work, eliminating the 2,200 miles I had placed between them and me. This was a crisis. They were stunned. I wanted to take care of them, protect them, like comforting hurt and puzzled children. These were strange new feelings for me.

As we were settling down after the cold, they called the Sanders Clinic for the treatment dates. They were shocked to learn that Dr. Sanders had no understanding of a definite arrangement to treat Dad. He said that he was waiting for FDA approval for new patients. He suggested they call back in a few weeks.

That was a blow. Dad was ready to begin. He had been ready since the meeting with Dr. Sanders in Boca Raton. I thought he should fight the disease however he could. I believed he should try the cobra venom serum. Probably should. Possibly should. Well, why not?

Actually, I didn't know what he should do.

But I knew what I had to do: find out if Dr. Sanders could and should treat Dad. I plunged into research on ALS, Dr. Sanders, and his cobra venom serum.

I made a first attempt to learn about ALS in the weeks following the diagnosis when I read pamphlets sent by the ALS Society, an organization for patients and families. I quickly ended that investigation as I became absorbed by Dad's actual ALS developments.

The period between my December visit to Skokie and the March visit to Florida had been a lull in the storm. Dad's disease was progressing, they had the MDA clinic for medical support, and they were coping with the ALS symptoms. I felt that I should be preparing for what was to come, but I didn't know what to do. Now, I had a concrete research goal: determine the effectiveness of the cobra venom serum.

I began with another investigation into this extraordinary disease. In repeated descriptions of ALS, I read that it was a neuromuscular disease, today referred to as a "neurodegenerative" disease, affecting the motor neurons. These were the mysterious nerve cells, extending from the brain to the spinal cord, that control the voluntary muscles throughout the body. For unknown reasons, probably genetic and environmental, the motor neurons gradually degenerated and died. They stopped signaling the muscles. The muscles progressively shrank and atrophied. They wasted away, leading to stiffness, slowness, and eventually paralysis. Literally, the acronym "ALS" stands for no (A) muscle (MYO) nourishment (TROPHIC) resulting from hardening (SCLEROSIS) of areas in the side portions (LATERAL) of the spinal cord where the motor neurons signal the muscles.

ALS is among the rare neurodegenerative diseases. About 5,000 Americans are diagnosed with it each year. An estimated 12,000–15,000 Americans may be living with it at any time.

This condition could make insidious progress for months and years without notice because other nerve cells would compensate for the lost motor neurons until a third to a half were gone. Eventually, the remaining functional cells became overloaded.

"Spinal onset" ALS involves the death of the motor neurons in the brain stem and spinal cord, the lower motor neurons. It begins with a variety of subtle symptoms: body fatigue, weakness of arms or legs, sluggish fingers, fasciculations of the muscles, stumbling, muscle cramping, and muscle atrophy. It can show up in difficulty grasping a pen, opening a food can, or stepping off a curb. Dad had first noticed shoulder stiffness while playing golf the previous summer, June 1979. There was no straightforward certain diagnosis at the beginning, but these symptoms and examination of the patient's body and the muscles, along with differentiating tests for similar motor neuron diseases, could lead to an accurate diagnosis.

To this day, over forty years after Dad's diagnosis, I monitor myself for these first faint signs of ALS. Any stumble—a possible dropped foot—any stiffness or muscle weakness, still gets my attention for this terrifying disease.

Another form of ALS, known as "bulbar onset," involves motor neurons in the brain, the upper motor neurons. The failure of these motor neurons affects emotional response, along with speech, eating, and breathing. It can begin with slurred words, swallowing problems, or uncontrolled excessive laughing and crying. I didn't give attention to this form of ALS at the beginning because Dad seemed to have "spinal onset" with prominent weakening of arms and legs. But bulbar ALS soon presented us with a staggering set of other problems affecting Dad's vital functions like talking, eating, and breathing.

Today, thinking about Dad's volatile emotional responses from the time of his diagnosis, his frustration, anger, and crying, I wonder if the bulbar form was actually prominent through the entire course of his ALS.

I learned that the disease progressed in varying, seemingly capricious ways. Sometimes, ALS begins with muscles in the extremities, the hands and feet, gradually working toward the trunk. In other forms, it starts with the muscles that affect speech, swallowing, and coughing. Either way, ALS means progressive muscle weakness and paralysis, and it usually spreads to other parts of the body. Most victims are eventually unable to move their arms and legs, lose the capacity to speak and swallow food, and begin to lose the ability to breathe on their own. ALS is devastating, but you have to witness it develop to grasp the destruction of its victims.

In the final stages, ALS often weakens the skeletal muscles responsible for breathing. ALS patients typically die of respiratory failure from the weakness of those muscles, like stopping breathing during sleep, or from a secondary respiratory ailment like pneumonia.

Life expectancy also depends on the rate of deterioration of swallowing muscles. Weakening of those muscles can lead to an earlier death through malnutrition and dehydration.

Strange to me, ALS did not affect involuntary muscles controlling the eyes, the bowels, the sphincter, the bladder, sexual functions, or internal organs like the heart muscle and liver. It did not affect the senses: the ability to see, hear, taste, smell, and feel.

Also strange was that ALS, a devastating disease, is largely painless. That somehow increased the horror for me, like a silent scream in a nightmare. *How could it inflict such misery*, I thought, *without pain?*

The cause of ALS was not known at the time of Dad's diagnosis, and it still is not known. For the 10 percent of ALS that is genetic, various mutated genes have been identified as causing an accumulation of abnormal proteins in the brain, leading to the death of motor neurons and neurodegenerative disease.

Environmental factors were also identified as causes, giving me much speculation about Dad. Exposure to heavy metals like lead, mercury, or other toxic substances is regularly identified as a possible cause of ALS. Although Dad denied any such contact in his long career as a chemist, this was my prime suspect.

Smoking was another possible contributor. Dad had this habit since childhood, one that he never completely kicked, as I was surprised to learn in December when we first visited his workplace. Looking at our family pictures today, I am surprised by how many show Dad with a cigarette lodged between his fingers, ready for the next puff.

Head trauma has also been considered a risk factor for ALS and other neurodegenerative diseases. These are diseases that afflict retired football players with brain injuries from playing the game.

That brings me to speculation about what actually happened in a mysterious auto accident Dad and Mom had suffered months before the diagnosis. "Mysterious" because their car was totally destroyed without any involvement of another car. Dad crashed it when he hit a guardrail on a Florida freeway. Apparently, they had walked away miraculously unharmed. But did Dad bang his head, precipitating the ALS?

Looking back, I think ALS had already weakened Dad's arms on the steering wheel, without him telling anyone, causing the accident. At the time, Dad attributed his loss of control of the car to being tired. But years later, I learned that a few weeks before the auto accident, he had fallen while walking down the basement stairs. He missed a step, another health secret kept from his kids. His shoulder weakness playing golf, the auto crash, and the fall on the stairs all seem to me like pernicious early indications of failing muscles in his arms and feet. *ALS.*

ALS most frequently struck white men over sixty. Dad was a typical case with diagnosis at sixty-four.

There was no known cure for ALS, then or now. There is no known way to stop its progression. That was the most difficult feature for me to absorb. There was no way for us to fix this problem and save Dad. That's what led me to Dr. Sanders and his cobra venom serum.

In 1980, the ALS survival rate typically was two to five years from diagnosis. It is the same today.

ALS is an extremely variable disease. Among those with spinal onset ALS, some 10 percent survived longer than ten years with a very slow progressing form. Steven Hawking, an anomaly, lived with ALS for over fifty years. Mom and Dad hoped for ten years at the outset.

Hawking had an extraordinarily active mind and a positive mental outlook, exactly what Mom wanted from Dad. However, there is no evidence that lifestyle or psychological well-being added to Hawking's unique longevity.

When Dad was diagnosed in 1979, there was no drug treatment for ALS. Since FDA approval in 1995, the medication Rilutek has been used for ALS and may increase survival by a few months. Radiclava, another drug treatment approved by the FDA twenty-two years later, is also thought to slow ALS progression by a quarter to a third for some patients. Today, I regard several more months with ALS as cold comfort for ALS patients and their families.

Like the present, when Dad had ALS, it was treated as a medical management problem, addressing symptoms and support to improve quality of life and prolong survival. ALS symptoms varied among patients and developed unpredictably. Treatment was usually through multidisciplinary teams of medical professionals like Dad had at the Evanston MDA clinic. It included neurology, physical and speech and occupational therapy, social work and psychology, devices to assist with body movement, nutrition and diet, feeding tube options, help for respiratory weakness, and palliative care. Good management of ALS could improve the quality and length of a patient's life.

Treatment also included early discussion of end-of-life care to avoid unwanted interventions and allow a peaceful death. When I later met Dad's neurologist at the MDA clinic, Dr. Nicholas Vick, I learned that my parents had some early discussions with him about the end stage of ALS. In July 1980, during a visit with my parents, I had my own startling discussion with Dr. Vick about Dad's end-of-life options.

It's not surprising that many doctors simply wrote off ALS patients as goners they could not help. Shirley Knight, in *A Journey Through Fire*, a nurse's memoir of her husband's death from ALS, recalls his neurologist prefacing disclosure of the diagnosis with a nervous joke: "I hope you are a religious man" (Knight 2011, 12). Archie J. Hanlan, in *Autobiography of Dying*, recounted an initial week of hospital testing with no explanation for why, and then at discharge, receiving a brutally precise account of the forthcoming atrophy of his muscles and how it would affect his bodily functions (Hanlan 1979, 15-16).

Mom, like me, was irate toward their family physician. He had given Dad the death sentence diagnosis over the telephone. We considered it a cold, cowardly act, one that neither of us ever forgave.

Dad never complained about that communication. Dad might have invited it with his desire for the truth about his condition, his courage from the outset, and his insistence on being realistic. But after his initial pride in having been seen at the famous Mayo Clinic and pride in the immensity of his disease, when he understood that he would receive no help to cure or halt ALS, he became contemptuous of doctors, ridiculing their white coats, technology, and strange medical language. For all their inflated importance, doctors could not help him get rid of this thing.

Dad rarely spoke with contempt about his own doctors, perhaps because they were so responsive to help with his ALS symptoms. He approved of his neurologist, Dr. Vick, as blunt and to the point, and he liked discussing ALS with Dr. Vick. When they requested that Dr. Vick give Dad the injections of the cobra venom serum, he refused, citing studies he believed had shown conclusively that the cobra venom serum did not work. That frankness didn't disturb Dad.

Dad was angry with the doctors in our own family, whose support he expected. A young nephew, who, correctly, had first suggested that Dad see a neurologist about weakness in his legs, never visited Dad after the ALS diagnosis. Another nephew, an eminent surgeon, never even called to express sympathy. Dad repeatedly told the story of how both these doctors were at a family gathering with him a few months after the diagnosis, and neither came over to speak with him about ALS.

ALS was a test for everyone. Lack of family loyalty over ALS was unforgivable to Dad.

With a better grasp of ALS, in April 1980, I called the Food and Drug Administration for information on Dr. Sanders's cobra venom serum. I soon discovered it was a "modified neurotoxin," a biologic that derives from a living source rather than a drug manufactured from chemicals. Its effectiveness and safety fell under the jurisdiction of the Bureau of Biologics, a department of the National Institute of Health. The FDA regulated the use of biologics.

At the Bureau of Biologics, I reached a Dr. Elaine Esber, who was alarmed about my inquiry into the cobra venom serum. According to Dr. Esber, Dr. Sanders had been administering his cobra venom serum for some eighteen years—to over 1,000 patients—without following "clinical protocol." He had conducted no controlled trials, that is, no double-blind tests in which one group received the neurotoxin and a control group received a placebo. Dr. Sanders's patients, after an initial six weeks of direct contact with him about using the cobra venom serum, went home. They received the serum by mail and administered it themselves.

The serum contained venom from two snakes: the cobra and the krait. The theory, according to Dr. Sanders, was that his modified neurotoxin protected the motor neurons that were under attack by an unknown agent. Dr. Sanders claimed that his neurotoxin prolonged patient survival and could improve functional capacity. He had not claimed a cure.

Dr. Esber told me the NIH sponsored the first two double-blind studies of Dr. Sanders's snake venom serum in 1978. These two studies found no evidence of any patient benefit from the neurotoxin: no increased longevity and no improvement in body functions.

The FDA immediately followed in 1979 with a request that Dr. Sanders take no new patients for uncontrolled studies and banned interstate shipment of his neurotoxin. It did not prohibit Dr. Sanders's 100 remaining patients from continuing their cobra venom serum treatments, but most discontinued treatment after the FDA contacted them about the two studies' findings and Dr. Sanders's treatment practices.

I asked Dr. Esber whether Dr. Sanders could provide treatment for my father in Florida, without interstate shipment of the neurotoxin. I thought Dad may want to try the cobra venom serum despite the negative findings. She seemed to evade my question by repeating that the FDA had requested Dr. Sanders take no new patients.

She was more forthcoming when I asked why patients claimed to feel improved when they received Dr. Sanders's neurotoxin. She explained that it could be a placebo effect, a self-induced optimism resulting from any treatment, or the result of Dr. Sanders's caring attitude. But she insisted there was no scientific evidence that the modified neurotoxin led to longer survival rates or improved condition.

Dr. Esber referred me to a transcript of the previous year's FDA workshop on Dr. Sanders's cobra venom serum and the recent double-blind studies. When I gave her my office address at UC Berkeley, she surprised me by initiating another discussion.

In the future, she said, I should use my "professor" title when seeking medical information. I actually was not a professor—my official academic title was visiting lecturer, the lowest possible rung on the UC faculty scale, a remote relative of professor. But she began speaking with me in a more conversational tone as if I was an errant colleague who simply needed some straight talk to get back on track. She suggested that I contact neurological research institutions and place my father's name on the lists of ALS patients available for legitimate experimental drug programs.

I decided to reserve judgment on the cobra venom serum until I read the FDA workshop transcript. I was satisfied just to have been treated as a credible inquirer, and I vowed to use a professor title in the future.

But I felt sick over not having investigated mainstream ALS experimental drug testing programs. How could I have ignored it? By now, I could have entered Dad into some legitimate drug experiment to cure ALS. I realized that's what I should have been doing after the diagnosis five months prior. But it wasn't too late.

I called Dad that evening to assure him I was investigating the cobra venom serum. I urged that we also explore mainstream experimental drug programs. Knowing his desperation, I thought he would be enthusiastic.

He immediately rejected the idea. He did not want to participate in a double-blind study, in which he would not know if he was receiving the actual experimental drug. Even if he did receive the drug, he did not want to be the subject of an experiment.

"It's too dangerous," he insisted. "I'm too weak to take risks."

That surprised me. I had read about ALS patients willing to accept great risk in drug experimentation because the disease was so deadly. But Dad's desperation had brought him to self-protection, not to risk.

However, Dad's desperation, I thought, was causing him to ignore his own scientific rigor in assessing Dr. Sanders. He was convinced that Dr. Sanders knew more about ALS than anyone else. He believed the snake venom serum had proven power of widespread use over many years to improve ALS patients. He did not consider it experimental. While I was finding Dr. Sanders less credible and his serum doubtful, Dad's faith in him was not shaken.

Waiting for the FDA workshop transcript, I found a 1979 scientific article by one of the investigators, Dr. Richard Tyler, about the double-blind study he had conducted on Dr. Sanders's modified neurotoxin. He concluded, "We did not find any objective, meaningful improvement in the course of motor neuron disease . . . and we saw no effect on longevity in patients who received neurotoxin" (Tyler 1979, 80).

Dr. Tyler ended his article with a sharp criticism of Dr. Sanders for uncontrolled research methods and unsubstantiated claims. Patients with "hopeless progressive disabling disease," Dr. Tyler noted, will learn "through the patients' grapevine and press reports" of any medication that offers stabilization or improvement. These patients will want that treatment as soon as possible. "Physicians who believe they have a medication of interest," he continued, "must accept the responsibility for seeing that valid studies are performed prior to making unsubstantiated statements that precipitate crisis." He concluded, "To raise false hope, which results in economic and social sacrifice by families and patients, and removes patients from the supportive care of their primary physician and neurologist, cannot be condoned" (Tyler 1979, 81).

Strong stuff for a medical science paper, I thought. *That could be our family Dr. Tyler was describing, the potential patient victims of Dr. Sanders.* But I needed a treatment for Dad. I was not ready to give up on the cobra venom serum.

Then, I received the transcript of the 1979 NIH workshop on Dr. Sanders's neurotoxin. There before me in the transcript was our story again, from the scientific perspective, in accessible language: the essential features of ALS, formerly called motor neuron disease; the grim outlook for men in their sixties with the disease; the unproved theories as to the continuing mystery of the cause of ALS; the centrality of respiratory failure at the end of ALS lives; the healing properties of snake venoms for the human neuromuscular system; the characteristics of Dr. Sanders's modified neurotoxin; the two recent double-blind studies of Dr. Sanders's serum.

Dr. Sanders was a speaker for one hearing session on his clinical experience with his modified neurotoxin treatment for ALS. In this gathering of largely neurology medical scientists, Dr. Sanders was notable among the speakers for expressing his feelings for ALS patients. He characterized ALS as "cruel, gruesome, and heartbreaking." He described the typical ALS patient as "a very fine person" and lamented, "They do not know what hit them." His neurotoxin, he believed, had significantly inhibited the advance of ALS in his patients. He argued that his neurotoxin, while causing no harm, offered the only available treatment for ALS (Bureau of Biologics, Workshop on Modified Neurotoxin, 80-104).

Reading the transcript of the 1979 NIH workshop on the cobra venom serum, I admired Dr. Sanders's sympathy for ALS patients. It reminded me of our visit at his office, the sympathy he had shown for Dad, my feeling he was a healer, and our desperate hopes for his help.

However, I knew that the FDA and these scientists were scrutinizing the most recent evidence, the two recent double-blind studies, not sympathy. The evidence at this meeting offered no support for Dr. Sanders and his cobra venom serum. The FDA summarized the workshop findings in a sentence: "The vast majority of participants concluded that there was no evidence that MN [modified neurotoxin] treatment improves patients with ALS or comprises even a partial treatment of the disease" (Bureau of Biologics, Executive Summary, Workshop on Modified Neurotoxin, 3).

In a 1979 letter to Dr. Sanders's patients, the FDA described its long history of differences with Dr. Sanders and the findings of these two recent double-blind studies of the modified neurotoxin: "Neither doctor had observed functional improvement, stabilization, or prolongation of survival in the treated as compared to the placebo group." The FDA reported telling Dr. Sanders, "The continued expansion of inadequately monitored, uncontrolled clinical trials is unjustified." It allowed the continuation of treatment only for those current patients who elected to continue after hearing from the FDA (Meyer to patients of Dr. Murray Sanders, May 23, 1979).

I had read and heard enough to conclude that we should not proceed further with Dr. Sanders. But I needed something, anything, that might help Dad. I still would not give up on the cobra venom serum. Here was my desperation. I had no other treatment option.

I made another call to the Bureau of Biologics. Given Dad's belief in Dr. Sanders, I had to clarify if there was some way for him to receive treatment from Dr. Sanders as a new patient.

Specifically, I wanted to know if Dr. Sanders could treat patients in Florida despite the FDA's request that he take no new patients. I also wanted to see whether there was an FDA arrangement for Dr. Sanders to conduct further experimental treatment, as Dad and Mom believed.

This time, I reached a Mr. Cipriano, some kind of FDA bureaucrat, I figured. He was not a bit collegial on this second call, even with my professor title.

He insisted that the NIH was not reconsidering its position on the modified neurotoxin, that the hearing was final, and that no new evidence was under consideration. He repeated that the FDA had asked Dr. Sanders to take no new patients for uncontrolled study and prohibited the shipment of his neurotoxin across state lines. But, on my close questioning, he reluctantly conceded that Dr. Sanders could administer the snake venom serum under Florida state law.

I called Dr. Sanders and reviewed my discussions with the FDA. He urged me to request a copy of his critique of the workshop on the neurotoxin, which neither person at the NIH had mentioned. He insisted he had new data pending before the Bureau of Biologics, he planned to take on new patients, and Washington bureaucrats were disorganized. Besides, he was considering moving his program offshore, perhaps to Bermuda. Dr. Sanders told me he had a new monkey experiment in the works, and he was investigating another drug for the treatment of ALS. As for FDA approval of his administering the neurotoxin in Florida, my report was the first he had heard of it. If I could get that in writing, he assured me he would treat my father.

This was, finally, as far as I would go with Dr. Sanders. I saw no likelihood of him treating Dad soon. I was left in the position of lobbying the FDA to allow him to administer the cobra venom serum to Dad. His talk of going offshore with patient treatment in the Caribbean and trying another drug inspired only my skepticism.

I was surprised by my own persistence amid all these "NO" signs when seeking Dad's treatment by Dr. Sanders. But I knew the reason: Dad wanted that cobra venom serum. I had nothing better to offer.

I called home to report my findings to Dad. I was proud of my quick, effective investigation, fearless calls to the FDA and Dr. Sanders, and carefully balanced conclusions. This one time, I used my historian's research tools to help Dad. But I was apprehensive. This was the worst possible news about Dr. Sanders.

On the other end of this telephone call, Dad was dissatisfied with how Mom was holding the phone for him. Welcome back to our real-world ALS. He quickly lost patience with my detailed report about who I spoke with, what I read, and how I evaluated it. "Just yes or no. Will he treat me?"

Startled, I hesitated. That, after all, was Dad's question, not what I did, not even whether the treatment would be effective. I did not want to disappoint him. But I could not feed his hopes about Dr. Sanders.

I replied, "It's unlikely. I don't think the FDA will approve more treatment with the snake venom serum. And I don't think Dr. Sanders has a plan for a new study or new patients."

"That bastard."

They hung up.

This was a terrible blow for Dad. It was his final hope for treatment. But I did not see how Dr. Sanders's snake venom serum could help Dad. The FDA had found no evidence that it had any beneficial effect on the treatment of ALS patients. After Dr. Sanders's long use of it on hundreds of patients, I thought it unlikely his neurotoxin would be harmful. But I concluded there was no chance the FDA would authorize Dr. Sanders to take Dad as a new patient for treatment with the snake venom serum. There would only be more disappointment for us. We had to break off contact with Dr. Sanders.

I did not follow up with a request for written permission from the FDA for Dr. Sanders to treat Dad in Florida. I did not believe I would receive that written permission, nor did I want it. And I did not search for another experimental drug program. Dad did not want to be in an ALS experiment. And, as time has proved, in 1980, Dad did not miss any effective new drug treatment.

I asked Mom to shield Dad from any further well-intentioned suggestions by relatives and friends of experimental cures for ALS. Those suggestions continued, and Mom passed them on to me. I followed up on them all, including a chiropractor offering holistic healing and a doctor who had a high-tech spinal implant in place of dying motor neurons that emitted electrical surges to stimulate nerve impulses to the muscles. I continued to search current ALS publications for any new treatment that was promising and possible.

I accumulated a thick file of information on current human experimentation for ALS. But I never again discussed a drug treatment with Dad.

Dad gave up hope for a cure or a halt to the advance of his ALS. I'm not sure Mom ever had that hope. I felt awful about ending this possibility with Dr. Sanders. But I didn't believe he could stop the ALS juggernaut. And I didn't believe he could treat Dad. I owed Dad the truth.

After the crisis with Dad's cold and the snake venom fiasco, Dad seemed to decline even faster. Speaking with him on the telephone in early May, I realized his voice sounded oddly raspy. Mom thought it was the evil cold lingering. I thought it could be the onset of respiratory problems.

I was shocked that the disease could already be moving into this new area. It seemed just a short time since the diagnosis, though over half a year had passed. I thought we needed more time to recover from Dr. Sanders and the events of recent weeks. This wasn't fair. But ALS presented nothing but relentless, nasty surprises to my notion of justice.

Within days, I learned that Dad was having difficulty clearing phlegm from his throat. The problem did not go away over the following weeks. At the MDA clinic, they reported to Dr. Vick that Dad was constantly clearing his throat and spitting up phlegm. Dr. Vick responded that he saw no significant change from previous visits. The throat-clearing problem was irritating, but it did not seem to weaken Dad. They returned home reassured.

I received other reports of different parts of Dad's body weakening. One day, it was the legs. They tried a cane, which did not help, and quickly found its way to the basement. Mom ordered a wheelchair designed for Dad's body for his mobility away from home. While it was being built, they received a loaner wheelchair that Dad refused to use and banished to the basement.

Another day, his right arm was weakening, with the left arm "close to gone." He still could "sort of eat by himself," with Mom half-feeding him. He was eating heartily, but he continued to lose weight as his muscles wasted.

Then, for me, came a report of another unimaginable problem: his neck had difficulty holding up his head. Those neck muscles were dying too. *How can that be?* I wondered. *What is it like to be unable to hold up your own head?* I couldn't imagine it. But this was nothing unusual for ALS. The MDA clinic gave him a neck brace that helped.

Everything was becoming more difficult, even sleep. Now he needed help rolling over in bed with tangled covers, temperature fluctuations, and taking a pee and another pee two or three times a night. There was no sound sleep for Dad or Mom. The nights had become difficult.

I had read about these problems in the ALS literature, but the words on paper did not help me grasp what they meant in real life. Hearing about them on the telephone, with graphic descriptions of the limitations that accompanied each body loss, helped me more. But I needed to see these problems to grasp them.

The clashes between Dad and Mom increased. The battlefields were often bizarre, that is, strange ALS fights over Mom's assistance, that he never found satisfactory. They had a furious dispute over how she buttered a bagel for Dad. I never did understand what happened, but he yelled at her, while she nonchalantly brushed it off as frustration. "This will pass." From California, at the other end of the telephone call, I could not picture what I was hearing.

Dad needed more and more assistance, and Mom found it restricting. She still didn't mind cleaning him after those "acts of nature," but she resented his detailed demands for how to do daily grooming with teeth, shaving, hair, and cleaning out his ears and nose. Their days and nights were becoming geared to Dad's needs as his body shut down. He needed her help for everything he wanted to do, and he resented help that was not exactly as he wanted.

"I'm doing the best I can," she insisted. And she was. As he became more demanding, she resisted. She fought back.

He had been courageous for months after the diagnosis: searching out how to resist ALS, continuing his work, and talking with family and friends about ALS. But now he was becoming frustrated and discouraged.

Mom wanted him to be positive. She told him to be more cheerful, and he was some days. But he lashed out at his condition, angry over his slipping control and disappearing independence, with self-pity too. He told me, "What did I do to deserve this?"

I learned that Rabbi Stern from their congregation visited, and Dad had a good discussion with him about Jewish history. I also heard that Dad cried during the rabbi's visit. I was receiving regular reports from Mom and my brothers about his crying. I continued to wonder, *Why all this crying?* I suspected two answers: after the Sanders snake venom episode, he was encountering the terrible truth that he was dying, and, possibly, he had bulbar ALS, causing heightened emotional responses. I had to see for myself on the next visit home.

I still thought a resistance stance was best for him. I did not believe he could win against ALS. But fight the disease every day. Live your life however you can. Do your job. See family and friends. Enjoy what is possible. Don't give in.

That's what he was doing. But he didn't believe it would help with the ALS.

He still saw the homeopathist, who was giving him supplements for mineral deficiencies, but Dad never believed it helped. Nor did I. Now, after the collapse of the snake venom possibility, I didn't know how else he could resist.

Mom was digging in. She'd cry, sometimes a "good cry." And then, she would bounce back. "I'm not falling apart," she reassured me. She focused on what she could do now, on getting through each day. The future made her worried and unhappy, so she didn't think "too far ahead." I thought, *She will help him to the end. She knows what she has to do to survive.*

Longer-range problems about the future persisted: retirement, pension, social security and Medicare, health insurance and life insurance, and investments. Dad worried about reduced work projects being given to him at the plant, when to retire, the retirement benefits decisions, and what he would do in retirement. He was angry that two colleagues who "know nothing" were replacing him. According to Rob, "He's had it with the job."

We continued worrying over whether they should stay in Skokie, relocate to Florida, or take up my offer to move near me in Oakland. Chicago was home, with family and friends, frequent visits from Rob in nearby Madison, and their medical support at the MDA clinic, but they would be cooped up inside for the winter. Boca Raton meant Florida warmth, where he had done well in the February visit, but they would be more isolated and thrown together. Oakland, my recent proposal, offered warmer California weather and me nearby for help, an option that became more attractive with each crisis over his deteriorating condition. We went around and around discussing these options. Where was the best place to face ALS?

In retrospect, the strangest part of this residence dilemma was my assumption that we could try one of these alternatives for the coming winter and then make a permanent decision. I assumed that his ALS was a stationary condition, and we had a reasonable six months to decide where they should live. I could not have been more wrong.

In another compartment of my mind, I suspected ALS was charging ahead, now, in new ways I did not grasp. At that time, spring of 1980, I thought we were entering some kind of terrible new stage of the disease. Rob would call after a weekend visit and refer to "tremendous changes" taking place with Dad. Mark, on his June visit to Skokie, called it "major major changes." I didn't understand it, but I knew something big was happening.

Around that time, I read Gerda Lerner's 1978 book, *A Death of One's Own*. It's the story of her husband dying from an inoperable brain cancer, over a period of eighteen grim months. That book inspired me. His brain cancer was every bit as capricious and awful as Dad's ALS. Lerner's struggle to keep him at home and comfortable was hopelessly demanding. She was determined to stand by him. She had grit, toughness, and tenderness. Her account showed their commitment to each other, honesty, and integrity, particularly when she faced questions like whether to tell him the cancer was terminal and whether to stop medical interventions that prolonged his life. As a historian, Lerner offered a perspective from her family's own historical experience, including the Holocaust. And the book was a terrific read, powerful and eloquent, riveting as I faced my own challenges (Lerner 1978).

I wanted to write a story about Dad and ALS. I couldn't stop his ALS. I couldn't slow it. But I wanted to understand this extraordinary experience, search out the meaning if there was a meaning, and portray to others what happened. I started a journal.

But telling this story would be a task for another time. Now I was engulfed in our crisis.

I found comfort in recording what happened each day: Dad's condition, what we did, and what we thought.

I was still in disbelief about ALS. It was so different from anything I had expected in my life. I'd ask myself, "How can this be happening to Dad? To us?" But now was my time for action, not reflection.

When I worried or became anxious about our future, I simply repeated a comforting mantra to myself: "I will do what has to be done."

CHAPTER 5

Letting Go, Holding On

JULY 1980

Dad was waiting for me in the backyard.

Twenty-five years earlier, he planted the grass, shrubs, and large maple tree. He built the fence and laid the patio. He bought the barbeque where he held court cooking for family and friends. This trim suburban scene, his own creation, clearly would outlast him. Arriving from the airport in the sunny splendor of that July afternoon, I saw a sick, frail old man, a stranger in his own blooming backyard.

My father, weeping as I approached, unable to rise, barely gesturing with his left hand. I kissed him gently.

He poured out a deluge of information, problems, and worries. He darted between topics: declining body, approaching retirement, pending financial decisions, and conflicts with Mom. What should he do? He had been waiting for me.

He asked if I still wanted them to come live near me in Oakland. I said I did and repeated my reasons. But there was no need to convince him. He was ready to go! When do we leave?

My thoughts lingered over this momentous question, wondering if they really should move to Oakland, thinking we had to discuss it before they hopped on the next airplane to California, feeling his desperation to act. But Dad raced on.

Suddenly, he was explaining an agreement with his neurologist that no heroic measures be taken to prolong his life. I wondered, *What does that mean with ALS?*

I can't recall why, but next, I was assuring him that no matter what happened, we would not place him in an institution. We would take care of him at home. I knew what that meant. But, seeing how weak he had become, I worried, *Can we really do that?* Then I thought, *We have to do that.* But he had moved on.

He wept through it all. He wept about his declining health. He wept at the mention of any loved one. He wept for no apparent reason.

To me, his voice was different. It had a higher pitch, a weaker timbre, and a more excited tone. He lisped and slurred words.

He was completely different from when I had left him in Florida three months prior. The surroundings were eerily familiar: the backyard, the house, Mom bustling about as if everything was normal. But to me, Dad was a transformed man.

He had also suffered physical deterioration. It was a new level of weakness, a kind of feebleness, really. As I walked into the house, I watched Mom help him come in. She placed a walker in front of Dad's chair, lifted him to a stand, and raised his hands onto the walker. Then, they began a torturous journey to the house, Dad leaning on the walker and propelling his legs in slow, tiny steps. Mom held him under an armpit with one hand and helped maneuver the walker with the other. Together, they teeter-tottered toward the house, a few inches forward with each sideward rock.

I stared in disbelief.

How in the world, I wondered, *will they climb the five steps to the back door of the house?* I did not stay to watch.

In the solitude of my old room in the basement, unpacking slowly,

I tried to calm myself. *Dad has suffered a total collapse*, I thought. *A physical and emotional collapse.*

I had believed I was ready for anything. I had told myself I would do what I had to do. But I was simply not prepared—and could not have been prepared—for the upheaval of this visit. As my brothers had warned me, Dad was undergoing a profound transformation. And Mom was at her wit's end, caring for him and coping with him. They seemed to inhabit another world. It was the world of ALS.

For the first time, I saw my parents unable to take care of themselves. That's why I came home. I had to be a *mensch*, a man, responsible for my parents.

I had heard the word used many times. It was casual praise for someone else who stepped up and did the right thing. But now *mensch* was about me caring for my parents. Here, it was a big word that frightened me.

Each new glimpse of Dad was another assault. When I rose from the basement, Dad called me into his bedroom, where Mom was changing his clothes. He sat there in boxer shorts, spindly legs hanging down, ravaged arms dangling helplessly at his sides, ribs clearly outlined on his sunken chest. There was not a muscle in sight. Except for his animate face, he looked emaciated, like a concentration camp inmate.

I thought of one picture of him in the family album. He had been a high school athlete, a distance runner. That picture showed him in a bathing suit with a lean body and muscular shoulders, so healthy. Who would have believed that five decades later, ALS could decimate that beautiful young body?

I stared at him, stunned again, while he delighted in the spectacle. "The body bee-ooo-tee-fool," he droned, with a wry, pained smile, pleased with his macabre joke.

Dad's new physical limitations were staggering. Where he had helped to care for himself in Florida, now he was completely dependent on others for the most elementary tasks of living. His fingers, arms, and legs were dysfunctional. Whether eating or defecating, walking or sitting, reading or talking, he needed help somehow. He required constant assistance throughout the day, from sitting up in bed in the morning to being covered in bed in the evening. There was no rest for him or from him because now he had problems sleeping at night.

His care was taking a terrible toll on Mom. On my first day home, she bristled with nervous energy, immersing herself in cleaning and cooking while I was with Dad. She seemed remote from him, sometimes not responding to his requests for help, rarely assisting him with the precision he demanded.

It triggered bickering and startlingly ferocious exchanges. My first meal home was punctuated by Dad's repeated corrections of how Mom fed him: what foods, what utensils, how much, how fast. Suddenly, irate over spilling crumbs, he yelped, "Ann! You're dropping food on me! Use the napkin!"

She looked at him, puzzled, then tried a few two-handed passes as he wanted, holding a napkin under the moving fork. But soon, she became distracted and spilled more crumbs from another forkful. He howled out a protest in that odd new voice, sounding close to angry tears. Mom snapped back, "I'm trying, Sammy. Just relax."

In our first snatches of conversation, Mom spoke as if Dad was an unpredictable alien presence pervading her life. She dismissed my first attempts to discuss our big problems—financial, health care, and where to live—with an "Ah, whatever," as if events were entirely beyond our control, despite my good intentions.

Her energy seemed superhuman as she cared for Dad day and night, but her eyes looked tired and faded. When she wasn't quarreling with Dad, she seemed not to see or hear him, as if she was retreating into some private inner world. From the first glance during this visit, I was haunted by the possibility that she would break under the strain. What then?

As I reassured myself that there was no impending catastrophe, everything suddenly mutated. Right before my eyes, sitting at the lunch table, Dad's ability to swallow food came under attack from ALS.

The problem seemed simple at first: some food lodged in his

throat after a meal. He felt it deep down in that passage for air, food, and liquids. It was not a problem so much as an irritation, a foreign presence that he felt compelled to force out.

It had been happening for several months, along with his throat clearing to bring out phlegm. They had asked about it at the MDA clinic, where the doctors found no problem.

He had become adept at coaxing the obstruction up or down. He coughed, gulped, gargled, or drank. If those did not work, he ate some matzos, the unleavened bread of the Jewish Passover, a favorite food that he considered the best help to move it down. To everyone's amusement, he had been eating a lot of matzos, as if ALS had sanctioned a new indulgence.

This weird difficulty morphed into a nightmare the day after I arrived. Dad's efforts to clear his throat began to generate a thick, ropey phlegm that coated the inside of his mouth. Dad said he felt like the phlegm came from deep down his throat. Try as he might, he could not cough it up and spit it out.

Suddenly, Dad was requesting that someone swab the inside of his mouth with a napkin. It violated all our instincts, our fastidiousness, and our fears of contracting the evil disease. But there was no refusal. We would swab out his mouth with the napkin, swab again with another napkin, and then rush to find another napkin for another swab. Astonishing quantities of that awful, gooey phlegm came out of his mouth. I couldn't scrub that stuff off my hands fast enough.

All the while, Dad would cough more forcefully to bring up the original obstruction in his throat. His most strenuous coughs were eerie, for they sounded weak, but they triggered his body into fits of coughing, heaving his chest and vibrating his frail frame. It went on and on, building in intensity through involuntary reflex and his own obsessive determination to clear his throat.

The coughing paroxysms cut off his air supply, and he would start gasping, gagging, and choking. His eyes would roll back and forth, round and round. At the peaks of airlessness, his body froze in exertion as if it would explode. His eyeballs bulged, and his eyes stared up into nowhere. It was a deathly stare as if he was gazing into the next world.

Sooner or later, he would bring it up: a little globule of phlegm mixed with bits of food. Then, he would sag with exhaustion, utterly relieved, grinning proudly over his accomplishment.

Such horrors. I never imagined the human body doing such things. As I tried to calm Dad during these swallowing episodes, I had to fight down my own terror. It seemed like he actually was choking on his own phlegm and his frenzied struggle to exorcise it. And I thought this was not just my imagination, for I had read bland reports in the ALS literature of patients who had choked to death on their own saliva.

Dad was seized by a galloping panic. "We've got to do something. I can't live this way."

I was irate that his doctors had not prepared them for this approaching terror. At the clinic, Mom and Dad had reported weeks of throat clearing, and the doctors assured them of no significant changes. But now the disease seemed to be careening along, gathering momentum, making unexpected, capricious attacks. This newest plague inflamed our feeling of crisis beyond control.

I searched my ALS literature for a remedy. I knew that difficulty swallowing food was characteristic of the disease, but I could not believe that Dad, that we, could continue like this.

Indeed, I found recommendations that ALS patients avoid foods that thicken saliva, particularly dairy products, and avoid dry, crumbly foods, like matzos, I thought. There were drugs that controlled saliva flow, home suction machines for clearing throats, and, I did not mention to Dad, the surgical insertion of tubes for feeding directly through the nose or stomach.

Dad was exuberant over my findings, offering extravagant praise for my medical knowledge and insisting I was more helpful than his doctors. He immediately banned dairy foods from his diet, and he became suspicious of all food as dangerous. He latched onto the possibility of a drug that would make his saliva normal again. He became obsessed with getting pills immediately and stopping this thing.

Even as I basked in the glow of Dad's praises, I cursed myself for intervening. I believed there would be no simple solution to this problem. But I had to do something about it. As I embarked on telephone calls to Dad's doctors, I lashed out, "Don't expect any miracle cure!"

He dissolved into tears that quickly transformed into peals of laughter. "Maybe the cure will be another one of my favorite foods. Maybe sauerkraut will do it!"

I stared at him, puzzled, wondering how this childish joke came out of my father's mouth. I was scared to death.

Eventually, I reached Dad's internist, the infamous physician who had delivered the ALS diagnosis by telephone. It occurred to me that I should give him a piece of my mind. I didn't. We were in a crisis. I was relieved he called me back on a Saturday. I was angry, but I also felt grateful. Gratitude prevailed. And prudent caution. I thought, *We may need him ahead.*

He concluded that Dad had an infection. His prescription of cough medicine for the mucus and penicillin for the infection did not inspire my confidence. After all, this phlegm from hell was ALS, not the sniffles. But these medications did ease the problem over the weekend. On Monday, I reached Dad's neurologist, who prescribed medicine to dry up secretions and said they could provide us with a suction machine for removing phlegm from Dad's mouth and throat.

The problem eased, temporarily, but it was just the beginning. Difficulty swallowing food, excess saliva, and related choking, known as dysphagia, is a common ALS problem when muscles of the tongue, cheeks, and throat are weakened. As these muscles weaken, food and liquids regularly go down the "wrong pipe," down the windpipe to the lungs rather than the food tube to the stomach, causing tightening of the throat, spasms, blockage of air, and choking. Or, also in Dad's case, weakened throat muscles cannot push food down the food pipe, and it would stick in his throat. Excess saliva flow, dribbling down his chin, and drooling also come with ALS, often caused by insufficient swallowing of saliva.

We eventually learned there were many actions we could take to ameliorate these problems, from "tips" about food choice to medical interventions to avoid the need to swallow. No one told us, but we also slowly learned that Dad's swallowing and drooling problems would persist, not disappear. There was no cure for his weakening muscles. Get used to it.

And we did. We adapted to the unthinkable as we tried to continue our normal lives. Within days, we placed a slab of napkins near the kitchen table, ready for Dad's outpouring of phlegm at our family meals. Mom and I soon were swabbing the inside of his mouth and his drool as if nothing could be more normal. At meals, our initial stunned silence during Dad's coughing fits passed. The fear passed. We continued chewing and chatting while he choked and drooled.

There appears to be no limit to what people can suffer through with the illness of a family member, and we adapted to this new affliction. But our tradition of family dinners together, enjoying the food and discussing the day, became torture. That swallowing problem marked a transformation of our lives. It was a constant reminder of how Dad might die at the kitchen table, choking before our eyes. Looking back, I recall that weekend as the beginning of a state of permanent crisis. ALS always seemed ahead of us.

With despair, I recognized Dad's swallowing problems and voice changes as symptoms of another phase of the disease: bulbar ALS. It occurs with the dying of upper motor neurons in the bulbar region of the brain. Along with affecting the muscles for speech and swallowing, it could also change cognition and behavior. My ALS literature casually mentioned that bulbar symptoms did not necessarily indicate rapid degeneration or imminent death. But I regarded these new complications of vital functions as ominous.

For me, the most cryptic symptom of bulbar ALS was what my ALS literature called "inappropriate emotional response." That is, the patient has emotional reactions far beyond what is "appropriate" for the situation. My ALS pamphlets offered little attention to this strange and disturbing ALS symptom, only wooden assurances that it was not a sign of derangement. The patient simply lost control over emotions.

Today, patient information about ALS recognizes cognitive and behavioral changes as common characteristics, known as pseudobulbar affect, affecting up to half the patients. These changes range from minor symptoms to full-blown dementia. They include language dysfunction, executive dysfunction, and lability. The ALS literature for patients offers little discussion of the cause. But today, these symptoms are recognized as another set of problems for patients and caregivers.

"Lability," the loss of inhibition and rapid change of mood, described Dad. His emotions were spilling out in tidal flows. He raged over trifles, sank into silent depressions, was plagued by anxieties, fixated on ideas, argued over getting out of bed, negotiated about taking pills, made odd jokes accompanied by his own rollicking laughter, and showed new flashes of biting humor. Most of all, he cried. Almost anything, happy or sad, friendly or hostile, could trigger a binge of tears.

At the time, in 1980, I considered these emotional displays to be Dad's idiosyncratic reactions to having ALS rather than symptoms of the disease. I held him responsible for this emotional roller coaster as his way of coping—or not coping—with the terrible disease. Despite my awareness of "inappropriate emotional responses" as an ALS symptom, I had difficulty understanding that his unusual moods and behaviors were the terrible disease itself. Looking back, I wish I had been better educated about ALS and more tolerant of Dad's emotional display.

It was difficult to be tolerant. That first weekend, with the swallowing and saliva problems, we had dinner guests, Esther and Ziggy Klein, old friends dating back to the prewar West Side. They brought takeout Chinese food, a big treat at previous visits. In the middle of the dinner, during a break from swabbing his mouth and choking, Dad called Ziggy "stupid" for no apparent reason, repeating it several times and then insisting on leaving the table immediately. I helped him into the living room and kept him company till everyone joined us later. I had never heard him be so rude, but he didn't notice anything strange had occurred. Even as I recognized it as an evil symptom of the disease, I was embarrassed for him and all of us. But Esther and Ziggy just shrugged it off, and they returned for future visits.

Mom noticed another feature of Dad's runaway emotions. "He has no defenses anymore," she told me sadly, quizzically, after one of his crying jags. She said it with a hushed voice as if pointing out an embarrassing oddity, knowing she shouldn't. She didn't understand it, nor did I.

Mom despaired that she could not please him. Occasionally, without much hope, she would try to ease him back to normal. "Be rational, Sammy," she'd exclaim, warmly, sensibly. "That's what you always told me. Follow your own advice."

She was talking about the many times he had steadied her with rational reassurances against cancer fears.

Dad would shake his head up and down in solemn agreement, without the slightest ability to follow through on his old advice. For him, there was no going back to that rational scientist, husband, and father he was before ALS.

For me, it was an extraordinary transformation. I placed Dad among a generation of men, children of Jewish immigrants, who wore protective armor of rationality and certainty. Immigrant parents, growing up in the Depression, the American promise had launched them in a single-minded lifelong pursuit of business and professional careers and affluent suburban family lives. The goals were clear, the paths were open, and the landmarks were intact; they never swerved to examine deepest feelings or question their own motives. They did not even change residences more than once in twenty years, let alone switch careers or wives. They were the Greatest Generation who survived the

Depression, won World War II, and built postwar prosperity. There was no reason to question themselves.

Dad would "tell the facts" and skip the feelings. "I'm not introspective," Dad once told me, proud that he had avoided this path of fatal irresolution. "I don't second-guess myself."

He had been a pre-Freudian mystery to me. I could pile up a stack of sociological explanations for his generation's values and behavior. But I still could not understand this celebration of his self-ignorance.

I was a baby boomer, a generation of second-guessers. We had merrily indulged in what our parents had denied. We had rebelled in the 1960s, and in rebelling, we had questioned everything: the government, the universities, the suburbs, and most of all, our own families. We had challenged into oblivion our parents' way of life. When the smoke cleared at the end of our rebellion, we could rely on nothing but our own selves and feelings. In the 1970s, we had morphed into a "me generation," away from social responsibility, now preoccupied with our own psyches, lifestyles, and self-realization.

We knew too much about ourselves. Like others of my generation, I could mull over emotions and interactions for days or years, particularly when they involved Dad and me. And despite all my attention to who I was and how I felt, I never understood how I sprang from Dad.

Years ago, when my parents visited me in California, I had a memorable exchange with Dad about picking up a rental car. I had made an offer to help, which he immediately dubbed "stupid." I had dropped my head into my hands, despairing at the insult, while he continued discussing the rental car as if nothing had happened.

"I teach at one of the greatest universities in the world," I raged to a friend that evening, "and *no one* calls me stupid."

"University, shmuniversity," reminded the friend. "To him, you're still the same *schlemiel* of a kid."

His insult left me stewing throughout that visit. Mom had tried to patch it up. "That's just the way he is," she pleaded. "He won't lose any sleep. Don't let it bother you."

But it had been bothering me for years. These little explosions loomed as large emblems of his inability to accept me as another person, his adult son. He would not, could not, recognize another way, my way. I regarded him as blind to emotions, oblivious to himself, insensitive to me, constantly irritating my exposed sores, and incapable of navigating the emotional storms he triggered.

Instead of confronting Dad, I convinced myself that he was fragile behind that façade of rational certainty and suburban propriety. He would crack the moment I assaulted him, and then I would have to pick up the pieces. Even as he mellowed with airport hugs and California visits, I maintained a cautious distance and nursed my grievances.

But now there was no escape, for him or for me. ALS was turning him inside out, exposing his private thoughts and hidden feelings. Now, the emperor stood bare for all to see, especially me, his angry eldest son.

This reversal scared me. It was frightening to witness his loss of control, first physical control and now emotional control. He became too weak and vulnerable. I was too powerful, too responsible for what would happen.

As Dad's defenses crumbled before me, I also witnessed something unexpected. Instead of finding a hollow man with no internal resources, I discovered that Dad had ideas and feelings that touched me. Paradoxically, at this moment of greatest vulnerability, Dad never seemed more sure of who he was.

I saw it with Dad's reminiscences about his life. At first, I thought it was Rabbi Stern who had visited and triggered this reminiscing with the suggestion that Dad tape-record his story of our family history. But as I listened to Dad day by day, I thought he was doing a recap, a reckoning, of his own life: where he had come from, the challenges he had faced, what he had accomplished and where he had failed, and the people he knew. It was a life summary for himself and our family.

I would listen, surprised, as Dad told his history. Each morning, he would position himself in a corner of the living room on the single chair he preferred, and he would call me in for a conversation. I never knew him to talk so much.

At the turn of thought, he would be sobbing, transported by memories of Grandma and Grandpa, their little grocery stores, their extended immigrant families with eccentric characters, and the old Jewish and Italian neighborhoods of his Chicago youth. It was a pure vision of a Jewish immigrant family living in a few squalid back rooms, all working to keep open the store's front door eighteen hours a day, seven days a week. He described it through a child's eyes: the sweet colored candies (Mary Janes and Green Leaves and Bullseyes and Hershey bars), the exciting new *Superman* comic books, the rich milkshakes Grandma made for him at their soda fountain, the time Grandpa bought and sold a store within a week, the cars he drove around Chicago on store business. These were familiar tales of my immigrant roots, told with Dad's new passion to recite his life story and pass on our family history to the next generation.

Dad told a new story about contracting scarlet fever in 1927, age twelve, the year he became the family driver. He was quarantined at a contagious diseases hospital, where he was treated for a month. I have postcards the nurses gave him to write home every day. Those postcard messages show a serious American boy who felt responsible for his immigrant parents: assuring them he was being well treated in the hospital, worrying about the welfare of the family in his absence, directing his mother to stop bringing fruit for the nurses, and telling his father to start carrying American newspapers in their grocery store.

I listened with pleasure, again, to the old stories of his gang of friends and their adolescent exploits. The setting was exotic, the old immigrant West Side of Chicago, but the ruling passions were familiar from my own teen years in the suburbs. Every tale began in their club's rented basement rooms along Douglas Boulevard that he once had showed me on a West Side tour. Every adventure included a car, a Hudson or Packard or Studebaker, that carried them in the search for girls.

For a few weeks during my July visit, and only then, Dad spoke like a street-smart kid growing up in a Depression immigrant neighborhood. There was not a trace of Yiddish, the language he grew up speaking with his parents at home. He swore in English, used old American street expressions, and was flippant, sarcastic, and cocky. The rawness was accentuated by his new speech impediments, lisping and slurring, and I wondered if he had spoken this way as a kid with his friends. I felt like I was peering through a window into his past, seeing him for the first time as a half-formed, ambitious, untamed son of immigrants, confidently striding into American life with his generation.

Dad spoke with pride of his marriage to Mom, the postwar years of building a family, his three sons and their achievements, the good jobs, and the financial success. But wait. I was surprised. That was me he was celebrating among the accomplishments.

He recounted failures too. It pained me to hear him review them again and again as if he could place them in perspective through sheer repetition. There were business ventures he had not dared and careers he had not pursued. He wished he had lived a more carefree life, with more great adventures and more simple daily enjoyment. "Take our friends Edith and Ralph," he explained. "They go to the bathroom for a shit and find something interesting along the way." He spoke wistfully of the pleasures he had missed, the places he had not seen, the Florida retirement that could have been and never would be. Suddenly, unexpectedly, his life had screeched to a halt, up against this relentless disease. Now it was too late to reach for more.

I could not just listen to these recriminations and regrets. I repeatedly interrupted, insisting on the completeness of his achievement. I wanted him to be satisfied with his life. For me, who would live on, his pride of accomplishment made his ALS suffering and this abrupt encounter with his mortality more tolerable.

One of those mornings, out of the blue, he turned to the future of his sons, particularly me. Only now, ailing, could he speak about his worries over my unsettled life at thirty-five: no wife, children, house, or secure job. He despaired that he no longer could do anything for me.

It had been that way for a long time. I was an adult, making my own life in California. But it was difficult to hear him speak those words of regret about me.

This was a rare breach of our long silence about my life. He had tried before, during a California visit in 1978, when he had apologized for not teaching his sons how to work with his tools. At first, I had been amused when he insisted on buying me a television as if that might help me along the road to suburban normalcy. But when he had openly expressed concern about the direction of my life, I was both touched that he cared and outraged by his implication that I was not finding my own way.

I had sidetracked that discussion, but now I assured him I was optimistic. My first book would be published at the end of the year, with another to follow. More than that, I had a new girlfriend, Stephanie. True, she had been a girlfriend for only a month, but I thought this was different. I was different. I had brought her picture to show him.

"I didn't think you had the inclination," he said, staring at the picture, surprised, happy, crying.

I thought that something significant was happening with Dad. His unbridled emotions and lush remembrances were not just the mysterious workings of bulbar ALS. He was crossing a threshold, a great divide, from the world of the living to the world of the dying. Nine months after his ALS diagnosis, I thought he was recognizing that he would not beat this disease. He was coming to terms with his suddenly stopped life, with his impending death.

Dad wanted me to join his mourning. I did not understand at first, when he requested that I listen with him to records of Enrico Caruso, Luciano Pavarotti, Mario Lanza, and the great tenors of opera. He had developed a taste for opera as a young man when he appeared in operas as an extra, and he listened to it on his work commutes. Rob had brought those records for Dad's entertainment in retirement, but Dad would dissolve into tears with the first strains of the music.

Day after day, I listened to that music while Dad sobbed, reminisced, or sat quietly, lost in thought. I knew nothing about opera, but I was swept up by the power and charm of those sweet voices. I was stunned by the sentimental beauty of Dad's lamentation for his fading life.

Most surprising to me, Dad displayed a powerful religiosity with the playing of Richard Tucker, the great Jewish tenor. Although Dad grew up in a Jewish immigrant household, he had a largely secular upbringing. I had long considered his strongest tie to Judaism as the B'nai Emunah men's bowling league. But I knew better from my parents sending me and my brothers to Hebrew schools for years, the annual family seders and Hannukah parties, and the elaborate bar mitzvah celebrations for each son. I remembered back to when we lived on the West Side, attending Rosh Hashanah and Yom Kippur services with our family, walking to synagogue in our finest clothes on crisp fall mornings. In my memory, these had been special occasions.

Now, when cantor Richard Tucker bellowed out those Hebrew prayers on Rob's records, Dad wept uncontrollably. I felt like I was sitting through Dad's home-improvised religious service of mourning for himself. By my presence, I was assuring him that I knew he was dying and that I would remember him after death. It always ended with a surge of Dad's tears through the singing of "Kol Nidre," the haunting prayer chanted every Yom Kippur, the holiest day of the Jewish year, the Day of Atonement when you ask forgiveness for your sins.

Mom came from a Jewish orthodox family, with a difficult father who peddled used clothes for a living and spent most of his time praying in *shul*, synagogue. She had a saintly mother who everyone loved and who kept a kosher household and found ways for the family to get by. Mom had rejected orthodoxy for her own family with Dad. Now she refused to listen to that music with him, particularly Richard Tucker, and soon I understood one reason why. I became exhausted with the intensity of emotion, his and mine. I joined the family conspiracy to distract him with amusements. Anything to hold back his mourning.

In the past, in the long-ago era before ALS, Dad had spent much of his free time watching television. Now, with nothing but free time, he had no interest in the tube. I would describe the intriguing possibilities of a cop show or an old movie, and sometimes, he would humor me by watching it. But he craved more intense experience with people.

I was surprised by how little he was interested in the newspaper and the world beyond our house. If the daily *Sun-Times* was properly positioned on a tray in front of him, he could still turn pages with a rubber finger grip and a slight motion of his right hand, one of his final self-help actions. He might read an article on Israel or a business item with bearing on his investments. But he glanced through most of the news as if it was folly unworthy of his attention.

He saw everything differently, particularly the house. The basement, no longer accessible to him, existed only in memory, but it was still in his mind because it had not yet been fully cleared out as he wanted. He had not been in the back bedroom for weeks, simply because he had no compelling reason to travel that distance. He entered Mom's province, the kitchen, less and less, as he had a growing dislike of the odors, noise, and cooking heat.

Dad rarely visited the back patio because of those five steps to leave the house. He would no longer spend time in his den. I thought he found it too dark, too enclosed, too removed from the central axis of the house. He stationed himself in the living room, where he could watch life pass by on the street outside and monitor events inside the house. He seemed to know everything that happened in the house, including hushed conversations at the other end. He missed nothing in his new circumscribed world.

More than anything, Dad craved close contact with the immediate family, and at the best moments, we all found pure, warm pleasure in our own company. We were content to be together most evenings in the living room, Dad in his chair in the corner, me stretched out on the couch, classical music in the background. He listened, I read, and we chatted. Sometimes, we played a musical that Dad would follow with visible delight. If it were his favorite, *Fiddler On The Roof*, he would provide a running commentary on the Yiddish words and Jewish traditions.

After a long hot evening bath, Mom would drift into the room with her sewing. Still eager to comfort Dad, she would offer him a snack, a cushion, a glass of water, anything. Then, she would snuggle up in a large chair, sinking into her knitting. The family circle was complete; we were content.

By 8:30 p.m., Dad's body would be aching from the long day of sitting. He would check his watch, starting the countdown to bedtime and relief. I would offer to massage him, and sometimes he let me work on his aching calves, or Rob could warm his cold toes. This physical contact was unusual in our family, small signs of the ALS transformation of our lives together.

One evening, Mom told him, "Don't be angry, but try this." We were all careful with Dad. She didn't want to set him off, anger or sentimental tears or wild laughing, but she raised his feet onto a stool for relaxation and better circulation. "What's the difference?" He shrugged, giving me a look that meant he would humor her and the rest of us. But I thought he liked her attempts to comfort him.

The later he stayed up, the fewer problems in the night, so I would read aloud to help him pass the final hour. My most successful reading was from *The Pushcart War*, a book Rob brought for Dad. It was a warm, wry children's story about a battle for space on New York City streets between plucky little pushcart peddlers and the big bad Mammoth Moving Company. Evening after evening, Dad listened to chapters of that tale, engrossed, following the tribulations and triumphs of the heroic pushcart peddlers with a child's delight (Merrill 1964).

I had to fight down disappointment at the end of those evenings. No matter how sweet the hours had been, at exactly 9:30 p.m., Dad would insist upon beginning his elaborate bedtime preparations. Dad's ALS and Dad's routine always prevailed.

Only in retrospect have I understood the paradox that ruled our lives during my July 1980 visit. As Dad began to let go, to accept dying, he also mounted a ferocious struggle to tighten his hold on life. His attachment to the 9:30 bedtime was but a small skirmish in his monumental battle to master his faltering body, overcome his disabilities, and control his household world. He might reminisce about his life, calculate the final returns on accomplishments and failures, and prepare himself and us for his death. But on a day-to-day basis, he would not yield an inch to ALS, even if he drove the rest of us crazy. This was not graceful aging.

All of Dad's courage and determination, all his infuriating, stubborn pride, came into play with his continued insistence on walking. When I left him three months prior in Florida, he was on the brink of disaster with those terrible falls. He had puzzled over the problem until he thought out his own solution. Upon return to Chicago, he requested the MDA clinic construct a walker with wheels on the front legs and tennis balls on the back legs. After much insistence on his part, they had done so, and it worked. The front wheels allowed him to maneuver the walker without lifting the full weight while the back legs with the tennis balls offered steady support for balance. (Twenty years later, I saw many similar walker devices, by then called rollators, when Mom lived in assisted living, but Dad's 1980 invention was the first such walker I've seen.)

This ingenious device had allowed him to continue walking alone, and his independence had been sweetened by his pride of invention: "I'm a problem-solver." But now he had become so weak that he could no longer maneuver the walker with his arms. He needed another person.

I had never experienced anything like helping Dad walk. I would face him across the walker, holding one hand under his shoulder and the other on the walker, lifting and stepping backward with his moves forward. He would bend over the walker, struggling to hold himself up, inching ahead with a sideward-swaying, forward-rocking motion.

This exquisite slow-motion pas de deux demanded complete

concentration by both partners. To walk, Dad explained, he had to consciously send orders from his brain to his sluggish muscles, telling them what to do. When he was tired, when the thirty-foot journey from living room to kitchen loomed large, he strained at the effort, beads of perspiration streaming down his face. With the final steps, he would grunt aloud, "Walk. Walk! WALK!"

If I kept to his rhythm, our journey with the walker would be easier. But my mind would wander during these tedious excursions. Then, I would be jolted from my revelry by a shriek from Dad, indicating that I was holding him back or tipping him over, that some ground obstacle blocked his way, that he wanted to detour, that some damn thing was wrong and I was not paying attention. That shriek, the product of his changed voice and exploding temper, filled me with guilt and anger, with determination to be more attentive and with an impulse to flee.

Dad had another problem that seemed more bizarre to me. He sat the entire day but chose not to sit in a comfortable chair.

He refused to sit in our chairs with the softest cushions because he sank so deep that he had to be lifted out as deadweight. He hated that state of dependence, where he could not participate and direct his own body movements.

He spent much of the day sitting stiffly in a hard, low-backed chair that was placed against a living room wall so he could support his shoulders and head. From that chair, he could lean forward, position himself on his center of gravity, and use his remaining leg strength to help someone stand him up. He insisted on sitting in that rigid chair on the edge of the room as if it had been dictated by a law of nature.

Naïve, I urged him to experiment with other seating arrangements. Little did I know that I was blundering into the complex world of sitting and rising with ALS. Dad's problem involved not only the softness and shape of the cushions but also the height and width of the chair, the angle of the back, the size and position of the armrests, and even the texture of the outer fabric.

If that was not enough, Dad also insisted the chosen chair should not look odd and violate the integrity of the living room decoration. This time, he explained, after growing up with shabby old chairs and tables in the junky back rooms of their West Side grocery stores, he would not tolerate weird-looking concocted furniture in his nice home today. I understood.

As I began to despair over the Herculean task I had proposed, Dad became intrigued by the challenge of solving his sitting problem, just as he had done with his walker on wheels and tennis balls. He grabbed onto the problem and would not let go. Resting in bed that afternoon during a break in our work, he did not at all rest. His mind was churning over the components of a chair and how best to maneuver up from one.

We worked together in the living room. Dad directed my good hands to meet his mechanical and design ideas as we modified chairs, fabricated special neck rests, and concocted cushions. There were some familiar clashes over his rigid instructions and my clumsy craftsmanship, but that was subordinate to my satisfaction watching Dad's mechanical ideas become reality again and the surprising pleasure of our collaboration.

But nothing met his exacting requirements for comfort, autonomy, and appearance. Only a telephone conversation with Dad's occupational therapist at the MDA clinic convinced me that we had not lost our senses in this quest for the right chair. Turned out, this was a problem for many ALS patients, though I could not believe any other was as particular as Dad. However, after days of labor, if only to please me, he began sitting part of his days in one of our modified chairs placed in the middle of the living room. I was satisfied.

At the beginning of the visit, I thought that a wheelchair would solve all these problems. Dad already had one on order from the MDA clinic, a wheelchair that would be constructed specially for his body size and ALS problems. I imagined him sitting comfortably in that vehicle, gliding easily about the house, ending our strange chair experiments and agonizing walking journeys.

That was fantasy. Dad already had a temporary wheelchair that he refused to use. Being pushed by someone else, by Mom, was contrary to his instincts, his codes, and his conception of himself. He had banished it to the basement, where it stood as a proud new edition to the now legendary $750 shoes and his other unused devices for the ALS patient.

When I asked Dad about using the wheelchair in the house, he explained, "No, I don't want to give in. I want to walk as long as I can."

I was moved by Dad's courageous struggle to continue using his body however possible. And I was exasperated by his stubborn refusal to use supports that could make life easier and enhance his autonomy. There was no halfway with him. He would struggle beyond reason to do things himself. Once he could not, he would collapse into passivity, demanding that it be done for him, irate if it was not done exactly as he wanted.

Caring for Dad had become a relentless job, morning through evening and into the night, day after day after day. There seemed to be no end to his needs and no limit to the powerful reactions he inspired in his family helpers.

Each morning began with a wrench as I saw Dad lying in bed, frail and helpless, waiting for someone to assist him. Sometimes, he would be ready with a warm smile and a funny, odd thought. He seemed like a gentle, hurt child, bravely eager to start another day. No matter how many times I saw him like that, no matter how many times I cradled him in my arms to sit him up, I felt engulfed with anguish that my father had become this sweet, feeble old man.

That feeling would pass quickly as I became subject to his tyrannical morning routine. Everything had to be done according to his exacting requirements: when and how he was dressed, the temperature of his orange juice, and the amount of milk and bananas with his shredded wheat. He kept track of an incredible number of tiny details for each task, each one with its own good reason in his scheme of things. Any deviation, accidental or deliberate, was met with firm corrections, angry protests, and repeated orders. In the end, it was easier to submit than to challenge him.

I found little satisfaction in caring for Dad, even by midmorning after several hours of feeding, cleaning, dressing, and grooming him for the day ahead. He might be satisfied, but he still did not look right to me. No matter how carefully I dressed him, his clothes hung askew on his skeletal body. My best attempts to shave him always left some stray protruding bristle. I would comb his hair one moment, and the next, it would be mussed. I fussed with his appearance throughout the day in a futile effort to make him look right again.

My sense of time changed with this stage of ALS. Looking back now, Dad's illness ran its course in the flash of fifteen months. But during that July visit, the days slowed to a snail's pace, crammed full of Dad's requests for help walking, sitting, eating, cleaning, and countless other things he once did himself without thought. And every half hour, without fail, he still insisted that he be lifted to a stand so he could loosen his few remaining functional muscles.

His watch was the first thing he wanted after sitting up in bed each morning. Armed with that watch, he enforced his schedule as if all existence depended on it.

Dad had a maddening need to control his environment. Every day, he would joust with the air conditioner, requesting changes of thermostat, air vents, windows, and clothes, in a never-ending search for the right temperature. He noticed open doors, lights left on, and pictures hanging crooked, and he would not forget it until you made the adjustment he wanted. Because he walked leaning on the walker with his head hung down, he would see things no one else saw—a scrap of paper on the floor, a bit of lint on a carpet—and he might interrupt the most strenuous journey with a startling request that it be picked up immediately.

I never fully adjusted to his unique perspective on our world. He could not move his hands to protect himself from flies, and if he saw one in the house, he yelled for it to be swatted. The movement of an ant was an insulting reminder of his own helplessness, and he would order it squashed immediately. He was obsessed with the removal of bugs from the house.

The going-to-bed routine had its own unique choreography. Following a final bathroom stop, it began with a change of clothes through bewildering, precise movements of body parts and garments. Then, you laid him back on the bed, picked up his feet and swung them into the bed, and began the arrangement of legs and feet, arms and hands, with straightening of his left fingers. Next was the placement of pillows and covers. Then, he wanted final adjustments to the house—air conditioner, air vents, windows, doors, and locks. And, finally, a chair by the bed with a plastic covering, ready for use as a portable urinal in the middle of the night.

Every evening, once Dad was settled in for the night, I felt exhilarated. Come ten o'clock, Mom and I would meet in the kitchen for root beer floats, a kind of mini celebration of our release from him.

It was only an interlude because Dad no longer slept through the night, even with valium. Now, he slept alone because he could not get comfortable with another body in the bed. Mom had begun sleeping across the hall in the den, awakening when he called for assistance. Neither of them had gotten a full night's sleep in weeks.

I alternated with Mom on the grueling night shift in the den. Dad usually made a first call at 1 or 2 a.m., his feet tangled in the covers, unable to roll over. A second call would follow at 3 or 4 a.m., this time to urinate. Then, I had to clear my mind and wake my body to help him into the chair, where he could pee in a small urinal. That short journey between bed and chair required holding Dad under his shoulders and rocking along as he stepped and rotated. Mom called it "the midnight dance."

One night, I became furious when he woke me a fourth time with a call for help. I rarely showed my anger at him for the endless demands of ALS. But this time, I came stomping into the bedroom, muttering my annoyance, only to discover he had to urinate badly. He must have been lying awake a long time, holding it in to avoid calling me again. I returned to bed with guilty hope that he had not noticed my foul mood. But the next morning, when Dad first saw me, he broke out crying and abjectly apologized: "I'm sorry I was such a bother last night." He had become sensitive to other people's feelings, to my feelings. I felt awful.

Over thirty years later, I was reminded of Dad's nighttime predicament and my limited ability to grasp it by the English historian Tony Judt, who wrote about nights with his ALS. In his essay, "Night," Judt described ALS paralysis as "progressive imprisonment without parole." "Imprisonment," that is, in your own body, "confined to an iron suit, cold and unforgiving." He described a nightly bedtime routine that included a precise placement of torso, arms, and legs in specific positions, hooked up to his breathing device, allowing no body part to be misplaced or "I shall suffer the agonies of the damned later in the night." Through the night that followed, unable to move without help, unable to scratch an itch or shift a hand or pee, he was "obliged to lie absolutely motionless" for seven unbroken hours. Only the morning brought "respite," which was the prospect of transferring to a wheelchair for the next seventeen hours and the new opportunity to communicate with the outside world his "angry words, the bottled-up irritations and frustrations of physical limitation." "Helplessness is humiliating," he wrote, particularly with ALS where it is "a life sentence."

Judt conjured up his own survival mechanism for the nights, a mental discipline: "solace and recourse in my own thoughts," thinking about events, people, and narratives that captivated his attention and encouraged sleep that would rescue him from "an almost insufferable nocturnal ordeal." But, he explained, "Even the best meaning and most generously thoughtful friends or relatives cannot hope to understand the sense of isolation and imprisonment this disease imposes upon its victims." Judt with ALS, I thought, might have been every bit as difficult as Dad (Judt 2010).

I was one of those best-meaning relatives who ultimately could not grasp the enormity of Dad's ALS. I never did ask how he made it through those nights. I think I stopped trying to understand his experience with ALS in that July visit. Living with Dad required superhuman stamina to help him. I no longer speculated about how I would act in his situation or how my generation would face this death. Dad, as his body continued to shrink its movement, had inflated beyond my sociological categories and imagination. Confronting the end of life, he had become an elemental force who triggered my own tumultuous feelings about him. Around him, there was no escaping him—and no escaping yourself.

I desperately feared that Mom could not last in this hothouse of emotion. The acrimony had become too intense for the affection and courage that had sustained her and Dad through the first half-year of the disease. Now they were fighting bitterly. I sympathized with both their grievances.

Dad had a catalog of dissatisfactions over Mom's clumsy handling of him, her inability to follow his exact instructions for assistance, and her tuning out his words. I sympathized with him. I would watch with silent distress when Mom set him down with a thud, dropped food on his chest while feeding him, or did not hear his calls for assistance. Helplessly dependent on her, he would grimace with despair or yell out in fury.

Where Dad demanded agonizingly slow and deliberate assistance, Mom seemed to be moving faster and faster. "It's like she's on roller skates," he said to me bitterly one morning, explaining he was afraid of her fast movements. She had just fed him breakfast, periodically leaving to check food on the stove and laundry in the basement washing machine. "What's the hurry?" he asked, dripping with sarcasm. "Is she going to a party this morning?"

I sympathized with Mom's immersion in other tasks in other rooms. I thought I recognized a semiconscious, self-protective mechanism when she shut out his words. She always heard him when necessary, even his faint calls for assistance in the dead of night. I understood her need for distance from him because this visit gave me a taste of his constant inflexible demands.

"It's a nightmare," she told me. "No one could understand it."

I thought I did understand. As a spouse caretaker for Dad, Mom had no relief except visits from the three sons. ALS was no temporary condition, with no possibility of future improvement. It only became worse. Dad only became more demanding. As a caretaker, all you could do was push on without hope.

But no matter how awful things became, leaving never was a consideration for Mom. She was living on grim determination to endure. I found that reassuring, even as I squirmed over how she sometimes expressed it. "I won't let him drag me down," she insisted. "I'll survive. I'm a survivor."

Sympathize as I might, understand as I would, their fiercest battles were beyond anything I had witnessed before. It happened during my visit. I'd hear angry voices from another room, a dispute that flared over how Mom lifted, dressed, or fed him. Suddenly, Dad would be staggering into the living room as fast as he could with the walker, which was very, *very* slow, moving only with Mom's help, yelling that he had to get away from her.

It was that terrible temper again. Now it was fueled by frustration with his unresponsive body, by his inability to do anything of his own volition, even get away from Mom.

Pale and sobbing, Mom would hand him over to me and flee into the back bedroom. Dad would rant about his awful existence. He would rave about how he should have committed suicide when he had the chance. But after one of those fights, weeping, he also acknowledged that after looking out for Mom for forty years, it was difficult for him to accept her help.

They held two worldviews that repeatedly collided in the confines of our house: dying and living. I found myself mediating their differences, affirming grievances, encouraging sympathetic understanding of the other, reminding Mom that Dad was dying, and reminding Dad that Mom had to live.

I felt like I was trespassing on forbidden ground: their marriage. I was meddling in a taboo: how they coped with this terrible disease that engulfed everything. But I was determined to hold everything together, as ALS threatened chaos.

By the end of my first July weekend home, I felt like I had been swallowed into an alien world where I had huge responsibilities and no power to act. "Like a nightmare," as Mom described it, this world was wholly self-contained with its own rules, rhythms, boundaries, and tensions. It was familiar because it was home. But everything was distorted by the crazy disease and its mad flux.

I discovered that life is never more intense than at a time of dying. At thirty-five, I had no experience with death. When I was fifteen, Grandpa died after a crippling stroke, but my parents had shielded me from the ordeal, and his death was a fleeting surprise. Thousands of my generation had died in Vietnam, but I was protected by social class and student deferments; I knew no one who fought, none who died. I remained among those in the baby boom generation who did not really know or believe in death.

Preparing for this July visit, I had reassured myself with the vow that I would do what I had to do. But what to do was often a mystery.

I still thought about dying in abstractions. Either you went quickly or slowly, with fear or courage, gently accepting or raging against it. I did not understand that it could all happen together, with terrible confusion over what to say and what to do. And I still believed that something could be done about it.

What to do? Throughout this visit, I was consumed by what to do. That's what led to my most agonizing moment, an exchange with Dad that echoed for months and years to come.

It occurred in the bathroom my first weekend home. Dad could still use the toilet to pee, but he needed help. I had to maneuver him with the walker in front of the toilet, remove the walker and hold him steady, pull down his zipper, and help him wiggle his penis into dangling hands. Sometimes, I had to place his penis in his hands.

This was enormous labor for a pee. The assistance of another person, his wife or son, was a terrible violation of Dad's sense of dignity.

It all must have struck him that moment as he stood peeing, steadied by my hand on his shoulder.

"Skip, I'm starting to feel really helpless," he said.

He spoke in his old voice, strong and full, with a sober desperation that seemed to spring from his old self, before ALS, before dying.

I reassured him, "We'll be here to help you."

"No, no . . ." he whispered as if I had not understood. And then his mind wandered off, or he decided against explaining to me.

That night, and for long after, I agonized over having missed his message. Much as I vowed to do what had to be done, the hard truth was that I often didn't know what had to be done.

Today, over forty years later, I think I know what Dad meant: "I'm becoming someone else, helpless and dependent. I don't want your help. I want to be me."

Today, I realize there was nothing I could have done except understand and sympathize.

But that afternoon in July 1980, I thought crazily, if only I had understood him, if only I had reached him with my reply, I might have held him with us in the land of the living, with his real voice and true self. Instead, I had let Dad slip out of my grasp.

CHAPTER 6

Retirement

JULY 17, 1980

"But how will we get down those steps?" I asked Mom. Five front steps.

"He knows how to do it."

Dad agreed to use the wheelchair he had banished to the basement for this trip. But we had not yet built a ramp. There was no avoiding those steps.

We used his ingenious walker to shuffle our way to the front porch. There, he encountered the steps like a rock climber descending a cliff face. He plotted each perilous step, then maneuvered at a glacial pace, deliberating after each slight movement downward. He grabbed familiar handholds he had devised on the iron railing these past months and located familiar foot placements as he negotiated the precipitous eight-inch drops between steps. Here was my Dad, the high school athlete.

He sweated under the intense summer morning sun as he struggled to shift weight and maintain balance with his weakened limbs. I got a whiff of his body odor, sweet, not unpleasant.

I strained to help. I supported him under his shoulders. I moved with his lead, following his rocking rhythm as he toiled downward. I struggled to prevent a disastrous fall and to avoid causing one. There had been no falls on these steps before, and we wouldn't start now.

As we descended, I puzzled how he had done this for months without me—down those stairs daily to go to work and back up too—until he stopped going to work just a few weeks ago.

Mom had helped him many times, but she refused to watch. It was easier to help than to watch.

Dad and I labored downward, oblivious to the world, but the world noticed us. Our slow-motion ballet down the steps was so tortured that a passing motorist stopped his car. He ran over and helped us.

That morning, my father would retire. I was taking Dad to his workplace. He wanted to say goodbye.

How do you use your remaining days when you learn you have a dreaded disease? When your statistical life span is a few years?

Me? I imagined visits to my Sonoma County ranch. Another walk in the vast expanses of Death Valley. Rome again? But you don't know until you face the unimaginable choice of what to do with your precious remaining time. Why do anything? What matters?

Dad was single-minded: continue his work. He would not retreat into the quiet comfort of his Chicago suburban home. He would not disappear to the warm leisure of their Boca Raton condominium. No grand journey to Israel.

He wanted to continue his job for TRW Cinch. He worked at a western suburban plant near O'Hare Field, the workplace he had showed me at the close of my December visit.

Dad and I had driven together many times to another of his TRW Cinch workplaces. During my college summers in the 1960s, I worked for his company at its factory on the gritty industrial South Side of Chicago.

Dad drove in the mornings, and I drove in the afternoons. We'd talk about the best driving routes, the factory, and sports. When he snoozed on the afternoon return trip, I felt entrusted with the responsibility of bringing my father home.

That 1960s plant was a massive old five-story manufacturing building that stretched over several city blocks. Dad worked at the far eastern end in air-conditioned administrative offices and laboratories. I was on the western side in stockrooms, filling orders of manufactured parts for delivery to customers through the truck bays on our end. In the vast in-between, amid thundering machinery and sweltering heat, they produced whatever they produced, some kind of airplane parts.

Was it important? Did we keep aircraft aloft? I never asked.

I worked in that stockroom for three summers with the same groups of young men and older women. The ladies packed manufactured parts into boxes all day. The guys stored the boxed parts on stockroom shelves and gathered boxes to fill orders.

Throughout the day, we guys invented games and goofed around. We had to do it to relieve the boredom of the mindless, repetitive work. And we did it, I learned, to preserve our jobs. If we all had worked steadily, the company could have eliminated half those stockroom jobs. I'm an enthusiast, and I like to accomplish. I only worked hard, even then as a teenager, and the guys got on me about it. They slowed me down and taught me how to look busy for our supervisor.

One of the guys, Harold, was as smart as anyone I knew. We became friends through our passions about the Cubs, the Bears, and the Blackhawks. But, never mentioned, Harold would remain in the Cinch stockroom, and I was a college boy passing through.

The ladies regularly warned me, "You finish college. Don't end up packing parts like me."

I didn't need urging. When I began working at TRW Cinch in 1962, the first summer before college, I had already decided on a career change from my father. College was a given, like summer factory work to earn money for college. But I planned for two professions after college: a tax attorney and a certified public accountant, sure to be a good combination. And without a thought to the costs of two professional educations. This was the prosperous, optimistic 1960s. Launching from an ascending middle-class family in a comfortable middle-class suburb, I could become whatever I wanted.

Science and technology—chemistry and metallurgy—had been my father's route out of the tiny neighborhood grocery stores of his parents on the immigrant West Side of Chicago. He graduated from high school in 1932, at the bottom of the Depression. He obtained a college degree in chemistry in 1940, after eight years in and out of night schools: Crane College and Lewis Institute. He was among a rising American-born generation, children of Eastern European Jewish immigrants, leaving their fathers' shops and pushcarts and needle trades, charging into mainstream American business and the professions. They were the Jewish Greatest Generation.

Through his teens, Dad supported himself by working in commercial laundry, peddling clothes, selling shoes downtown, and helping in his parents' stores. Then, he found jobs working with metals in machine shops and plating in electronics companies, leading him to chemistry. I think of him in those years as earnest and hardworking.

He emerged in the 1940s as a chemist and metallurgist, exempt from military service. During the war, he worked at Thor Power Tool Company, supervising line workers in the heat treatment of steel for power tools and then the electroplating of valves for airplanes. He was unusual, a Jew in heavy industry, ambitious to get ahead. In the 1950s and 1960s, he worked for a series of companies developing industrial products with printed circuits and semiconductors. As a child, I thought Dad had invented them, and I wondered why we weren't rich.

My father was a man of science applied to technology who wanted the independence of his own business. When I was young, he seemed perpetually dissatisfied with his employers, changing from one to another every few years, working with different metals and products at each: Apollo Metals Inc., Scientific Control Laboratories, Independent Pneumatic Tool Co., The Dole Valve Company, Zenith Radio Corporation, Bastian-Blessing Company, Methode Electronics.

Or perhaps he was just restless. I never heard him complain of anti-Semitism, but now I wonder.

He had tried his own enterprises. First there had been a business with my mother's sister's husband, featuring a special procedure for electro-polishing stainless steel watches by the thousands. Dad walked away with large profits in the late 1940s.

With the money from that business, he and a high school friend had leased a North Side bowling alley at Lawrence and Milwaukee streets from his cousin Irving Tarnopol. It was rough, with everything from hiring Skid Row bums as pinsetters to operating a cocktail lounge, an unlikely enterprise for an ambitious Jewish family man. As a child, I delighted in the thunder of bowling balls crashing into pins, the cool low lights, and the strange smells.

My father gave it up and defaulted after four years on a five-year lease. He had battled his cousin for rent relief without success. At the bitter end, Cousin Irving refused to give him a break and return the $20,000 one-year security deposit and instead gave free rental of the alleys to his daughter Dolly. Then, he sold the building for a large profit.

That lost $20,000 was a huge sum in the early 1950s, money my father might have used to start another business. He never again spoke with that cousin. Years later, on a balmy summer evening in the early 1960s, when our family strolled at Lake Michigan's Belmont Harbor, Dad pointed out a small luxury boat, a yacht, belonging to the infamous Irving Tarnopol. Dad cursed him, "my own blood relative," as an unscrupulous, greedy man.

Other schemes followed throughout his life. I discovered during a home visit from graduate school in the 1970s that Dad was inventing things in his basement workshop. He had ideas for making money and elusive dreams of self-employment. He had taken out patents and sold his inventions by mail order, metal-plated things I never understood. But after the debacle with the bowling alley, he never again ventured full scale into business.

Dad took a job with TRW Cinch in 1961, and he stayed with

them until his retirement in 1980. It was a high-tech, heavy-industry conglomerate with divisions for automobile parts, electronics, space, energy, and communications. He worked with metal plating of parts, particularly gold plating for electronics. It was five days a week, 9 a.m. to 5:30 p.m., a sports coat and tie every day. "The job was good," he told me. "I was on my own. I selected my projects."

I charted another course from my father. Leaving high school for college in 1962, my goal was still that potent combination: tax attorney and certified public accountant. Despite my father's career path out of the Depression through scientific work in heavy industry and the national preoccupation with Sputnik and science education, I had no interest in science and technology. Nor was I attracted to business, my own or run by others. I thought those two professional degrees, law and accounting together, would bring me wealth and independence from the employers who had constricted my father's work life. I was tracking an American middle-class social bargain: accept the existing system, get your education, work hard, and become a successful self-employed professional.

At the University of Wisconsin–Madison in 1962, I inadvertently found myself in a great university that was one of the hothouses of the student upheaval. I discovered the rebellion during my second semester, just when the instructor for my introductory accounting class told me I had an aptitude for the profession. It was at the start of my brief fraternity membership when, as a pledge being hazed one evening, I suddenly realized this was silly. Sophomore year, I joined the uprising: the struggles for social justice and the big wide world of learning.

No more accounting, no prelaw preparation. I had a new plan based on courses with electrifying left-wing professors. I would become a historian, a radical historian of European working-class movements. That, I realized with absolute clarity, was the way to understand the past, the present, and the future and to change the world.

My world expanded. I did my third college year in Scotland at the University of Edinburgh. That was the time of the Free Speech

Movement at UC Berkeley, a student insurrection that I followed with rapt interest in the international press, much like my daughter Julia immediately enlisted in the Occupy Wall Street insurgency almost fifty years later. The young recognize the big historical moments of rebellion.

My new trajectory was clear. At twenty-one, I set my sights on graduate school in history at UC Berkeley. I hadn't thought about accounting for years. I didn't consider law school. I didn't apply anywhere else.

And I was right. Looking back now, higher education was enjoying a growth explosion with idealistic baby boomer students like me. University campuses were driving national and international social change. Berkeley was a leader in both the university and its student movement.

The bounty of the sixties and my own diligence provided. I won a Woodrow Wilson Fellowship, a prestigious scholarship large enough to finance my first year of graduate study. I was accepted into the history graduate program at Berkeley.

I never asked Dad what he made of it all. My steady, reliable father, son of immigrants, child of the Depression, problem-solving chemist, family man, creator of postwar suburban affluence, and purchaser of a new Chevrolet every two years had provided me with every advantage. I had the intelligence, work ethic, and family support to succeed in any career path I might choose. I declined the choices of my Skokie friends who pursued business and familiar professions. Instead, I selected student, rebel, and scholar. With scant information, I opted for years of graduate study and living on a pittance along an unknown path to a mysterious career as a university professor. And on the other side of the country, in unknown, unpredictable, glittering California. I knew it was right, but how could Dad get it?

And what did he think about my next transformation to freelance popular historian eleven years after I had enrolled in graduate school? That was the detour from the university professor career in 1977, just when I completed my PhD degree, my hard-earned passport to an academic job, a salary, and the end of an already extended adolescence.

By then, I had become preoccupied with the history of a left-wing Jewish chicken ranching community thirty miles to the north of San Francisco. First, it would be a book on the community. Then, there'd be a second book, on the life of one of the community's Communist trade union organizers. For these books on chicken ranchers, yet to be written, I gave up my hard-won academic career.

I was not politically far from my father. He was a lifelong liberal, a supporter of Franklin Roosevelt, Adlai Stevenson, and Martin Luther King. We both opposed the Vietnam War and supported the civil rights movement. We criticized Lyndon Johnson and Mayor Daley.

But I was not haunted by the Depression. I took for granted the affluence of the postwar era. I dismissed Dad's suburban world of "do your job, earn and consume, support your family, and live in a tidy house in boxy postwar neighborhoods." I didn't think much of the comfortable practical suburban world that launched me to Madison and Berkeley.

I emerged in the late 1970s with my PhD and new career: freelance popular historian. It was no job Dad could recognize: no workplace, no boss, no dress code, no paycheck, and almost no income. I scrambled for writing grants and temporary college teaching gigs. Others might have said my career path was downward mobility, from becoming an upper-middle-class professional to a wandering part-time teacher and wannabe writer, that is, an academic migrant worker.

At the time of the ALS diagnosis, when I was thirty-five, I didn't have to ask what my father thought of my work. I knew: "All those years in school. What kind of job is this?"

Dad ended his work life over three hours the July morning that began with the descent of our front steps. I wheeled him through the TRW Cinch offices as he X-ed the retirement papers, all his atrophied fingers could do. We went on to the laboratories and production areas for more goodbyes. An emaciated figure in a wheelchair, pushed through by his son, everyone could see he was a dying man.

Dad wanted a simple departure with no ceremony, but he insisted on this final visit. I had arranged it with the personnel office. They'd been relieved to hear from me. They'd been wondering how long he could continue working.

I had told a few people we were coming, but news of his presence spread. As I wheeled him through the building, colleagues spilled out of offices and laboratories to say goodbye.

I watched the reactions. Some of the clerical workers handling the retirement papers were officious, barely looking up as they processed his papers. Several executives were cautious as if a strong word or fast movement might cause him to expire. A couple of engineers seemed thrown, at a loss for what to say. Others simply denied what was happening, speaking as if he would return in a few weeks after a brief vacation.

A few people had avoided my father during the months of decline, and they remained behind closed doors, shunning him again this last time. "I don't understand it," Dad said later. "Some people are afraid of a dying man."

Others were wonderful. One office worker, Irene, had a warm understanding of what was happening from early on. She had joked and commiserated with my father over the months of his physical decline. Now I watched as she hugged him goodbye, and they laughed again.

There were coworkers who had helped him overcome ALS disabilities so he could work those last few months. They had supported him in the great struggle I had missed, the struggle to continue his normal work life. They said warm goodbyes, a joke here and there, a touch on the shoulder, and shared a few tears. I felt thankful for their decency and friendship.

With some, he spoke about his ongoing work. He had projects to continue and ideas to pass on. It was difficult for him to leave his work behind. "My body is shot to hell," he told them, "but my mind is good as ever."

As we traveled through the building, I could see he was proud that I was with him. He was not alone as he said his goodbyes. I was proud to be there for the final day of his public life. I was an assurance that Dad's life would continue at home, that he would be cared for by a loving family, and that there would be continuity through his son.

When he cried, he explained it was "this crazy disease" that made him emotional. He continued on, despite the tears, focusing on his colleagues and projects.

We did not stop at his laboratory, but I was certain it remained as I had seen it in December, crammed full with his projects. He hadn't even cleared out his desk, and his assistant asked me what to do with his belongings. All his energy had gone into continuing the job.

We passed the bathroom where he had taken that terrible fall from dropped foot. He shook his head again, remembering he could have died in there.

In a funny exchange with his immediate boss, my father expressed his gratitude for leaving him alone with his projects all those years. That independence had meant everything.

In a meeting with the company president, Mr. Sostek tried to talk about Dad's health, his family, and the son behind the wheelchair. But Dad wanted to discuss his current projects. He offered proposals for new approaches to metal plating processes. He had ideas for future technologies and business directions for TRW Cinch.

Dad wanted a consultant position with the company after retirement. Mom pushed him for this new job. He should be needed and valued, she thought, and have a purpose in this forced retirement with the great uncertainty ahead. At Mom's urging, he had already suggested it to his boss, and I had reminded an HR executive by telephone while arranging his retirement. In those days, I was never aggressive on behalf of my own employment. But as the meeting with Mr. Sostek ended, I raised it again. And then Dad chimed in, saying he should pay TRW to do it, and we all laughed. Mr. Sostek promised the company would get back to Dad.

Watching Dad with his colleagues, seeing his devotion to these people and projects, and seeing their respect and affection for him had me thinking about my work. I worked alone, without colleagues or common purposes or an institution that commanded my loyalty. And without much reward either; I was barely able to support myself, let alone a family. I believed in my work: those books I was writing about chicken ranchers. But I was isolated and poor. Here was my father, on his final workday, showing me another way as he was retiring and dying.

We concluded the visit with an inspection of the new building they had just erected on the site. Dad had helped design the electroplating machines inside.

We went with Steve John, the plant superintendent and one of Dad's oldest work friends. I had known Steve fifteen years earlier, the big boss when I worked at the South Side Chicago plant. He ran those factories with authority and a friendly word for everyone. I admired him.

Steve and my father gave me a tour, with Dad riding in the wheelchair beside Steve. They explained the hulking electroplating machines inside and the installation below ground of huge state-of-the-art equipment for pollution control. Then silence.

It was a cavernous building filled with machinery—massive, hard, bright machinery. The building was empty of other people. It was as if we were in a science-fiction movie, Earthlings on a strange planet, inspecting immense, unfathomable technology left behind by an ancient alien civilization, dwarfed by the technological world before us.

Dad sat in his wheelchair, quietly inspecting the scene, engrossed, intent, drinking it in. The contrast was painfully evident: my father, with his atrophying body, surrounded by that perfect, pristine, unyielding machinery whose life was just beginning.

Steve was quiet, pensive, grim. I felt tears trickling down my cheeks.

"In appreciation for the consideration shown to me and my son on our visit to Cinch," Dad wrote several weeks later, "I would like to offer some thoughts, both philosophical and actual, that might be a benefit to the company." What followed was a four-page, single-spaced letter. Attached was the technical paper I helped him rewrite in April in Boca Raton, now scheduled to be presented at a conference in September. He directed the letter to five company executives he had worked with on these programs.

The letter presented his key ideas for the company's plating operations and related manufacturing, sales, and business practices. He identified innovative plating techniques and the supporting science. He showed how these technological innovations would reduce costs, serve customers, and increase profit. The arguments were precise and brief. The tone was all business.

Dad's letter was dated a week after I left Skokie at the end of July. I believe he dictated it to Mom, and she typed it. I heard about this "thank-you letter" at the time but didn't see it until decades later.

The letter is a beautiful piece of business writing. Dad did it when he was facing the cataclysmic failure of his body, a gloomy retirement, and death. I don't know how he marshaled the mental discipline for this kind of organized and sustained technical business writing in August 1980. There was no hint the author was dying from ALS.

Why did Dad write the letter? Perhaps he was auditioning for the consultant position. But I don't think so. He was humoring Mom and me, who wanted him to be offered that position because we thought he had earned it, and we didn't know what else he would do in this ALS retirement. But Dad, I think, knew he was through with his work life. Like he often said, he was a realist.

No, this letter was about finishing his job. It addressed the big issues on his work agenda directed to the decision-makers he worked with. These were ideas he had labored on for many years. He had continued for months after the ALS diagnosis, knowing the end was coming. These projects would continue after he was gone.

Here was Dad wrapping up his past work and making his final contribution to the future. He was completing his job the way he knew, not by cleaning out his workshop or his desk but by offering his final ideas. That was what he had to give his colleagues at TRW Cinch. That was the right way to end his job.

Dad knew what was ahead for himself: all ALS.

CHAPTER 7

On My Own:
Facing the Business of ALS

JULY 1980

As a teenager, I daydreamed about what would happen if my parents were struck by a disaster. I'd imagine an act of fate, like an auto accident that left them injured. Disaster threatened until I stepped in. I would find a job and earn our living, take care of my parents, and raise my brothers.

I found a helper in these daydreams. I would turn to my father's friend, Maysh, for advice. Maysh, a Yiddish name translated to Maurice, was the leader in my parents' group of high school friends from the old Jewish West Side of Chicago. A thick man with a lumbering gait, close-cropped hair, and heavy facial growth, Maysh had a weighty physical presence. He was clever and funny, a delight to children and adults, with a magnetic warmth that tempered the sharpness of his jokes. Behind that merriness stood an old-fashioned patriarch, a self-made businessman, and a bedrock conservative. In my adolescent imagination, Maysh loomed as a substantial figure I could depend on.

I had long been intimidated by Maysh and the other men in that group of my father's friends. Through high school and college, I felt uneasy among them, as if I could be exposed at a whim by a dirty joke I did not understand. Later, when I visited home in the 1970s as a hippie radical graduate student, itinerant teacher, and aspiring writer, I was wary of them. My scruffy beard, shabby clothes, and radical politics were inviting targets for gentle ridicule. Among them, my freewheeling lifestyle left me feeling perpetually adolescent and unworldly. I regarded their smug suburban fraternity with a mixture of childhood awe and New Left contempt.

Even from the distance of California, I had been stunned when Maysh died suddenly from a heart attack in 1978, a year before Dad's ALS diagnosis. Dad's shock and grief at the time, his assurances that he did not fear death, had made me uneasy. Maysh's death also caused me to consider who I could turn to for advice if my imagined family crisis arrived. Although I had not seen Maysh in years, his death had been like losing a father-in-reserve.

Now, with Dad dying, I could not look to his old pals for help. Maysh was gone. Seymour had stopped visiting, admitting he could not bear to witness Dad's terrible deterioration. Charlie came with fear in his eyes, cautious, as if Dad was so delicate, he would shatter under the impact of a mistaken word or a wrong touch. Ziggie came with warmth and high spirits, but he froze, staring, bewildered, at that first meal when I was wiping the gooey phlegm coating the inside of Dad's mouth. Witnessing Dad's ALS, these awesome adults had become scared old men. I was on my own with the business of Dad's disease and our family's welfare.

The storm I feared had arrived. In the first days of my July visit, I was staggered by the pending issues. Dad had been waiting for me before making decisions about his retirement, pension, Social Security, investments, and life insurance. These decisions were connected to other pending issues with health insurance options and Medicare coverage. Everything seemed predicated on estimating expenses for home nursing care. And what about the coming costs of hospitalization? Underlying it all was a need to protect Mom's future financial security.

Dad was obsessed with placing all his business affairs in order, with *me* placing his business affairs in order. It was the first subject he raised with me each morning and our final discussion each evening. He was at it incessantly, scheming to reap every possible cent, prodding me to act quickly, and worrying about possible mistakes.

He wanted the most for his family, and he wanted it secured now before he suddenly died. But he was preoccupied with the little stuff, like competing bank interest rates and immediate check deposit. Or he would propose unnecessary big new projects, like selling their Florida condominium. With more at stake than he had ever handled, with too much time to think about it and too little strength to do anything about it, he was obsessed with our money.

Occasionally, he recognized that he was losing all sense of proportion. "Foolishness," he told me one day about his fixation on minuscule variations in comparative bank interest rates. I'm talking foolishness." I tried to persuade him otherwise, not simply to bolster his self-esteem but because I desperately wanted his help with important decisions.

From the time of his diagnosis nine months before, I had urged him not to make any major financial decisions without consulting me. I wanted to ensure that, with the distortions of terminal illness, he did nothing rash and silly. And I wanted to be part of the decision-making, sharing the great responsibilities for family finances. But now, suddenly, I was horrified to discover that he had done nothing. He had left it all for me.

Mom, who worked as a bookkeeper, had a precise mind for business matters, but I would not realize her excellent skills and judgment until I helped her after Dad's death. In 1980, she was coping with Dad and his struggles with ALS. She could not focus on our family's business problems.

I was scared. All my life, Dad had kept me away from family finances. He had been generous, underwriting me for a year of undergraduate study in Europe, buying me several cars, paying for my airplane trips to Chicago, and sending me cash when I was in a pinch. But he had been stingy with responsibility, shielding me from problems, which was the way of their generation. They always seemed to have everything under control. But now, at this perilous moment, he suddenly turned everything over to me.

"Why?" I asked myself.

I had an explanation. Faced with so many large and novel decisions, Dad must have procrastinated for months while he searched for medical treatment. Then, he must have simply ignored it all as he became preoccupied with his plummeting health and the daily struggle to continue working. The failure of his body, I thought, was worse than anything he or I had imagined. It was incapacitating, consuming, and scary. And I reminded myself that he was dying, that death held his attention.

Looking back today, over forty years later, I believe something else was happening in July 1980. One of the effects of bulbar ALS can be changes in cognitive ability, including weakened executive function. The contemporary literature is clear that ALS can diminish a person's capacity to organize information, interpret it, and make decisions. It can cause people to become fixated on single ideas, have difficulty remembering what they intend to do, and be unable to follow instructions. The current patient literature cautions that people diagnosed with ALS should make end-of-life arrangements "while they are still able to think clearly."

I understood bulbar ALS in July 1980 only for Dad's "inappropriate emotions," not for its impact on his capacity to make business decisions. As I searched for explanations for his giving up on tackling these problems, I also condemned Dad for not taking care of his business while he could. I would have done it differently, I told myself.

Of course, I had already done it differently, and that was my problem. At thirty-five, I had never handled a financial transaction larger than a small auto purchase. I had never held a full-time job.

I lived hand to mouth, on the margins of middle-class life. I was completely unprepared to handle the finances of a middle-class family.

I felt like I was being called to account. It seemed like my life had been a flight from responsibility and adulthood, from stable work, secure income, and worldly involvement. Despite holding a PhD, ten years of teaching experience, prestigious scholarship awards, and a publication contract, I had lived on a patchwork of academic grants and part-time teaching. I had no experience with the most conventional middle-class financial responsibilities and transactions.

Although I was irate about Dad dumping this unfinished business on me, for the first time, I appreciated his years of steady labor, patient saving, and cautious investment. Just as he had raised a family in middle-class comfort, supported three sons through advanced degrees, and took care of aged parents, now he seemed financially prepared for this catastrophic illness. Worried as I was about his declining income with retirement and rising medical expenses with ALS, studying our family's business papers again, I was surprised by the size of our assets. I suspected we had the resources to absorb the costs of ALS without a financial crisis.

This was a revelation. I never understood my parents' preoccupation with financial security. As a historian, I had explained it as the residual fears of their generation, as emotional baggage leftover from impoverished childhoods among immigrant families in the Depression. As a baby boomer, viewing America from the suburbs and the campuses during the postwar economic boom of the 1950s and 1960s, I had considered their fears silly.

Even as a radical—a socialist—I always believed that capitalist America would provide well for me and my family. Like others in the sixties New Left, my economic critique of American life had been directed against the manic enterprise and mindless consumption of the middle classes, based on everyday life in the suburb where I grew up. True poverty and economic want, what you might encounter in the 1960s War on Poverty, never seemed real to me. Not until now, facing Dad's ALS, did I grasp my parents' generation's belief in the possibility of unexpected economic calamity.

I shuddered to think what we would have done without their ready cash in the bank, the long-term investments, and those insurance policies. What if there had been no comfortable house where we could cope with Dad's bizarre new ALS problems? Just a few degrees change in temperature sent him shivering or sweating. The absence of central heating and cooling would have caused him enormous hardships.

I wondered how I would cope with catastrophic illness. Such things happen to men in their thirties. I had zero savings, investments, or resources. I had avoided the problem through a simple trick. I thought of myself as in my twenties, still invincibly young and healthy, still cushioned by my parents.

However, I was not in my twenties, and the 1960s were long gone. I was thirty-five years old and healthy. But my father was dying, and I faced decisions about family business arrangements and my parents' welfare.

Of course, my father's need for me was not a complete surprise. Not so long ago, I had confided to a therapist a fear that my father, self-assured and overbearing, always in control, was weak and would become dependent on me. Dad's ALS confirmed my worst suspicion: that what you fear most in life is bound to occur, like the emergence of some irrepressible part of your own self. Now it was happening, and I was not ready for our crisis with ALS.

I vowed never to allow this to happen again. Next time, I promised myself, whatever the crisis, I would be ready for it. I would have my life in order, I would have resources, I would know what to do, and I would not be scared.

During the first days home in July, as I prepared to tackle the employment, financial, and medical problems, I reassured myself by repeating my mantra: "You'll do what you have to do." To which

I added, "Forward. Don't look down." That's what I knew I had: willpower and gumption. Those resolute slogans comforted me.

I prepared to handle these problems as if I were beginning an academic research project. I identified the issues, reread the documents, established files, and prepared to-do lists.

I decided to represent myself as "Professor Kann" in these business dealings out in the world. This was a takeaway from my investigation into the cobra venom serum. I hoped the title would encourage others to take me seriously, even if I had doubts.

No one brushed me off, notwithstanding my self-designated title of professor. On the telephone with the Social Security Administration, the Muscular Dystrophy Association, and social service agencies, people didn't break out laughing; they responded at length. When I met with bankers, insurance agents, and health-care administrators, they received me as a man with responsibilities. I was, I soon decided, a credible representative of Dad and our family.

I was occasionally startled when reminded of this new role I had assumed. Calling the Jewish Welfare Federation for advice about home nursing, I was referred to a special program for "the Jewish aged." "Aged?" I thought of Dad as ill but not aged because if he was aged, then I must be his adult son.

Strangers helped. They responded to the nightmare ALS story. Within a few minutes on the phone, the Skokie town nurse, a welfare worker at the Jewish Federation, an insurance agent, and even a voice at Medicare would be deep into Dad's case. They were sympathetic, explained what I wanted to know until I understood, and volunteered other sources of assistance. I was grateful. They wanted to help me, and they did help me.

Within days, I was engrossed in this new world and began to enjoy it. At the end of each day, as I reviewed new information and sorted through decisions with Dad, I felt satisfied.

Conducting this business gave my life at home a weird dual nature. I was living from minute to minute with Dad, exhausted by his needs, wrenched by his struggle to hang onto his life and let go. At the same time, I was planning, calculating the costs of his illness, and making decisions that assumed he was dying. Even amid the gloom of Dad's suffering, I was excited by my newfound ability to handle our family's medical and financial planning.

I wondered if Dad was pained to watch me assume these responsibilities. No. When I reported my progress to him each evening, he was visibly relieved to hear me explain what I had learned and how I thought we should proceed with our various decisions. He had always been stingy with recognition of my accomplishments, but now he praised my work. I felt proud.

I took special satisfaction in unraveling our most nightmarish knot of financial and medical issues. From the time of Dad's diagnosis, his potential medical expenses had assumed huge, opaque, and worrisome proportions in my imagination. His health insurance had seemed like a precarious platform of help with the astonishing ALS needs—for moving, eating, talking, breathing—and the unnerving unpredictability of what was yet to come.

I had long feared the prospect of weighing the costs of Dad's health care against Mom's future financial security. How could I find a dollar balance between the needs of the dying and the needs of the living? That moment of accounting seemed to arrive on this July visit. And like many of life's moments of accounting, in the end, it was no big deal.

The problem began with estimating the likely costs of ALS treatment. I squirmed with discomfort over the prospect of inquiring into the costs of Dad's health care, but I had to know. I arranged to speak with a social worker from his MDA clinic.

I blurted out my question. "Since my father wants no heroic measures to prolong his life, then there should be no long hospital stays with huge bills. Is that right?"

"Yes."

"Even if his ALS takes the worst possible course?" I had vague ideas of what that could be, and I did not ask for details.

"Yes, no large hospital bills."

I could have hugged her.

"Then our greatest expense will be home care?"

"Yes."

More joy.

I thought home health care was what we needed, as soon as possible. Mom had to stop acting as Dad's nurse. She was taking care of him, alone, day and night, without a break unless one of the sons was visiting. It was exhausting, stressful, and lonely. Dad had become too difficult for her or any of us to care for alone. I thought we needed professional help.

I expected home care for ALS to be expensive. But here was some strange, good news. Speaking with home care agencies, I learned that we had minimal need for professional nurses because nothing could be done to treat Dad's condition. He would require "maintenance care"—cleaning, dressing, moving, feeding. Weird as it seemed, considering how sick he was, Dad only required unskilled home health aides. They were much cheaper than nurses.

I was appalled to discover that Medicare offered no support for this kind of home maintenance care. Medicare offered extensive coverage for institutionalizing the sick and aged in a nursing home, but it would not pay a cent for the cheaper, more humane alternative of home health care. Our government, building arsenals of multibillion-dollar weapons systems, did nothing to help families care for their own members facing a catastrophic illness like ALS.

But, wait, before blaming the US government, there was also Dad's private insurance plan. And there, reading and rereading his policy, I thought I discovered he qualified for extraordinary benefits. Because Dad was retiring under conditions of disability, I thought he was eligible for an extra year of coverage under the company's group plan before he had to convert to an individual policy to supplement Medicare. In my reading of the group plan, the benefits for retirement with disability included coverage for unskilled home health aides.

In telephone calls with his company's HR department and then with the health insurance company, I was astonished to learn that my reading was correct. Continuing group health insurance would cover most of Dad's home health maintenance care for the first year following retirement. I was swept with gratitude again for Dad's company and now its generous group insurance plan. And I was impressed with Dad for earning these benefits.

Looking back now, I understand why I was so worried and excited about insurance coverage for home health care. Even as I celebrated the good news about low medical expenses and extensive insurance coverage, I worried about what would happen after a year, when we would have to pay for those home health aides entirely by ourselves. Worrying about a year into the ALS future was like fretting about another galaxy, but I fretted.

My fears were justified. We would discover that the costs for home aides to care for Dad around the clock, every day, were astronomical. If he had lived on with ALS for five or ten years as he and Mom originally hoped, we would have encountered the financial crisis I had feared. I thought we were lucky with Dad's insurance coverage for home aides that first year. And even then, it never occurred to me that in the murky future, I would have to fight the insurance company to cover the cost of those home health aides we did use.

I checked out home health-care agencies. I identified two that seemed competent, friendly, and reliable. With Mom's collaboration, I selected one and confirmed with the insurance carrier that this agency's home health-care services were covered. We chose a start date a week before I would return to California. That was a huge accomplishment.

Where the health insurance problems seemed deadly serious, I found the life insurance problems to be macabre and funny. At retirement, Dad had the option of converting his company group policy to an individual plan at the same high benefit level if he was willing to pay a whopping annual premium that discouraged conversion. I still remember his company's benefits administrator raising an eyebrow when I said we would do it. I was betting that Dad would die within a few years before the high premiums would swallow a policy payoff.

The life insurance company's agent approached our transaction with continued pitches to buy other insurance. At the final meeting with Dad and me in our living room, when I hesitated over whether to pay the new premium annually or in installments, he turned to me in an aside, voice hushed but not really very low, speaking as if Dad's ailment prevented hearing, and he assured me that we would receive a prorated return of the annual premium if Dad died before the end of the premium term. It was so crass that I almost laughed, except that he had answered my unspoken question. That decided, we completed the transaction, and he left with a final pitch to buy his homeowners' insurance. When the door closed, Dad and I laughed out loud. Our sense of humor about ALS—about life continuing as normal in the midst of disaster—had not entirely disappeared.

Dad did tell me what to do about another matter: a bill collector was badgering us about some persisting squabble from an old auto accident case that had been settled. When he called again one morning, Dad said, "Tell him I'm dying," as if we could drive him away with gallows humor. I did just that, with a description of ALS. We never heard from him again.

———◇———

I found an adviser for insurance decisions: Bucky Levin, the brother of Dad's deceased friend Maysh, who ran an insurance agency. I was on the edge of tears when I met Bucky. He not only looked like Maysh, but he had Maysh's gruff, kind, and assured manner. It was as if my adolescent fantasy had come true. Here was one of those thick, responsible, experienced older men who would guide me.

Bucky was a calming influence. I felt reassured by his solid advice about the various insurance problems. He told me what to do, and I happily did as he said.

Then, as I was feeling secure with the resolution of the insurance issues, Bucky stunned me with a warning: "You should be ready to place Sam in a nursing home. It will be better for everyone. There is only so much you can do for him at home."

Bucky's advice violated my promise to Dad that we would care for him at home. It was contrary to all my convictions and planning. I felt terror at the mere mention of a nursing home. It was unimaginable: overriding Dad, finding the nursing home, placing him in some unfeeling institution, leaving him helpless with strangers. No.

I pushed Bucky's advice from my mind as an unthinkable betrayal. That was how his generation handled their aging parents. That was Dad and Grandma, not me and Dad. Let Bucky place his own father in an institution. We would take care of our own.

Of course, that was Mom doing the taking care of Dad. But on this matter, I knew her wishes. I never discussed Bucky's advice with her.

I had another adviser, this one from a younger generation, my cousin Neil. Several months earlier, I had urged Dad to have his will reexamined. Dad had turned to Neil, who was an attorney with a law firm that specialized in estate planning. He prepared an estate plan for my parents that would save us money, along with avoiding a probate proceeding when Dad died.

I remembered Neil and his two brothers as teens with strong professional interests, and now in their twenties, they were all established in successful careers. Mickey, a surgeon, had recommended Dad to a neurologist when he reported weakness in his legs. Bob, a general practice attorney, had handled that 1978 auto accident case for Mom and Dad. And now Neil had prepared my parents' estate plan. None of them would accept payment in return for their services. I felt like I should have been doing the work they handled for my parents. But I knew I was just a historian—no use for these real-life problems.

I wanted Neil to explain the estate plan he had prepared for my parents so that my arrangements for investments and insurance would be consistent. More than that, I wanted to see how Neil operated as a downtown lawyer. I was curious.

I made an appointment to see Neil at his LaSalle Street office in the heart of Chicago's financial and legal district. Several days later, I was ascending in a fast, high-rise elevator. I walked into a handsome lobby with sweeping downtown views, my first entry into the world of law.

I had not seen Neil in over ten years. When he came out to greet me, I was surprised to find the same boyish face I recalled from when he was a kid. And yet, mysteriously, he was comfortable in this downtown law office, complete with a dark suit, white shirt, and sporty bow tie.

Neil explained the estate plan he had prepared for my parents. He was friendly, businesslike, clear, efficient, and entirely at my service. He described what I would have to do to fund the trust he had established. He was receptive to my urging that his law firm accept our payment for all costs incurred in preparing the estate plan.

Neil closed the meeting by praising my actions in bringing order to my parents' affairs. "When the going gets tough," he said, "the tough get going."

That platitude seemed right for Neil to say and for me to hear. I left impressed, appreciative, and more confident. Three years later, I remembered that meeting. That's when I applied for law school. Thank you, Neil, for your generosity and career example.

My cousin Norm became my closest adviser, a true friend and confidant. Norm, my mother's sister's son, was between Dad's age and mine. He was a CPA and a shrewd businessman with whom I'd been arguing politics since I was radicalized at the University of Wisconsin in the sixties. After Dad's diagnosis, I began meeting Norm for dinner every time I was in town. He was sharp on financial matters, with unfailing common sense. I learned that I could review every important decision with Norm. He was my reality check, my Maysh.

Norm had known Dad for decades since Dad was in a wartime business with Norm's father, and Norm admired Dad as smart and capable. Norm accepted reality, unblinking, and called things as they were. I thought he understood our family problems, whether financial, health, or human, and he was unfazed. He would commiserate with

Dad about ALS: "Sam, you were dealt a hand from the bottom of the deck. Just bad luck." For Norm, that bad hand was what Dad had to live with, and I had to play. He gave me practical, sensible advice. With Norm, I felt confident that everything I did would turn out okay, except Dad's ALS.

Norm helped me with one other problem: whether to move my parents to Oakland near where I lived. I had raised the idea several months before my visit, and Dad was ready to go by the time I arrived in July as if a change of scene would improve his health. Within a few days after my arrival, considering Dad's physical and emotional condition and his bulbar symptoms, I wondered if these transitions were already too much change for him to absorb. I began questioning whether a change of residence was preferable or even possible. Could they travel cross-country? Could I really help them in Oakland?

Norm recognized the benefits for them in Oakland, having me close by. But he thought they were well set up to grapple with ALS in their Skokie home where Mom was managing the ALS challenges, they had the necessary medical services, and family and friends were nearby. He also questioned whether Dad had the strength for a cross-country flight.

Listening to Norm, I suspected it was already too late for them to change residences. My parents would have to entirely reestablish themselves in Oakland, with only me for help. And what Norm didn't say outright but encouraged me to consider was that my own position in the Bay Area was tenuous at best, with no solid job or stable income.

We settled the issue after I found a promising Skokie home healthcare agency whose services would be covered by Dad's insurance. With that home help, I thought we would be set for the coming winter in Skokie, even though Dad would remain inside for months. I thought we could reevaluate in the spring, simply assuming Dad would be alive in the spring. Mom and Dad both agreed.

Over those months of ALS, I formed a deep, lasting friendship with Norm. We later visited each other in San Francisco and Miami.

We spoke regularly by telephone for many years, particularly later when Norm was ill. We discussed family, politics, health, his Florida retirement, and his tennis game. He followed my new career as an attorney. In the end, we talked about his own terrible disease, multiple myeloma, another fatal hand dealt from the bottom of the deck. I miss Norm.

I received advice from another person during my July visit: Dad's neurologist at the MDA clinic, Dr. Nicholas Vick. At my request, I met with him at Evanston Hospital a week after I arrived in Skokie.

Dad, who had contempt for "useless" doctors since his diagnosis, spoke highly of Dr. Vick: "He's no-nonsense. He tells it the way it is." Dad preferred frank talk about his condition.

Dr. Vick was familiar with Dad as a patient. He knew Dad's struggles to continue working over many months with ALS. He was aware of Dad's labors to continue walking. He knew about the ingenious walker Dad had designed and Dad's satisfaction in seeing his mechanical ideas realized. They had many discussions about ALS. He admired Dad.

Dr. Vick described other families that had endured ALS. He told me, "Your family will survive too." I thought he meant this: *ALS is awful, Sam will live and die with it, and the awful will end*. I wanted him to understand our suffering and assure me of our family's life beyond it.

Dr. Vick spoke about his opposition to some extreme measures to prolong life. It was a morality lecture, very preachy, about what he would do and not do to his fellow man. He gave the example of invasive ventilation for patients no longer able to breathe independently because of weakened respiratory muscles, the most frequent cause of death for ALS patients. This intervention required a cut in the trachea, the windpipe, and the insertion of a tube attached to a mechanical ventilator, a breathing machine that forced air into the lungs. It left the patient alive, but likely in a nursing home, entirely dependent on the breathing machine and around-the-clock aides, breathing but no longer able to eat, drink, or speak, at risk for becoming "locked in," unable to move or communicate. Dr. Vick insisted this intervention was something he would not inflict on a patient. He said he had spoken with Mom and Dad about refusing such extreme measures to prolong survival, and they had agreed. That, I realized, was what Dad was speaking about on the backyard patio when I arrived for this July visit: "No heroic measures." It was not until many years later that I read about some ALS patients with tracheostomies who were grateful for their prolonged lives with breathing machines.

I asked Dr. Vick for his opinion of how long Dad would live with ALS. I thought Dr. Vick would have an informed estimate based on statistics, his experience, and his familiarity with Dad's rate of decline. I didn't expect a precise answer, but I wanted his approximation of when this ordeal was likely to end for Dad and the rest of us.

Today, on the internet, you can find functional measures that tell you how far a patient's ALS has progressed, but in 1980, I only had my own opinion. My view was that Dad's ALS was developing fast. I thought he was at the low end of the life expectancy for men diagnosed in their sixties. I thought he would last under two years from the diagnosis in October 1979.

Dr. Vick offered nothing specific. But he told me that Dad could die from ALS any time. Dad simply might stop breathing in his sleep. That surprised me. Dying now, as a possibility, not even a year after his diagnosis, was much sooner than I had expected.

Dr. Vick surprised me again by raising a related topic: suicide. This was not something I had expected to discuss with him. Again, he explained his policy. He would not assist an ALS patient to end his life. But he thought suicide was okay if an ALS patient wanted it and the family could arrange it. He said he thought suicide happened with ALS patients more often than people thought.

Thinking about the meeting later, I wondered if Dr. Vick was giving us some kind of license for Dad to end his life. But without any help from him.

How, I wondered, *did a family arrange a suicide for an ALS patient physically unable to help himself? And how can Dr. Vick just leave this to a patient and family to figure out?* I was puzzled and irritated by Dr. Vick's laissez-faire approach, where he approves of suicide, or at least does not judge but does not help. *Fine for him*, I thought. *He maintains his own principles. But how about us? We're left to find a way on our own.*

I spoke with Mom that afternoon about my conversation with Dr. Vick. She was shocked by his acceptance of suicide. If she had had a similar end-of-life conversation with Dr. Vick, she certainly did not recall it. I had let her know that these things happen. Extraordinary measures to prolong life could be rejected. Suicide was possible.

Dad and I had already spoken of suicide. No long or detailed discussion. When I first saw him in December, he said he had considered suicide after the October diagnosis. But he said he had worried about the possible disqualification of a life insurance payout for our family. I did not try to learn how seriously he had considered suicide. I simply listened.

Dad also spoke about suicide on this July visit after my meeting with Dr. Vick. I didn't tell him what I heard from Dr. Vick. Independently, one afternoon, he told me he took no pleasure in living with ALS. He said he should have ended his life right after he received the diagnosis—when he still could. But, he continued, now he was too weak to do it himself. And if anyone helped him, he said, it might be considered a crime.

I just listened again. He seemed to be ruling out suicide, but, like Dr. Vick, he was thinking about it. I thought Dr. Vick may have known that Dad's current condition, when patients begin to grasp the horror of ALS, was when some patients thought seriously about it.

Dr. Vick's discussion of suicide, and then Dad's, had me thinking about it too. Suicide was a fearsome subject: so big, so final, so unimaginable.

I didn't know my own views. I thought I had no ethical scruples against suicide. I didn't consider it wrong. Not after witnessing Dad's suffering with ALS, with worse ahead. But an ethical belief, I thought, was different from our real-life situation. Real life was Dad with this terrible, unstoppable disease, his considering suicide, Mom shocked by the mention of suicide, his neurologist on the sidelines, and all the social and legal prohibitions against taking life.

At times, exasperated with Dad, I had thought he should have ended it all. I had thought he should have spared himself and our family from his terrible decline, from this suffering.

But, I thought, how could he have committed suicide when he was diagnosed last October without understanding what was ahead with ALS? His suicide months ago would have been devastating for the rest of us. Not yet having lived through his ALS, we might have felt deserted and even considered him a coward. And with an early suicide, I would not have had the opportunity to live through ALS with him. I would have missed his heroic struggle to continue his life, Mom's great struggle to help him, and the family and friends who supported him. I would have missed Dad reviewing his life history in the face of death. I would have missed the sweetness along with the frustration of helping Dad live with ALS. His early suicide would have been an easier death for him but terrible for the rest of us.

Now that Dad would need assistance to end his life and was thinking about it, I wondered, *Will I help Dad if he asks? How much misery does he have to be in? How much more misery can he suffer? How does someone paralyzed by ALS, a quadriplegic, commit suicide?*

After Dad retired, his life at home became richer. The house hummed with activity. Friends and family continued visiting in large numbers, most fellow migrants from the prewar Jewish West Side of Chicago, their dense historical ties of neighborhoods and families living on in our Skokie home. There was a stream of telephone calls for the business I was conducting with finances, insurance, estate planning, health care, and home aides. The doorbell buzzed for the delivery of packages with ALS support gear. There was planning for work on that wheelchair ramp. Dad's barber came by for a home haircut. Everyone wanted to help.

It was touching to see Dad happily pass an afternoon with a niece, neighbors, or old friends who continued to visit for a few hours with an ailing man. When Dad cried while reminiscing about the past, dwelled on his disease again, and slobbered as Mom or I wiped the phlegm from inside his mouth and down his chin, they took him as he was with no sign of embarrassment. Much of the time, Dad was on the edge of the conversation, unable to push in, no longer caring, content to be surrounded by people who knew and loved him.

We tried to continue normal life. We sat down for dinners together, sometimes with a guest, and we all ate as Dad choked and drooled with his separate, soft, easily digestible food. Sometimes, his mouth didn't become "thick" with the dense saliva, and a meal could be successful. More often, he insisted on being taken away when the food became too difficult for him to swallow, the kitchen temperature got too high for his comfort, or some other ALS thing disturbed him. When he issued those peremptory orders to move him immediately—before I had completed my meal—my long-standing resentments over his arbitrary demands bubbled up from childhood. But now that quickly passed, and I would help him leave for the living room, swab out the gooey saliva, wipe his face, and talk with him until everyone was ready to join us.

I was exhausted by the succession of visitors and the constant activity. But Dad needed that life inside our house. He was too much in his mind, unable to do anything but think, mainly about ALS. He needed people and talk and ideas. And the people came as he wanted.

Those visitors made me wonder again what old age and illness might be like for me and my generation. Despite our preoccupation with "community," we were a generation on wheels, with fleeting friendships and communities. I had good friends, but I was not anchored in a network of family and community ties or in a shared history that would sustain me through something like ALS. *Bleak prospects*, I thought at the time, *for my own old age*.

One day, great news! TRW Cinch hired Dad as a consultant. Triumph! For Dad, Mom, and me.

Through many telephone calls, Mom arranged for the telephone company to provide a speakerphone for a disabled customer. This was innovative technology. The company sent three men who spent a morning setting it up. We practiced and called them back for adjustments.

I happily took notes at Dad's first consultant telephone conference. I was afraid that something would happen on the call that would humiliate Dad. I never knew what problem ALS would bring. But Dad was absorbed in the call, concentrating on the problem at hand. He gamely pushed into the discussion with his own ideas. Here was my problem-solver Dad at work.

But the speakerphone was clumsy, and the sound was unclear. Dad did not have endurance for an hour meeting, and ALS was weakening his voice. He could barely be heard by the end of the call, and his participation became marginal.

A month later, in California, I was not surprised to learn that Dad's consultant job had faded away. I thought of all our discussions about it, our strategizing over how to persuade his company, our conviction that this was important work for his retirement, and our hours dealing with the speakerphone and telephone company. We had believed that Dad might have something resembling a normal retirement with some satisfying paid work in the mix. We were wrong. Nothing could be normal with his ALS.

One thing that did stick was Dad's preoccupation with the weather. Sitting up in bed, his second request every morning, after his wristwatch, was to hear a weather report. He listened to weather reports throughout the day, with a final check for tomorrow's weather before bedtime. He was so interested that Rob bought him a weather radio, a terrific gift that he used.

I never understood Dad's fixation on the weather, particularly because he rarely went outside farther than the front porch. Rob thought it was left over from when Dad was twelve, in 1927, driving Grandpa around Chicago on store business. The weather, like rain or snow, would have been a big factor in the success of those driving errands. And then there was his driving across the city to work for decades. Weather had been a lifelong daily concern for him.

I had my own theory. The weather, after all, was beyond everyone's control. Notwithstanding Dad's paralyzed limbs, everyone else was just like him with the weather: powerless. I thought he found some comfort there.

One Sunday, just for pleasure, we decided on an afternoon expedition to the shores of Lake Michigan. Dad agreed to use the temporary wheelchair. But, in the absence of a ramp, we still had to negotiate those five front steps, another ominous reminder that we were lagging behind the disease. He needed a ramp to leave the house. It was planned but not yet done.

Everything about this journey was a problem. Transferring in and out of the car required yet another intricate system of strained movements, cautious steps, select handholds, daring swings, and my helping hands. Mom had to pack for all eventualities: damp washcloth to cool his face, soft food, napkins for wiping drool, even the urinal—as if she was bringing a toddler.

We struggled to maintain our optimism that we could do this little expedition. The inclusion of a new passenger, the wheelchair, presented special challenges. Dad was tense and bossy about how it went in and out of the car, especially how I set it up for his use. Deviation from his instructions or fumbling with adjustments brought a flurry of irritated new directives.

I thought I understood his anxiety. He was approaching a public appearance on a device he could not control, and I was not certain I would behave any better. For once, I managed to maintain my good humor and confidence during his orders and complaints.

The mood changed once Dad was sitting in the wheelchair. It was a bright, warm Sunday afternoon. On the promenade at Evanston's Memorial Park, we joined a parade of strollers, joggers, cyclists, skateboarders, and roller skaters. The wheelchair was just another mode of transportation, not drawing a glance. The green grass was filled with lazy bodies basking in the sun. Lake Michigan stretched out in endless blue to the horizon. The skyscrapers of downtown Chicago loomed large and clear in the distance.

We parked ourselves on the grass, looking out toward the lake and the magnificent Chicago skyline. Mom stretched out on the grass and dozed in the warm sun. I sat alongside Dad in his wheelchair, chatting with him and simply gazing out at the scene.

It was Dad's last expedition for the simple pleasure of public urban life. I remember it as a perfect afternoon, perfect because it was so normal, like many other Sunday expeditions during my visits home. This is what people do on a summer Sunday afternoon. For a few hours, we stepped outside the confines of our house and ALS. That was a sweet taste of our former life.

A week later, we went to pick up Dad's specially constructed wheelchair. I had no remaining illusions that it would transform our lives moving him around the house.

It was heartbreaking to watch Dad at that MDA workshop when the proud mechanic wheeled out the new chair. It was a spooky-looking thing, narrow enough to cradle his body, with a high back to provide support to the top of his shoulders, higher yet with the attachment of the headrest that would support his neck and head, and multiple features for containing dangling feet. It emphasized his body's frailness and the weirdness of his disease. Dad looked at it quietly, trying to maintain a brave front, despondent over his new transport and day chair on wheels.

When we reached home, he immediately banished the offending device to the basement. He preferred to allow his world to contract to the confines of the house rather than appear in the public world as a disabled man. He did not even want the wheelchair in sight. He did not want the appearance of disease in the house or for the house to hint at a hospital. He was ready to resist that wheelchair.

Mom was frantic that Dad would never use the wheelchair and that she was fated to continue her supporting role in his excruciating efforts to walk. "I can't do it anymore," she insisted. "You've got to talk with him."

Like Mom, I was exasperated by his refusal to make our lives easier with a few concessions to the disease.

A day later, I asked him to begin using the wheelchair when he was tired, for Mom's and my sake. He agreed. He seemed relieved. That evening, he bravely requested the wheelchair for his final trip to the bedroom. After that, the weird wheelchair resided in the den, out of sight, ready for occasional transportation between rooms and even for just sitting.

Nonetheless, I urged Dad and Mom that he continue walking as much as he could, as long as he could, however much time and assistance it required. I was beginning to understand that the weaker he was and the less he moved, the more often new complications would develop. His lack of movement was already causing problems with his blood circulation and bowel movements, and some patches of skin were irritated from the many hours inert in bed. There would be no shortcuts. There was no escaping the toll of the infernal disease.

Mom told me that no one ever offered to stay the night with Dad so she could get away for a rest. Well-wishers would ask Mom, "What can I do to help?" But they never offered specific help, and Mom did not know where to begin with what she needed. "No one," she said bitterly, "can understand what I am going through."

Of course, none of these friends and relatives could have taken care of Dad for several days while Mom vacationed, if only because he would not have tolerated it. Mom and the three sons were the only ones who could do it.

My July visit included a plan for me to care for Dad while she went away for a few days. I offered it, and to my surprise, Mom accepted. At first, it would be a week's vacation at their Florida condo. But she worried that would be too long for Dad and me. She changed it to four days with friends at a Wisconsin resort. The day came, and she actually left.

It was a grueling four days. Dad's routines and needs prevailed, morning through night.

Dad and me, alone together, were at our worst several times. Once, after dinner, while I was helping him move from the kitchen to the living room, the phone rang, and he directed me to answer as if he could continue walking or standing on his own. We snapped back and forth until I yelled at him, "Ignore the phone and continue *walking*." He did, but he was exhausted by our clash and told me to take him to bed for the night. It was 7:30.

Worse was a clash just before bedtime. I didn't place the water for the night in the right spot. He yelled, I yelled, and he became hysterical, shouting multiple directions. He became hot and agitated.

Lying in bed, he began gasping for breath. He looked like he would stop breathing. I lifted him back up to a sitting position, where he calmed himself, and we started over with the bedtime routine. As we finished, when I turned out the light, I began thinking about his failing respiratory system, the weakened diaphragm muscles that assist with pumping air in and out of the lungs, and Dr. Vick's statement that Sam could stop breathing and die anytime. Meanwhile, Dad, still absorbed with the sleep arrangements, called out to me with one more set of instructions for opening some windows and adjusting the house temperature. He was too warm.

I wondered how much longer Mom or any of us could cope with him. For the first time, I wondered if we would need to place him in a nursing home.

Dad and I also had sweet moments together. Most evenings, we made our way outside on the front porch. We would watch cars pass by and talk. One evening, he told me, "Thanks for putting up with me all day," and another, "Thanks, Skip, for making this a nice day." He melted my anger. Another evening, we ate watermelon—I fed him pieces—and watched a summer lightning storm in the distant sky.

Dad reflected on his health one evening. He felt himself becoming worse. He spoke of his weakening arms and legs, now paralyzed. Even his right arm, which he still used to flick newspaper pages, was all but gone. The fasciculations, the strange twitching of his muscles that had amused us all at the beginning of the illness, were largely over. His motor neurons had mostly died, the twitching signs of disruption of the motor neuron signals to the muscles had ended, and his forsaken muscles were largely atrophied. He could still find fasciculations here and there on a few remaining muscles, and he showed me some on his thigh. I found nothing funny about those anymore. I thought of them as death tremors, sinister when they appeared and more sinister when they were gone.

He didn't mention the problems that scared me most in July: swallowing difficulties, weakening voice, and compromised breathing. All were symptoms of bulbar ALS. All perilous, developing fast.

Nothing was stopping his decline. He pondered his homeopathic treatment. "Holistically speaking, maybe ALS is my fault." Here was the patient blame that Susan Sontag had noted in her critique of holistic medicine.

Dad acknowledged that he didn't have a "positive attitude" as holistic medicine called for and Mom wanted. "I can't help being realistic," he explained. He recounted the homeopath's most recent treatment, running a low electrical current through him for forty-five minutes. Dad, a metallurgist and electroplater, could tell what would happen with this minuscule current: nothing. And, indeed, nothing had come of it.

One evening during Mom's vacation, he volunteered another explanation of why he had not committed suicide: he simply had not understood what was coming with ALS. He couldn't imagine this utter devastation to his body and how helpless and dependent he would become. That was exactly what the pamphlet had warned me when I first began reading about ALS. I had not grasped it either. For the first time, I said if he ever wanted, we could discuss suicide.

And another evening, in a surprise to me, he spoke of how he would be remembered after he died. He feared it would only be with ALS. He wanted to be remembered for his entire life.

One of those evenings, I asked Dad if he might want to speak with a psychotherapist from the MDA clinic, someone who understood ALS. I thought he might have things on his mind he'd want to discuss: the ruination of his body, his total dependence on others, worries about family, and death. He was clashing with Mom, the sons were not right for confidential thoughts about life and death, and his pal Maysh was gone. Surrounded by people caring for him and visiting him, he still seemed isolated and alone in his imprisoned body.

He replied that he did have many unspoken thoughts, but he had always been a private person who kept his thoughts to himself. He saw no reason to change now. He considered himself realistic about what was happening with ALS, without "hang-ups." He said he didn't need someone to speak with.

I admired his integrity. I thought, *There will be no confidential therapy about fears and wishes. He will die as he has lived, with his own counsel and his own way.*

Mom returned home after four days away, a relief for me. I was exhausted by my round-the-clock care for him, by the intensity of my emotions while living closely with him.

Mom bubbled with enthusiasm over her trip: the drive, the resort, her room, the relaxed days, the restaurant meals, her cocktail one evening, a Bloody Mary. I thought, *This is a trial run for being a widow.* And Dad must have thought the same thing. For days after, he referred to her as "your mother." His wife was gone.

———◇———

We began professional home care the week before I returned to California.

First was insurance coverage and the costs. Next was identifying the agencies and then talking with them about Dad's condition, his needs, and their services. I discussed it many times with Mom, Dad, and my brothers. And, of course, I had to select the agency.

Dad asked me to arrange for his home health aide to be a man. "It's my pride," he explained. The aide would be dressing and undressing him, helping him pee, wiping his rear end, washing his body, and feeding him. The help would be so personal, so intrusive. I made the request. All the agencies said they'd try, but none would promise a male aide. I knew the aides would be women; another piece of Dad's dignity would be stripped away.

We began with unskilled home health aides coming for the day three times each week. I thought we would increase the aide time as needed in the coming months.

The first day came. We wanted to put our best selves forward, with me giving Dad a washing in the morning and Mom cleaning the house. In the middle of our preparations, the agency's nurse supervisor turned up unexpectedly, two hours early, to initiate home care. I was irritated. She threw us off schedule. When the actual aide showed up on time, we were behind schedule. Dad was on the toilet. That's how they met. Welcome to the world of ALS and home health aides.

No problem. The aide joined right in with me, preparing Dad for the day. I was reluctant to give him over to this stranger, but she was good-natured, competent, and, best of all, took charge. She stepped right in to help Dad and hung in there with his detailed directions. She was not afraid. She assisted him with authority.

This will work, I thought, exhilarated.

It wasn't perfect. Two days later, one of the visiting nurse supervisors talked with Dad in a singsongy voice as if he were a child who couldn't understand much. Dad responded with sarcastic irony that she did not understand, and she continued her patronizing patter.

Mom was outraged, upset that he didn't tell her off. "He could run circles around her," she insisted, with an unfortunate choice of metaphors since his running days were over. But, wow, it was good to see her proud of him and ready to fight for him.

Week one with home care was a huge success. The aides were competent and reliable. They stepped right into the job, and Dad was working with them. Mom was freed from attending to Dad's needs when an aide was present.

As I was packing for my return to California, I heard Mom talking on the phone about the possibility of going to Florida for the coming winter. She said they could bring along one of the home aides to help them.

Impossible, I thought.

But good to see Mom dreaming of happy times together.

After a month of caring for Dad and arranging for my parents, I found it strange to think of returning to my own life in California. *Yes*, I assured myself, *I have that other life*.

I had arrived feeling unprepared for our ALS crisis. I left knowing that I had done everything I could to help Dad and Mom. Dad was retired and launched on life at home. Their business and legal affairs were in order. Their insurance was activated. They had the medical services and equipment they needed. The wheelchair ramp was scheduled for construction. They had new support with home health aides.

I was surprised by what I had accomplished on the July visit. I was departing with everything stabilized. In those final days of my visit, for once, I did not feel helpless before the relentless advance of ALS.

Before I left, Dad wanted to give me a gift. I brought up from his basement workshop all the good tools I could find: mallets and hammers, large wrenches and long screwdrivers, many pliers, crowbars, levels, measuring tapes, his electric drills, and much more. He wanted to give them to me and my brothers.

We went through the tools together, and he discussed each—its purpose and what he had used it for. He was in tears about giving away these tools, but he wanted his three sons to have them. And I wanted them.

Preparing to leave, packing his tools, I wondered, *Has Dad given me another gift?*

He had relinquished his responsibilities to me for end-of-life business and health care. He had waited for my return home to join him on his retirement morning, the goodbye to his world of work. He had requested that I participate in the mourning for his fading life by listening to the opera arias and the recollections of his life. He even joined me in a successful project to fashion a comfortable chair for his sitting. He had allowed me to face the crisis with him. He had praised my accomplishments on this visit, and this time, it was enough praise.

When I left Skokie at the end of July, I thought he had given me a huge gift. Dad had helped me grow up.

CHAPTER 8

"What More Could I Do?"

OCTOBER 1980

I hauled Dad's tools back to the Bay Area and brought them to my Sonoma ranch, where Dad and I had worked together one weekend. It was difficult to leave them in the toolshed. "Of course," a friend explained. "Those tools are your inheritance."

Today, over forty years later, when I am working at the ranch, I still come across some of those tools. I think of Dad and me.

We had an unhappy history with tools. It dates back to my doomed seventh-grade reorganization of his basement workshop. There had been all those failed attempts to work together on house projects. And there was that visit to my ranch a year before the ALS diagnosis when Dad tried to apologize for not teaching me how to use his tools, and I rejected the apology.

Now, at the conclusion of my July 1980 trip to Skokie, Dad was ready to give me his tools. I was ready to accept them.

———◇———

I bristled at the life I found awaiting me in Oakland. After the high intensity of my Skokie visit, after my success with Dad's business and health-care issues, I found myself mired in the same marginal job: a part-time university teacher with unstable employment and low pay, dependent on the needs of academic administrators to fill temporary teaching jobs. Before Dad's diagnosis, I had been proud of these jobs that supported me as a writer. But now, suddenly, I detested this work. I saw an endless struggle ahead as a supplicant teacher, with none of the compensation, rights, and respect accorded regular tenured faculty. I told myself, "I'm better than this."

Neither of my books was published. One was coming soon, but it was the life story of a Communist trade union organizer who became a chicken rancher. This book would not solve my employment problem.

I still did not have a house. Before I left for the July visit, I spoke with a friend about buying half her duplex. With no steady income or savings, I'd never qualify for a mortgage. Mom and Dad offered to stake me in the down payment and cosign for a loan, but I decided not to take money from them during the battle with ALS. When I returned to the Bay Area, I told my friend the sad truth: I couldn't afford the duplex. *Buy house* remained on my to-do list.

I returned to one bright spot—Stephanie, the new girlfriend I had revealed to Dad.

We met at my Sonoma ranch in 1977. Stephanie was with a group of friends that one of my partners brought for the weekend. I met her in our pond, where she was skinny-dipping with her friends. I spotted her curly red hair from across the water and jumped in. She was young and striking. She was a poet and literature student, taking time off from undergraduate studies for travel and exploration. She was smart, funny, interested in our ranch collective, and, I thought, *smashing*.

A year later, I saw Stephanie again on a spring weekend with another group at the ranch, the same summer my father came for that visit. After lunch, I invited everyone to join me for an afternoon walk down to an old apple orchard. Stephanie said she wanted to come, the only one. We locked eyes for a moment. Then, off we went, down the old path to those apple trees.

I knew Stephanie better by then because she was my student in a history course I was teaching at San Francisco State University. Now I knew she was just twenty-one, thirteen years younger than me. And now I knew she was brainy, ambitious, and adventurous.

How adventurous? I didn't know, but I was tempted to find out. As we walked along, talking about history and literature, I thought, *I want to kiss her.*

I considered how young she was. And she was my student, a no-no for romance. I thought some more about the kiss. Stephanie later remembered thinking on that walk, *Yikes. He's going to kiss me.* But the moment passed.

Stephanie left the Bay Area to complete her undergraduate work in Massachusetts at Smith College. Our mutual friend, my ranch partner, Sarah Crome, was a tough old-time labor organizer who liked matching people. Sarah provoked me with a letter Stephanie had sent from Smith on feminism. I made my own provocative comments about Stephanie's ideas that Sarah passed on to Stephanie. Stephanie responded with her own letter to me, describing her life at Smith as intellectually exhilarating and socially boring. We corresponded. I sent her my homemade chocolate chip cookies.

When Stephanie returned home to San Francisco for the summer of 1980, eight months after Dad's diagnosis, I invited her for a hike at the Point Reyes National Seashore. A few days later, it was dinner at a quiet restaurant. Next, we were seeing each other. The kiss finally happened, and more. We had a happy June together.

We kept in close contact through my momentous month-long July visit to Skokie. I regularly spoke with Stephanie by phone and sent her letters about helping my parents cope with ALS. She wrote about friends she wanted me to meet, a weekend away together, and her plans for my thirty-sixth birthday celebration. She sent poetry: Yeats and Roethke. Stephanie was a lifeline, a reminder that I had a California life outside ALS, a life with happy possibilities.

Stephanie was in San Francisco in August 1980 when I arrived back in Oakland. We had another terrific month together. Then, she returned to Smith.

I could hardly believe this clever, playful princess would build a future with me, an older man, half-formed, with an unsettled life, absorbed in a family crisis with a dying father. Indeed, Stephanie told me her plan after January graduation was to go on from Smith to try New York City. I couldn't see the path to our future together. But I hoped we would find a way.

Events in Skokie passed me by as I resumed my California life. I'd pick up the ringing telephone, and there they were, Mom and Dad, trying to assure me they were okay. As if they could still protect their children from bad news.

They were not okay, not even for a telephone call. Dad sounded weak and demanding. He'd howl at Mom with that strange fading voice when he needed her help with his telephone receiver, and I'd hear her trying to do what he wanted. Mom sounded scared and shaky. About what? Whether she could help with the telephone? With his disease? Whether she would survive Dad's illness? I'd immediately be transported back to our family's world of ALS.

Why can't they rise to the occasion to face ALS? Be heroic? I thought. *Like their early months with the disease.*

I knew better. I had witnessed Dad's devastating decline for nine months. How could they meet the merciless demands of ALS? The disease was overwhelming them with its unrelenting advance. How could anyone face this onslaught?

I heard everything, but I couldn't grasp it: Dad's new weakening, the eating problems, the breathing problems, the speaking problems, the skin problems, the sleeping problems, their attempts to adjust, Dad's gloom and fury, Mom's fears and tears, their quarrels, the agency's inability to provide additional home help, and more every day.

I had to be there with them, experience it, to understand. But I knew ALS was devastating them. It would not halt simply because I was absorbed with my life in Oakland.

How bad could it get? I often wondered. Every time I visited, I learned it was worse than I imagined. I had the same lesson in October when I returned to Skokie.

Dad was hardly sleeping. He couldn't turn by himself to find a comfortable location in bed. He had two pressure sores from prolonged lying in bed, at a hip and a rib, and those spots had to be avoided for sleep. He needed help every hour throughout the night.

Dad could still stand, but he could only manage a step and pivot from the bed to the wheelchair. His walker was gone, placed in the basement, a relic from when he had the leg strength for a few steps and some arm strength to maneuver it. Now he had to be pushed in the wheelchair for all his travels through the house.

When he stood up, he was bent over, his head just hanging down. His neck could no longer hold up his head. It had been a problem for months. He wore the neck brace to hold up his head when he sat. But I never became accustomed to his head just dangling down when his body stood up, like a broken body part.

Dad was a quadriplegic. He couldn't move his arms or hands, just a bare squeeze with his right hand. He could move only two right-hand fingers. He could barely stand on his legs.

No matter how much fussing I did, his clothes did not lay straight on his body, and he would not tolerate much. But we adjusted his clothes all day for comfort. Underpants with wrinkles in the wrong place were painful for him. And he was preoccupied with his belt: it had to be buckled to hold up his pants when he stood and unbuckled while sitting.

His hair was mussed, only sometimes off his face as he wanted, no matter how much combing I did. And there were stray bristles, no matter how carefully I shaved him. To me, he looked like a broken man.

Most meals were torture. The saliva problems that began in July as a horrific malfunction of his body, a cosmic mistake we could not live with, became a fact of life to be coped with. He ate separately now, fed by an aide. He seemed to swallow some soft foods easier: eggs, fish, mashed potatoes, and, strangely, a certain brand of frozen waffles. But at most meals, his mouth would become "thick" with that ropey phlegm from his saliva. He would try to clear his throat by coughing, but he only had a weak cough left, not strong enough to clear the gooey stuff with food crumbs from his throat. And always the choking. Eating was an exhausting ordeal.

The MDA clinic had given them a suction machine to help with the throat clearing, but it was down in the basement with other MDA devices. Dad said he didn't need it yet. I thought he still preferred having some control over clearing his throat.

I tried to help him with the suction machine one evening. After many attempts, I couldn't get the suction nozzle to the right spot in his throat. He became hysterical as I persisted in trying to clear his pallet. After half an hour, Mom said, "That's enough." And it ended.

Mom criticized me for indulging him in my search for the correct spot in his throat. As an occasional visitor, I argued I was entitled to indulge him. But I knew she lived with him and this alien phlegm. I mostly tried to stay out of their clashes.

He was losing the ability to speak, a condition known as dysarthria. His speech had degenerated into a murmur of slurred words. It was from a weakening of muscles in his jaw, lips, tongue, soft palate, and vocal chords, and weakened respiratory power too. I later learned of language therapists who might help retain the voice with techniques for breathing and speaking, but I think Dad was already beyond such help. Dad's thin, fading voice, with its boyish, hurt tone, made me feel like he was a wounded child you could not console, only hold his hand.

Those who lived with Dad could still understand his words in October 1980, and we could translate for visitors. I worried about future communications. What happens when he can't tell us what he wants? It was another nightmare bearing down on us.

In his ALS memoir, Charles Pendergast, a longtime ALS patient and activist, writes about the most "catastrophic" affliction he faced after twenty-seven years with ALS: loss of his voice. He considers it "the ultimate loss, isolating you from the world." He describes the era before the eye-controlled computer and voice synthesizer in place of speech, as used by Steven Hawking. Before that remarkable technology, the communication solution was the use of an alphabet board as a substitute for lost voice and handwriting. The board contained a grid with the alphabet letters. Through blinking yes and no, with two responsive blinks or no blinks, the patient could identify letters to a caregiver who held the board and asked about sections of letters, then rows of letters, and then remaining specific letters. "Letter by painful letter, word by tedious word, the caregiver methodically worked to unlock his message." As Pendergast explained, when he first saw this communication system, "I grimaced and cringed at the thought that would be me someday." Today, he still uses it, along with the eye-controlled computer, because the board with letters is "fail-proof." Thus, the title of his book, *Blink Spoken Here* (Pendergast 2020, 283-290).

That alphabet board, with blinking, was the communication system we were nearing with Dad's weakening voice. My father was smart and determined, and he might have managed with a letter board for occasional communication. But I could not imagine him and our family using it for all communications. The alphabet board required patience and cooperation, already badly strained for us after a year of ALS. Without his voice, I did not see how we could know how to care for Dad at the standard and precision he demanded. *How would we remain sane?*

"He's absorbed with little things," Mom explained. "He's particular about everything."

She was speaking about Dad and his body. When he sat down, he insisted that his frozen arms, hands, and fingers be placed in certain positions: hands in his lap, right hand, palm up, left hand, palm down, and each finger straightened. Personal hygiene chores were to be done to his specifications. And his maddening meticulous demands for morning and bedtime routines.

Life at home was organized around Dad's maintenance and the minimal comfort we could provide. Little else mattered.

He had become sensitive to all bright light. Even the reflection of sunlight from passing cars bothered him, so we kept the living room curtains closed. He could not tolerate rapid movements, particularly Mom's speedy movement: "It's like she's on roller skates."

And odors. Mom's cooking and cleaning bothered him. And loud sounds. He complained about water running out of the kitchen tap. He listened to opera at a low volume.

The house was dark and quiet. I thought, *He's closing down for dying.*

Now they had live-in help. Mom changed agencies after clashes with the one I selected. She added weekend help and expanded to live-in help. This round-the-clock assistance had come much faster than I expected, over weeks, not months. The new agency told her they could end all her maintenance care for Dad, and she could return to being his wife. I liked the sound of that.

As she switched agencies, both sent us a torrent of papers, and the insurance company and Medicare weighed in with more paper. I took over dealing with payment. The switch in agencies left me with a colossal insurance mess, but I was encouraged that Mom made the change. She had learned what we wanted, and she could be tough and demanding with the aides and the agencies. It was exactly what we needed.

Through the new agency, we had Veronica six days and nights a week, with another aide the seventh day and night. I arrived home early one morning after a red-eye flight and found Veronica sleeping on a mattress on the floor in Dad's bedroom. She had moved in there to assist him faster in the nights.

Veronica was terrific working with Dad, much more capable than Mom or me. I was relieved and irritated that Dad chose her help over mine. I was surprised by my difficulty in giving up being needed to help Dad. And I was scared by our reliance on her. *What if Veronica leaves?* I worried. But for the present—and the present was where we lived with ALS—Veronica was perfect.

Veronica's job was hugely demanding: helping Dad six days a week, twenty-four hours a day. She could do it because of her skills and strength and because the job of helping Dad did not make emotional demands on her as it did with family. She wanted round-the-clock work because her husband was abroad, and she needed the money for personal reasons.

Veronica was a mystery to me. She was a street-smart young Black woman, bright and animated, with a large Afro, heavy makeup, perfume that Dad would tolerate, flashy clothes, and a preference for fried foods. I learned to see more. She was an excellent caregiver, a professional. When she worked with Dad, she was all business: patient and caring, strong and intuitive, and firm. She understood his physical needs and how to help. She never patronized him.

Dad came to know Veronica, and he liked her. He gave Veronica a hard time about not being able to read well and not appreciating opera arias. I worried that he might be needling her too much, but I was happy to see their warm personal relationship. Veronica was resilient; she could handle him, physically and emotionally. She was proud of her skills and care for him.

Veronica also stuck to her job and let our family work out our own emotional dynamics. She was present for the suction machine encounter. She held back and stayed out of it.

Veronica taught me another lesson about the unexpected generosity of others as we faced ALS. I never understood her. She brought a different culture into the confined world of our house, and she was a blessing during my October visit.

Veronica and the home health aides made it possible for Mom to continue working part-time as a bookkeeper three days a week. It was a subject of conflict between her and Dad. Her boss knew about Dad's illness, and he accommodated any work hours she wanted, yet another person who helped as he could. But she liked to arrive to work on time. Dad complained that she left every day at 8 a.m. "like the house is on fire."

I urged Mom to continue her job. She had been working since Rob began kindergarten. In 1960, she hesitated about whether she could reenter the labor market. Dad encouraged her to do it, and she found a job with a plumbing supplies company right in Skokie. She liked earning additional income for our family. She was an excellent bookkeeper, valued by her employer. She had friends at work. She needed workdays out of our house, keeping busy, away from ALS.

Dad always praised Mom's work skills and said that time had proved him correct. But now he was bitter about her continuing to work. He was home alone with Veronica and an occasional afternoon visitor. These were long days for him.

Sometimes, he'd tell Veronica to reach me by telephone. "I took care of her for thirty-three years," he'd complain. "I stood by her." He felt deserted, helpless, dejected, and angry. He said he felt like a burden: "Everyone would be better off if I were gone."

That was painful to hear. We were all doing our best for him, but it wasn't enough.

He worried about Mom's future after he was gone. He thought she should sell the Skokie house now because it needed a man to be responsible for all the innovations he had created, like the summer screens and the winter storm windows he had custom-built. If he had his way, we would have sold the house before he died so he could pass on the house responsibilities.

He imagined Mom living at the Boca condo, but he worried that she would live alone and that a fortune hunter would prey on her. This fortune hunter would swindle the money he was leaving for her and the sons. There was nothing he could do except listen to my repeated assurances of Mom's good judgment and that the sons would be there to help. He could not tolerate those big unknowns in a future without him.

Dad was mostly living in the present, where he and Mom clashed.

She stayed away from him, protecting herself. Mom saw it differently. "He's obsessed with controlling things. It's impossible to follow his directions."

Dad complained that Mom did not slow down, speak with him, and discuss things. She complained that he was dragging her down. At home, she mostly stayed busy cooking and cleaning, just "passing time," as she once put it. She responded when he really needed her help, but otherwise, she did her housework and blocked him out.

"My nerves are shot," Mom said—from the constant attention Dad needed, his dissatisfaction, and quarreling.

More often, she told me, "I'm okay." She was getting through each day, each hour.

She was slow to acknowledge he was worsening. I told her he was losing his voice and soon would not be able to speak. She looked at me, surprised, but I knew she understood. And then she stopped our discussion with a "whatever," like many times before, as if the whole thing was beyond our influence. I hated to hear that response because it was so true.

There continued to be two world views in our house, and the house was too small to contain them. Dad was in despair over his failing body and dying, and he was angry at her. Mom was discouraged and angry that he was so negative and difficult to help.

Mom told me she had tried to get in bed with him, to comfort him. But he couldn't bear it. He was too sensitive to tolerate her body touching him. I thought how difficult that must have been for her. It was a painful story to hear.

During the visit, Mom again asked me to help Dad change his attitude. "He should be more positive, more cheerful." She wanted him to enjoy the time they had left together. And make it easier to help him.

She had lost so much to ALS: her partner, their life together, their intimacy, their plans for the future. Mom told me, "I just want a little sweetness."

Reading the ALS literature for patient families, I knew that many people lived with ALS differently than Dad. I had read accounts of people diagnosed with ALS who accepted the illness and moved on to how to continue their lives with it, including people like Dad, who was on a survival track for just a few years. Most described initial anger, puzzlement over "why me?" and "paralyzing loneliness." They often advised finding joy and happiness, living every day to the fullest, and helping others as much as possible. They found purpose in public activism for ALS patients, religious faith, mindfulness practice, participation in new drug trials, devotion to spouses and children, travel, and writing about their experience with ALS. One counseled lowering expectations to "mediocrity" and a "C+ life" as a patient, with credit for "just showing up."

I sympathized with Mom. People made the best of terrible afflictions with ALS. As one patient advised, "Find joy and happiness to fill your days. Time is too precious to waste." They remained positive and productive however possible. I knew Mom would support Dad and remain in this battle with ALS to the end. She would live on after Dad. She had every reason to make the best of their lives together with ALS, while they could, however they could.

I also sympathized with Dad. He had put up a brave fight over many months of continuing his job. He had shared his remaining time with visiting family and friends. He had tried to protect Mom from his struggle with ALS. But he was dying. Now it was coming hard and fast. He was preparing to die his way, with frustration and gloom and grief, still puzzling over why this was happening to him.

Earlier that year, I had read a recent book by a man who had died of ALS. Archie Hanlan's *Autobiography of Dying*, published in 1978, was about Hanlan's life with ALS from diagnosis in 1971 to death in 1973. Hanlan, a professor of social work at the University of Pennsylvania, wrote about his experience with ALS, particularly how he was perceived and treated by medical professionals and academic colleagues.

Especially interesting to me was the book's postscript, titled "Living With a Dying Husband," written by Archie Hanlan's wife,

Mary Hanlan, also a social worker. Where Archie wrote about his experience in the world with ALS, Mary wrote about their home life with ALS. As they began living with ALS, Archie maintained his independence through teaching and writing while Mary did her own significant work, and they continued enjoying each other. Then came their gradual estrangement "as his body wasted away." The disease worsened with Archie's gradual paralysis, falls, need for a wheelchair, sleep disturbance, and becoming a "bony skeleton," all familiar to me. Archie "slowly slid into what seemed like another distinct stage: that of giving up, the feeling that life was no longer worth it." Mary described how she withdrew from Archie physically and emotionally. He began to rage at her and at friends for seemingly inconsequential matters. "One of the most difficult things about terminal illness is seldom stated," Mary wrote. "That when one is most in need of physical love and affection, there is no means to express it."

Their relationship became so difficult that Archie stopped eating and demanded to be hospitalized for better care than at home. With help from a therapist, there was a "good ending after all this pain." They had a peaceful final month before Archie died at age forty-eight in July 1973. Their final time together was relaxed, they communicated better, and she wrote goodbye letters for him to their children and friends. It was a confirmation of the loving life they had shared together (Hanlan 1979, 112-123).

I knew there was nothing unusual about Mom and Dad's clashes. I thought I understood both perspectives. I often wished it was easier between them. I couldn't help thinking, *What happened to the hand-holding after the diagnosis?* But that time had passed. I didn't know how they could do better. As ALS continued to ravage Dad's body, they were showing up and getting through. It was the best they could do with ALS, at least C+. It was good enough for me.

I joined Mom and Dad for the October MDA clinic. It was awful, from start to finish.

Mom arranged for the hospital van to pick us up so we would avoid the difficulties of transporting Dad ourselves. Now we had a wheelchair ramp to roll him down from the house. But Dad was irritated when I had to remove the head attachment from the wheelchair, and he had to scrunch down to fit in the van on the automatic lift. The driver was a young woman, a tough Rosie the Riveter type doing hospital deliveries in this rickety clanking vehicle. Dad's wheelchair slid a few inches with each abrupt start and careening turn, country music blared from the radio, and he was too hot and too cold. It was something we might have laughed about months ago. But I knew he detested that van journey to the clinic, the very opposite of the slow, quiet, predictable world he demanded at home.

On this visit, the clinic provided little help that Dad would accept. Mom and Dad had some warm moments with the physical and occupational therapists who had been helping for months, and they had some ideas for Dad's daytime seating. Dad bawled out one of the doctors for the clinic's weak information about food and nutrition, which had become a constant problem. Every meal was a huge challenge with food choice, phlegm, swallowing, coughing, and choking.

They received some other practical suggestions at the clinic: a hospital bed, an airflow mattress for comfort, and bed rails to secure him in bed. I had read one ALS patient's account of his family placing his hospital bed in their living room so he was always in the center of house activity. But Dad refused anything that looked like a hospital room, even for his bedroom. He only agreed to the air mattress and stronger sleeping pills, and both helped.

Dr. Vick, Dad's neurologist, whom I met in July, urged the use of a suction machine to clear the phlegm from his throat at meals. They hadn't considered it for months until I tried it unsuccessfully. Dad still wanted his own control over clearing his throat. No suction machine.

Dr. Vick suggested a nasal tube inserted through his nose and esophagus to his stomach. This would allow nasal feeding directly into his stomach: no more solid food or swallowing, just liquid formula through the tube. Dr. Vick described simple procedures for installing and using the tube.

From reading patient accounts, I knew that a feeding tube, welcomed by many, could present an array of new problems: installation, formula options, and maintenance. And, as Shirley Knight noted about her husband Bill in *A Journey Through Fire: ALS – Memoir of a caregiver*, "Having the feeding tube inserted appears to have destroyed whatever fighting spirit Bill had left." As with most medical interventions, I feared that a feeding tube would bring new challenges with its benefits. There was no free ride with ALS.

I kept quiet. Dad immediately dismissed Dr. Vick's proposal. He wouldn't hear of it.

No feeding tube yet, I thought with relief. He was still fighting for some control over his body. But I knew something like that was not far away. Or he would choke to death trying to swallow scrambled eggs.

Rob, who attended the September MDA clinic visit, reported that Dr. Vick had told them how impressed he was by Dad's struggle to continue walking at home and had urged Dad to continue. By the time of the October clinic I attended, Dad's walking had ended. There was no more encouragement.

Rob had reported in September that Dad had put up a good front with Dr. Vick about his ALS struggles, even joking about it. But he had also asked Dr. Vick how long he had to live. Dr. Vick responded that the average life span from diagnosis was three or four years. But Dad, I thought, was on a shorter time track, closer to two years for older men. And I recalled Dr. Vick's response to my same question in July: Dad could die anytime.

Dad apparently thought the end was approaching. At that September visit, Dad had asked Dr. Vick when he could be admitted to the hospital.

"Anytime you need it," Dr. Vick responded. "Why would you go into the hospital?"

"To die."

At my October visit to the clinic, Dad started a familiar conversation with Dr. Vick about possible cures for ALS. I saw Dr. Vick lean back and relax for a longer discussion. He had these rambling discussions about ALS with Dad before. Dad covered some of his old suggestions: try interferon and try steroids. He explained his latest idea: they should get a good electrical engineer to solve the problem of how to transfer electrical impulses from the brain to the spinal cord to the muscles now that the motor neurons stopped working. "I've been solving problems all my life," he told Dr. Vick again, "and now there's one I haven't solved. But I'm still working on it."

I thought Dr. Vick enjoyed that discussion with Dad. To me, it seemed like the only value in that clinic visit for Dad was when he could consider some slight influence over his out-of-control body. But I learned from Mom that Dr. Vick took her aside and told her he couldn't give Dad this much time for talk at the Saturday morning clinic, with other patients waiting. He suggested they make an appointment to see him on a weekday at the hospital. Mom was upset about Dad commandeering Dr. Vick's time, which she related to me, and she became very quiet after the appointment.

Dad noticed. With ALS, he had become sensitive to how other people felt. I had long been critical of him for his obliviousness to how other people, like me, felt. But, as I had been told, be careful what you ask for.

Dad asked me what was wrong with Mom. When I described what had happened with Dr. Vick, he responded in despair, "I just can't please her."

I ached for them.

———◇———

Dad and I discussed history for much of my visit. Dad had a history tale for me, the historian. He wanted me to hear the tapes he made of his life story.

He said he recorded his story for "posterity." That meant future generations, starting with my brothers and me. I thought he wanted to be remembered, not just with ALS but his entire life.

Rabbi Stern had suggested this personal history project during his March visit. *It's a terrific idea*, I thought. *But why didn't I, an oral historian, come up with it?*

My own oral history project, my long-delayed second book, answered my question. I was telling the story of a California community of left-wing chicken ranchers over three generations. It began with the heroic immigrant settlers in the early twentieth century, with their epic tales of emigration from Eastern Europe and building a new life in America. Then came the American-born children, torn lifelong between their parents' Old World ways and the attractions of their American homeland. It ended with the third generation, my generation, who grew up in the 1950s and 1960s as assimilated Americans but separated from their Jewish community and history. It was a tale of lost ethnic identity over generations of American assimilation.

Like many from the baby boomer generation in my book, I had lost connection with my family's history over our generations and decades in America, particularly during my years away from Chicago in California. By 1980, I had become an experienced oral historian who had interviewed hundreds of people about their California family histories. But I didn't think about my own Chicago family as having history. In my mind, we simply existed, timeless.

And I had another answer to why I had ignored Dad's history. I was absorbed in our ALS battle, reacting to one crisis after another. ALS was so strange, so perilous, so overwhelming that I couldn't think about our family history. ALS had intruded from another galaxy and blotted out everything except our struggle for Dad's survival.

Rabbi Stern's tape-recording suggestion jolted me into recognizing that it would be the final opportunity to learn about our family from Dad. In July, I tried to tape-record him. But I was puzzled to discover that I stifled him with my interview questions. He had a story in mind that he wanted to tell, and my questions threw him off his track. Dad asked that I leave my tape recorder with him when I returned to California. He said he would record his own history.

I was disappointed by my failed interview. But that was my father. He would do it himself, even with oral history, my expertise. This time, I did as he asked without protest.

I did not expect him to accomplish anything. But a week after I left, he asked Mom to set up the tape recorder on a living room table. He still had the strength in one finger to press the switch for recording. That was all he needed.

Over several weeks alone in the living room, he narrated his life story. He hoped we would transcribe the tapes in the future. He proposed that Ann and each of the boys tape their own accounts so we would have a complete family history.

Years later, Rob transcribed the recordings into seventy-nine pages of Dad's narrative. My mother, brothers, and I never recorded our family accounts. Those tapes became our precious source for Dad's life and our family history.

Dad asked me to listen to the recordings with him during my October visit. We sat in the living room in the evenings, tape recorder spinning, listening to his history.

He started in the 1880s with Grandma as a girl in Minsk and Grandpa as a boy near Kyiv. Five full tapes and one hundred years later, he concluded with himself in Skokie, puzzling why he was stricken with ALS.

Dad's account was chronological and factual. He was a scientist reporting what had happened over his life: family, friendships, work, and neighborhoods. Dad's storytelling was planned, ordered, and deliberate. He was telling his story, the facts, a legacy for his sons.

Dad had a point of view. As he explained at the conclusion of his taping, this "is not the story of a person but the story of a person with people."

These were familiar tales told in new dense detail about our extended family members, Grandma and Grandpa's stores, his schooling, his friends, their West Side neighborhoods, his various employers and businesses, and our family's life in Skokie.

Mom joined us to hear his taped stories of their West Side lives and neighborhoods in the 1930s and 1940s. Those were sweet moments listening together in the living room, with their reminiscing and kibbitzing. Mom gave Dad a hug after hearing his account of their courtship, marriage, and young family.

Dad offered little comment on the meaning of this history, but toward the end of the recordings, he addressed some larger subjects on his mind.

One was regret that his three sons did not stay in the Chicago vicinity. Unlike the 1930s and 1940s when he and his friends had remained in Chicago as they became adults, his sons settled far away in the 1960s, two in California and one in Wisconsin. Our lives were remote from Mom and Dad, our larger family, his old West Side world, and his current Skokie life. "I felt a lot of jealousy in recent years," he explained, "seeing fathers and sons bowling together in the congregation league. I miss seeing the boys more often, especially now because of this illness."

I tried to imagine it: me in the congregation bowling league with Dad, me living in a Chicago suburb. I could not fill in that picture of my alternative suburban life: wife, children, suburban house, job, neighbors, mowing the lawn and raking leaves, and Sunday dinner visits with my parents.

On the tape, he said that he missed me and my brothers. I wondered if it had always been so. *I couldn't have lived in Chicago*, I thought, *but should I have visited more often? Not been so angry over our disputes? Accepted his attempts at a closer relationship? Yes . . . yes . . . yes.*

Dad summed up his life together with Mom on the final tape recording. "I think for the thirty-eight years, it has been mostly good.

Whatever we did, we did together. We were not individual people. We raised the boys together. We made a home together. We traveled together. When family and friends came over, we hosted together. We've had our fights like normal people. We've had some bad disagreements, mostly over how to handle our children. But in the main, it's been good times together."

I wondered about those disagreements over me and my brothers. My guess is that Mom thought he was too demanding and overbearing, too hard on us, and Dad thought she was too understanding, too permissive, too soft with us.

But even with the children, they mainly agreed: "We reveled in their accomplishments. And we always accentuated the positive with them. We didn't tell our children our problems. We were very private, even with the children."

In Dad's telling, the exception to their happy lives together was recent months: "Particularly since I stopped working in July, we've been thrown together twenty-four hours a day with my illness. Whether it's due to my particular condition now or our makeup or both, we are not enjoying life at present." Under normal circumstances, he thought, they would have had a good retirement together: Boca Raton visits, travel, golf, eat what they wanted, and do as they pleased. They had lost their future. "Now it's wishful thinking. It's not in the cards."

This was a "realistic" account. He accepted his condition with ALS. There was no regret over the past. There was no regret over the future he would miss. This was the account of a man who accepted his coming death.

He closed the tapings with speculation as to why this ALS affliction was visited upon him. It was like puzzling out the cause of a Biblical plague.

It's a common question raised by people who suffer from ALS. In a memoir about their young Christian family's first year with ALS, Kristin and Todd Neva struggle with the question of why God would inflict ALS on Todd and their good, happy family that follows God. Why make them suffer this terrible burden? Kristin, outraged, puts the question to God: "What are you doing? Why do you allow this unfairness?"

Over that year, Todd and Kristin did not lose faith in God. They deepened their faith that there is a purpose to ALS they may never know. They find inspiration in people who lead meaningful lives despite disabilities and because of disabilities. Todd and Kristin discover they have become more sympathetic people who can empathize with the suffering of others, who recognize suffering as part of the human condition. They can find inspiration and meaning in ALS, in the challenges God has put before them: Todd to face ALS and Kristin to love and cherish Todd. ALS has allowed them lives of greater meaning with "a godly response to adversity" (Neva 2014, 114-116).

Dad saw his ALS differently. In the August 1980 taping of his life story, when Dad speculated over the cause of his ALS, he did not try to find meaning in it like the Nevas. He was not seeking out guideposts to give purpose for his life ahead. Dad was facing the end of his journey with ALS. He was encountering death.

Dad wanted to understand why it happened to him. What was the cause of his ALS?

He had an answer. He thought his ALS might have been caused by pride: "I've always had pride in my wife, my kids, my job."

I was surprised when I heard it on the tape. That was me he had been prideful about.

He expanded on his life accomplishments in his taped narrative. There was our family, the achievements of the three boys, the extended family, old and newer friends, this suburban home in Skokie and a second home in Florida, the good job and professional accomplishments, the financial comfort, luxuries, and world travels. Coming from an immigrant family in Chicago West Side neighborhoods in the 1920s and 1930s, from those cramped rooms behind the neighborhood stores, starting with nothing, working all the way through, he had built this. I thought he was proud that he had achieved the goals of his lifetime, of his generation.

He reflected further, "Maybe I was just too prideful."

He continued, "Perhaps like the superstitious Orthodox Jews say, '*kein ayin hara*' ('without the evil eye'), to ward off the evil eye. Maybe it's my punishment for being too prideful in the past."

Had he flaunted his achievements to others? Had he not been sufficiently modest? Had he caused resentment? Had he caused a malevolent glare from someone? An envious glare that was a vehicle for harm by the evil eye?

"Pride goeth before the fall." He quoted the old saying. "Well, I'm taking the fall."

Even with the evil eye afflicting him with ALS, he kept his pride. He still believed in his life path. He ended his taped account by noting that Yom Kippur, the Day of Atonement, was coming. Jews would be asked to atone for their sins. "My own feeling is that I don't have much to atone for with God. That is how I conducted my life. Not as a religiously observant Jew but as a good Jew. I am not afraid to end this 'veil of tears' and meet my maker."

Nothing happened that struck me as funny during my October visit. When Dad had been diagnosed with ALS a year before, when I heard his boasts about his Mayo Clinic evaluation, when my brothers and I joked about his "enemies list" of those who avoided him after the diagnosis, when Dad and I went on that wild goose chase for his chemistry manual we had donated to the Salvation Army, I thought humor would carry us a long way through ALS. And it did. But, after a year of ALS, his condition was dire. His mood was grim. Dad was shutting down. Nothing about his life with ALS seemed funny.

The visitors dwindled as Dad declined and lost patience with others. The weekends and evenings were quiet and slow.

Mom and Dad's old friends from the West Side, Esther and Ziggy, came for another visit. Ziggy was one of those adult male friends I had always planned to rely on in a crisis. Now he spoke again of bringing Chinese food at a future visit. They had arrived with Chinese food at a successful visit months ago, back when Dad could eat without thick phlegm and choking, back when he liked to talk with visitors about ALS. Dad was silent this time. It was a short stay, the final visit from the wonderful old friends from the West Side.

Rabbi Stern came again just before my October visit. We had a lot of history at synagogue B'nai Emunah: virtually founding members when we joined in 1955, three boys in Hebrew School who were bar mitzvahed, occasional Friday night services, and the High Holidays services every year. And, of course, Dad's years in the men's bowling league. We were part of his congregation.

Rabbi Stern dropped in unplanned one day at noon, when Veronica was feeding Dad. His first visit had been in June, four months before, when Dad could still work. I had heard reports of a lively discussion about Jewish history. I had hoped Dad would have a confidant in Rabbi Stern.

This time, Dad was angry about the long absence. "Where have you been?" he told the rabbi, amid spoonfuls of pureed food and coughing, choking, and drooling. "I thought you left the country."

Rabbi Stern quickly departed. We heard that at High Holidays services, he announced Dad's courageous battle with ALS. This announcement seemed to me disingenuous because the rabbi had learned little about Dad and his ALS experience, and he provided no help or comfort. The rabbi did not return until Dad was buried and we were sitting shiva.

Dad still enjoyed visits with his inner circle. His sister Min and niece Eileen were frequent visitors. So was Mom's cousin Norm, my adviser. And a few neighbors who were close friends. They could pass an afternoon talking about family, the old Jewish West Side, and their lives together. Dad would promote my forthcoming book, telling all visitors about it. I was touched to see them help Dad through the long days.

His work colleagues from TRW Cinch planned a visit. After fiddling with him all morning, for once, I thought I got his grooming right, that is, almost normal: well shaved, hair neatly combed back off his face, nose and ears cleaned, clothing hung decently on his emaciated body. I placed him in his favorite living room chair, from which he could help with standing him up.

In they came, these three caricatures of fifties nerd engineers, filling our living room. They were tall and thick, with black slacks, white shirts, skinny ties, and trim crew cuts, as if the sixties and seventies never happened. Tucked into those white shirts were the inevitable plastic pocket protectors for holding pens, pencils, and small slide rules, my father's own work garb for all the years I could remember.

I could have hugged them for coming, for their straight-arrow kindness.

Dad sat with them happily, not saying much but listening to the news about colleagues and projects, nodding his head in agreement, whispering a few words here and there. They reported on the favorable reception of Dad's final paper on gold plating. They had presented it at a Boston conference. This was the essay I had spent hours editing with him in Boca Raton. That update was satisfying, at least for me. And, hearing about it from these colleagues, Dad seemed interested.

I sat close by Dad to attend to him, translate when he wasn't clear, and make the visit go well. They stayed an hour, just right.

They brought a gift, a request for Dad's help with a work problem. He was interested and discussed it with them. He thought about it after the visit. Two days later, he responded with a speakerphone call to one of them. He thought his opinion was well received.

That was the very end of Dad's work. It was the final visit by anyone outside his inner circle of loved ones. I thought it was a fitting conclusion to Dad's life in the world outside of home.

I went out for a walk every day. There was suffering inside our house. I needed the cold, fresh air.

Exploring our neighborhood, I was struck by how Skokie had changed. I still thought of it as the raw, new suburb we moved into twenty-five years ago: freshly paved streets, new houses, empty lots ready for more houses, new schools, young families, and kids everywhere. Now it looked settled and aged with fine homes, mature trees, manicured lawns, and luxury cars in driveways. And quiet. Not many kids in our neighborhood.

The streets were haunted with reminders of my teen years: softball games with neighborhood pals in Seneca Park, drag racing at high speeds on usually empty Kedvale Avenue, the Greenleaf Avenue home of Jan Gordon, who I had a crush on, the Devonshire rec center where I was once Skokie's number one ranked Ping-Pong player, Sam and Hy's Deli on Dempster Street, where I had countless corned beef sandwiches, the nearby off-limits gentile sanctuary in the Evanston Golf Club, and B'nai Emunah synagogue on Niles Center Road, where, on Saturday morning breaks from religious services, I could look across the prairie to friends playing baseball at my Sharp Corner Grammar School. My high school, Niles East, had already been demolished as Skokie downsized to the two newer high schools built after the large population influx of the 1950s.

Skokie was the postwar middle-class Jewish Promised Land that Mom and Dad had embraced in 1955 with their generation of Chicago West Side offspring of East European Jewish immigrants. Skokie was the place to raise their kids in comfort and safety, in sturdy new homes with good schools. Now, the kids, still on an upwardly mobile ascent, had returned to urban life in Chicago, moved out to higher-end suburbs like Highland Park and Northbrook, or, like me, departed to exotic locales like California. My parents' generation was now in their final migration to Miami and nearby towns along the southeast Florida coast. Jewish Skokie was fading. Mom and Dad had some new neighbors on the block, Filipino and Indian and Chinese, none that they had met, a mystery, the current migration to Skokie.

Dad would never know the emerging new Asian Skokie. He would not make it out of their old Jewish Skokie, though he had come close with their condo awaiting a retirement in Boca Raton. ALS had stopped him cold and froze him in Skokie till the end.

"The job of parents," I have been told, "is to help their kids out of home and launched in the world. The job of kids, once gone from home, is not to worry their parents."

By these measures, in October 1980, I had failed. After a year of Dad's ALS, I was painfully aware of my failure. I had no wife or children, no reliable job or home. At thirty-six, I was not launched in the world. My parents had long been worried about me.

Dad, at thirty-six in 1951, had been married almost ten years to his sweetheart Ann. They had two kids, parents they watched over, a large extended family, and many close friends from their years in West Side Chicago. Dad was in his new venture operating the bowling alley and also working as a chemist. A son of immigrants, responsible for his family, he was ambitious as he explored the opportunities of postwar American life. Not far ahead would be a third son, along with the house and the suburban life they would build in Skokie. He was long grown up.

I knew the direction Dad wanted for me. He wished I would get a real job. He was proud of my coming book but wanted me to have a job with a regular paycheck. And a wife . . . and a house, my own home . . . and a kid or two. He wanted for me the good life he and Mom had built in Skokie. He wanted me launched and his own life's work completed.

He didn't know that something had already happened since his ALS diagnosis. I had taken a huge step: I realized I needed to change my life. There was nothing specific I could tell him about. I didn't know what changes or how I would do it. But I wanted something new.

Dad did learn about one development in my life: Stephanie, my new girlfriend. Stephanie visited me in Chicago for a weekend toward the end of the October visit.

This was a brave journey. At twenty-three, Stephanie traveled a thousand miles from school in Massachusetts for a Chicago weekend with me. She missed me. She missed our life together the past summer in California. I thought she wanted direct contact to see if we were for real as a couple and help her decide what to do after graduation. After all, we had been together in person for less than two months, June and August of the past summer.

She also came to meet my parents, to meet my father, who was dying a difficult death. She understood the significance. This could be "hello" and "goodbye" to my father.

I worried. Stephanie was young and had never seen anything like ALS. My family was living in our own self-contained world with its own logic and tensions. I had witnessed my parents at their best with ALS many months ago. Now I could see them at their worst on any day. Even at his best, Dad was preoccupied with his mutinous body and approaching death. Mom was absorbed with helping Dad and keeping her distance. Anything could happen.

I found a separate place for Stephanie and me to stay. An old high school friend let us use his nearby Evanston apartment. Here was another person who wanted to help.

Everyone was at their best for Stephanie's visit. Dad looked small and gray, old and frail. He had little strength, and with a failing voice, he was difficult to understand. He seemed like someone who was at the end. Mom looked worried, at his side, there with him to the end.

But, for the last time I can remember, Dad smiled when he met Stephanie. He smiled through the afternoon. He was absorbed with our visitor, and Mom was too. They told stories about their past in Chicago and Skokie, about me growing up. We talked about Stephanie's life at Smith, my California ranch where I met Stephanie, and what to see in Chicago.

Stephanie's visit was a gift, my gift: the presence of this beautiful, intelligent, and well-mannered Jewish young woman who liked their son and wanted to meet them.

My parents were in good form that afternoon and happy with the meeting. They enjoyed Stephanie. They were not appraising. They were delighted by this unexpected glimpse into my possible future with this lovely young woman.

Stephanie wanted to get it right with my parents, and she did. She was comfortable. She was herself. She was not intimidated by the terrible ALS drama before her.

Stephanie and I enjoyed our weekend in Chicago. Dad treated us to dinner and the theater one evening. We saw the sights downtown and walked by Lake Michigan in Evanston. Stephanie knew that I was amid a profound family event, and I was relieved that she understood. We still had our romantic getaway weekend together in Chicago.

ALS intruded once. Unsolicited, I assured Stephanie that my Dad's ALS was not genetic and that I was not at risk for inheriting it. I would not become the withered, dying man she had met. She was surprised. Nothing of the kind was on her mind.

On the airplane, Stephanie wrote, "The state of the relationship is, I think, quite good."

A few days later, Dad said he had a gift for me. He gave me the diamond rings that Grandpa had given Grandma in 1911 when they became engaged and married. There was an engagement ring with small diamonds and a marriage ring with one large diamond—real diamonds. It was a fabulous gift in 1911 . . . and still fabulous in 1980.

Talking about Stephanie and me, Dad said, "I would like to see what happens." Marriage? Children? A life together?

And then he remembered: ALS. He was dying.

He shrugged. He could still do that. And he muttered, "What's the difference?"

That hurt. What more could I do?

Dad had something he wanted to discuss with me. He waited for a quiet afternoon when we were alone in the house. Mom out. Veronica out. Just him and me in the living room.

He wanted to end his life.

He said, "I'm not enjoying this life at all. It's too hard for me and for your mother. It will get worse. I don't want to continue living this way."

I knew he was right. "It will get worse." Eating, speaking, and breathing would worsen. I didn't know exactly what was ahead. I never did with ALS. It could be intolerable swallowing problems and nasal feeding tubes. It could be more compromised lung muscles and a device to aid breathing. Or the frightening loss of voice and a primitive communication system. Or bedridden, not far away. I thought he was reaching a scary stage of ALS.

He wanted my help. He was too weak to do it himself.

I was not surprised. By then, he had referred to suicide in front of me several times. He had spoken about his regrets that he had not taken his life when he could. He said it when he was angry, fighting with Mom. He said it when he was cool and collected, reflecting on his life and death. In each instance, I said little in response. I thought it was just a matter of time before he reached this point, the real thing where he needed help.

I told him about my discussion with Dr. Vick: he didn't disapprove of suicide but wouldn't participate. We would receive no assistance from Dr. Vick or the MDA clinic. We were alone.

"How do you do it?" I asked, as if Dad, the problem-solver, had the answer.

He had no idea. Despite his previous references to suicide, he had no plan. Surely, there had been a way when he was able-bodied, when he could use his hands and legs to serve his purposes. But not now. He could do almost nothing for himself.

I said I needed to think about it.

Helping Dad end his life was what I thought about for the

remainder of the visit. Dad ending his life. Could I say yes? Could I actually help him do it? I couldn't imagine it. I couldn't picture the actual acts of helping him end his life. That did not seem possible.

But there was another response that was more troubling: no. How could I say no? He was suffering. He was lucid. He was unequivocal. He was my father who needed my help.

I had no doubt that he feared what was coming with ALS, that he had had enough of living with ALS, and that he wanted to end it. This was no passing impulse, no momentary low spirits. He told me in a steady, clear voice. He had been thinking about it. He was entirely cogent and persuasive: the awful nights, the torment of hours to get through each day, the tortuous meals, the struggle to do the simplest things, never comfortable, the dependence on others for everything, the unrelenting misery, the horrors ahead. He was tired of it. This was not him, not his real life, not his true self.

He continued to try. It was his pride, I thought. He would struggle daily to do a few exercises and take a few steps. He tried to keep his hair combed and maintain his hygiene with help from the aides. He tried to exercise control in many small ways. I thought it meant that he would preserve his dignity as best he could while he was alive.

I didn't need convincing. I had witnessed his unimaginable decline since December. I knew his struggles and his suffering. I saw his dwindling interest in the people and life around him. But I did not know how to do it. How would I help him end his life peacefully?

I would need someone who did know. That would have to be someone back in California, where I had friends and might find help.

A few days later, Dad and I had another private talk in the living room. I said I would try to help him. I said I would have to find out how to do it when I returned to Oakland. I said I would get a message back to him from California about whether I could help him end his life.

That afternoon, Dad fell asleep sitting in the wheelchair in the living room. He was relieved and relaxed after our talk. When he awakened, he told me about his sleep: "I felt like I died. It was so peaceful."

CHAPTER 9

With Dad to the End

DECEMBER 1980

A week after I returned to California, I received a letter from Mom. At the top, she dated it "Black Monday":

Dear Skip,
I never thought I would ever feel the need to unburden myself with the following "heavy" thoughts BUT—
I seem to recall you once telling me that Dad has told you in the past that he would like to "end it all."
Although I do not blame him for feeling that way, I do want to say I am strongly opposed to any help he might have asked you to give toward this end. That is too much to ask of anyone! Do not ever consider this, please—it is too much to ask of anyone. (I repeat!)
The fact that he concerns himself with taking some vitamins, eating his three decent meals, makes sure his bowels are regular, does not want to catch a cold, etc., means he still wants to live. Take that for what it's worth.
Well, I said it and already I am indecisive whether this should have been written or said—but it is done!
Love, Mom

I didn't remember telling Mom that Dad said he wanted to end his life. It was possible. Dad had spoken about suicide with increasing frequency over the past year: how he had considered it, that he could have done it, why he didn't, why he should have, and, finally, in October 1980, that he had to do it.

I never heard him say it in front of Mom. But, after my October visit, perhaps he said it in her presence. He may have wanted her to know he felt this way, like with the burial plots he had wanted me to purchase a year ago. He did not like going around her.

Mom's letter startled me. It was a complete surprise, spooky in its timing. I thought she must have been agonized with worry to send it. I read it and reread it for her meaning. I thought I understood her opposition to my helping Dad end his life. She did not think it was the wrong thing for him to do. She was concerned about the burden on me. But she also wrote that he wanted to live.

The truth was, in fact, I really was investigating how Dad could end it all. I did not want to lie to her. But I didn't know if I could find a way. And if I did come up with the means, would he want to go through with it? And would I actually help him do it? So much was uncertain at that time. This was so unimaginable. Why dispute something that might not happen?

I never responded to Mom's letter. And she never raised it with me again. The letter remained, undiscussed, an eloquent plea to me and a blinking red light.

The news from Skokie only became worse after my October visit. I heard about it in telephone calls with Mom and my brothers. ALS continued its merciless conquest of Dad's body.

His limbs were useless. The muscles in his arms and legs, fingers and toes, were gone, atrophied. He could wiggle a finger or two, but otherwise, nothing. It was like an alien presence had encased his body in iron.

He spent more time in bed, longer in the mornings and earlier in the evenings. He still had pressure sores from his hours without moving in bed, which was another constant problem.

Rob explained how Dad had to be watched closely when you stood him up. I had seen his head sagging down since July. But now Rob described him almost toppling over from the lopsided weight of his dangling head as his neck and legs further weakened. Like so much with ALS, I found this new peril impossible to imagine without seeing for myself.

Dad now spoke in a whisper with slurred words. They could hardly understand him at home. How softly can a person speak? Too faint for me to understand on the telephone, I discovered. I just heard a murmur of low sounds. I couldn't make out his words.

The MDA clinic had given him a voice amplifier, but it didn't help much, and Dad didn't like the thing. It was just a matter of time, and not much, before he would be unable to talk to us.

That prospect had alarmed me for months, and now it was almost here. How could we care for him without communication? It was awful. But, like all the other ALS impossibilities, it was fast approaching.

Worst were the reports of his horrific eating problems. It was the same thing that began during my July visit. He'd eat, something would lodge in his throat, he'd try to clear his throat, and his saliva would generate streams of that horrible gooey phlegm.

I knew that evil stuff from my own experience wiping the inside of his mouth. When it began in July, Dad said he couldn't live this way. I agreed. *We cannot live this way*, I thought. We needed our once civilized meals, talking with each other, living our lives together. We could not be wiping up this horrible goo that coated his mouth and poured out as we ate. But the goo had become a fact of daily life. His ability to clear his throat had become feeble over the months. It still led to choking and gasping for air, worse than ever, until he would force up the impeding objects—strangely innocuous food crumbs coated in phlegm.

Mom described these throat-clearing sessions as disgusting, scary, and becoming worse. It was terrible for him and her. Dr. Vick's proposed nasal feeding tube was still out of the question for him.

This is how he actually could die, I thought again. *He could choke to death trying to cough up crumbs.*

He caught a cold at the beginning of November. It was a crisis, a repeat of March. He couldn't clear his throat or his nose, and no one could give him the help he wanted. It became so bad that they considered placing him in the hospital like they had considered in March. Mom and Dad were exhausted by Dad's day-after-day inability to clear his vital passages. They sounded desperate. But Dad preferred to struggle at home over being in the hands of strangers at a hospital. And then the cold ended—a relief—and they were back to the usual problems with swallowing and choking, phlegm and drooling.

Each day brought some new crisis, small or large—eating, sleeping, breathing, sitting, etc. Even without a crisis, he constantly needed help—with his body, clothes, food, bed, the wheelchair, the house. Nothing satisfied him. He was miserable.

He repeatedly complained about being "treated like a vegetable" by the aides. I hated hearing that. I knew what he meant. I thought the aides were competent and caring. But as he could do less, he felt like a vegetable, powerless and passive, his body moved around, completely dependent on others.

He was suffering. He had been independent his entire life, a helper of others: from decades back when his immigrant parents relied on him to navigate their car through Chicago, running on the track team in high school with that fit young body, supporting a family with three boys and his parents, problem-solving in his laboratory at work, improving his Skokie house, picking up people at O'Hare Field. Now Dad could not care for himself, not in the tiniest ways. He could only say what he wanted, and that, too, was ending.

We had two competent live-in aides who covered the entire week, day and night. These aides knew what to do and how to do it. Any change of an aide, even with a capable replacement for a few days, required new training to meet his needs and wants. Dad couldn't tolerate these changes. Mom struggled to keep the two regulars.

Mom found him weaker than ever, more dependent, and more difficult to assist. They were not fighting as before, but she was laid low by his dissatisfaction and despair. After all, she said, he was not in pain, and it was easy for him to get assistance from an aide for any need. After more than a year of ALS, she was exasperated with catering to him. He constantly wanted something when she knew that nothing would satisfy him.

I worried about Mom. On the phone, she sounded anxious, often on the verge of tears. The year with ALS had taken a terrible toll on her. She was sad and depressed since he was dying, living on a day-to-day, hour-by-hour basis, helping him get through ALS and dying.

Amid everything, she said Dad continued to "bug me to finish the taping," that is, to tell her life story on tape, a complement to his taped life story. He wanted that project completed before he died. Mom told me she couldn't focus her attention on telling her history.

Rob said he didn't know how she could "take much more." She was "on the edge of desperation." He worried that she would "crack." But she assured me she was resilient and would help Dad to the end. I thought that was so. Mom might be fed up with Dad and feel despair, but she was also tough, loyal to Dad in his misery, and committed to helping him through this terrible final phase of their life together.

I was relieved to learn that Mom was thinking about her future after Dad. She told Rob she had decided not to move to the condo in Boca Raton. She would stay in Skokie, among family and friends, and continue her job. She thought about doing volunteer work for the Muscular Dystrophy Association.

They decided to skip the MDA clinic in November. Though it was just a few miles away, it would be a grueling trip for them: winter clothes on and off, on and off, the jarring van rides there and back, Mom handling the wheelchair, and the people, noise, and intrusions. And what would they get from it? Nothing important, they thought. ALS would march on.

That was a bad sign to me. The clinic was their only source of medical help with managing the disease. Even as I sought out a way for Dad to end his life, I worried that they were giving up help, giving in to ALS, giving up his fight to live, and giving up all hope. That would leave us only with watching him succumb, minute by minute, and my search for an earlier end.

Dad knew ALS would kill him. But would it kill him soon enough? He repeatedly told Rob and Mark that he was "ready" to "move on." He asked Rob to help him "end it soon," to "finish it off."

Rob and Mark told him to wait for me. They knew about my investigation.

He complained to Rob, "There's no way out." I thought he meant there was no way out of his ALS predicament. Arms and legs paralyzed, he could not end his life himself. He was helpless.

I knew he was desperate, locked in his immobile body. He asked Rob for reports from me, and he sent a message: "I need it more than ever." I responded that I was working on the problem. Dad usually said, "I'll wait for Skip's return." But when he felt most desperate, he would talk about stopping eating.

And Mom? At the beginning of December, a week before my next visit, she greeted me on the telephone with her own macabre joke: "We're still alive."

Even knowing that Dad was relying on me to help him "finish it off," I found Mom's gallows humor funny and reassuring. Laugh at our absurd helplessness to stop this calamity. Laugh at our living on through this disaster. That's all we had left for comfort.

In Oakland, I faced my problem: how to help Dad end his life.

This was not like any other problem I had ever encountered. This was my father's life, his misery, his desperate wishes for a conclusion. And it was Mom's life too. It was her determination to care for Dad to his natural end whenever it would come. How could I summon the clarity and strength to decide what to do?

Back in April, during my Boca Raton visit, when I witnessed Dad's cursing response to the fall in their bedroom, I speculated on what I would do if I had ALS. I vowed I would not put my family through an ordeal with ALS like Dad was doing. No, I would commit suicide to spare everyone around me.

Now, a half-year later, I realized I had been cavalier, arrogant, and impatient with Dad's frustration. Now, trying to help Dad with his insistence on suicide, what to do was not easy or clear for me. How do you commit suicide if you are paralyzed? I had no idea. And was suicide the right thing to do? It was vast. It was dangerous. It was unimaginably final. Considering real suicide was entirely different from my previous frustrated reactions and loose thoughts.

I had no doubt that Dad wanted this finality and needed it. I knew his situation with ALS was intolerable to him, only becoming worse, and he could do nothing about it. I had to find a way to help him end his life. He and I could decide whether to do it when I saw him next in Skokie. I would face the risks of an attempted suicide later—if and when I had to. For now, I had to give us the choice: figure out how we could do it.

I was entirely on my own. In 1980, there was no movement for permitting what is today called "physician-assisted suicide" or "medical aid in dying." There was no way to choose death sooner, with medical assistance that is reliable, pain-free, and dignified. There was no legislation allowing terminal patients the right to die. It was a decade before the infamous Dr. Kevorkian, popularly known as "Dr. Death," generated public attention to his crusade for terminally ill patients to have the right to end their lives. The Hemlock Society, with its advocacy for the right to die and assisted suicide, had just begun. There were no "how-to" books or websites on the practicalities of committing suicide, which some later advocates called "self-deliverance." If there were organizations or people who could help me, I had not heard of them.

I had one direction to turn: people I knew who worked in the medical system. I selected the first to contact.

Here, I had astonishing good luck. Never underestimate luck. This friend knew a physician who might help me.

I met with the physician at his office. I explained my father and ALS. I described the advance of Dad's disease, his current enfeebled condition, and his misery. My father, I said, was desperate to end his life, but he did not have the physical ability to do anything about it. He needed my help. I needed a reliable means for a peaceful death that would not arouse suspicion. I understood that we were in the realm of the illegal.

The physician understood exactly what I was talking about. He knew ALS. He asked many questions about my father.

He wanted to think about it. He said I should call him in two weeks.

I called. We discussed my father's condition again and what he wanted. The physician said he knew what I needed. Call again in two weeks.

I wondered if this was a test of my will to go ahead. I thought again about Dad and me—his wishes and my options. I reached the same conclusion: Now, find a way to help him. Later, decide with Dad in Skokie whether to do it.

I called in two weeks. We made an appointment to meet again at his office.

This time, the physician handed me a bottle of liquid. "Two tablespoons," he told me. "Your father should take two tablespoons before going to sleep for the night. It's painless. He will fall asleep, and he will not wake up. It will look like he died in his sleep."

I questioned the physician closely about what would happen.

He repeated what he had told me, this time suggesting that I try a tiny dose at home and see for myself. He said a small amount would not harm me.

The next afternoon, I experimented with part of a teaspoon. I had to try it, and I quickly fell soundly asleep for several hours.

I thought, *This is it! I have the answer. Thank you, courageous physician.*

I called both my brothers and told them what Dad and I planned to do. I told them I had found a way to do it. I said I would not need their help. It would be too risky: Mark had a family, and Rob was young. I wanted their approval.

I told them I would not tell Mom. She would oppose it.

I had thought often about Mom's letter and what this would mean for her. I thought her greatest concern was the risk and the consequences for me. Yes, this would be perilous. But now I thought I could help him. No one else would know.

Mark and Rob considered it for a few days. They saw his misery and how badly he wanted to stop living, and they both agreed.

I made my decision. It was not difficult. It was the decision I thought I would make when Dad first made the request. I could not say "no" to him.

I told Rob I had a message for Dad that he would understand: "I have it."

When I arrived back in Skokie for the December visit, Dad's first words, faint but clear, were "Do you have the stuff?"

"Yes."

He nodded in satisfaction, and I saw his face relax. There was nothing left to discuss with him but how and when to do it.

For me, there was no going back. I knew it. I would help him end his life.

The house was dark and quiet on this visit. The curtains were closed, dampening the weak winter light outside. No one spoke much. He even seemed to be spitting up less phlegm, with less coughing and choking. There was not much sound. I thought that exhaustion had set in as we all waited for the end.

Most mornings, Dad was in the living room where he could look out the window. He would sit quietly and think. Sometimes, he listened to his opera recordings. But no more bursts of sobbing with the arias. He was past mourning.

Only the closest family visited. No more friends. Dad's niece Eileen read to him every afternoon. He couldn't tolerate the stimulation of most people.

Mom and he were getting along better. She let the aides do all the physical caring for him. Mom continued working, grateful to have a place to go three weekdays. At home, she continued to cook and clean. In the evenings, she kept Dad company in the living room.

Was he nearing the end, the natural end with ALS? Dr. Vick had told me Dad could die anytime. Now Dad was in miserable condition, much worse than July. He could not perform the most basic life functions: turning in bed, dressing himself, cleaning himself, feeding himself, swallowing food, and walking. His speech was disappearing. Only his breathing weakness did not yet seem critical.

I believed he could become worse yet, and his life also might be prolonged with greater medical interventions, particularly support for his feeding and breathing. I guessed he would not make it to the two-year average lifespan from diagnosis for older men. But I thought he might continue for months. More months of his misery.

We had one celebration during my visit. My book on Joe Rapoport was published. The press overnighted a copy to me in Skokie. At last, I showed it to Dad, a real book. My name was in large letters at the top of the front book jacket. On the back of the jacket was a picture of me and my tape recorder with Joe. And inside, on the page before the table of contents, was my dedication: "For My Mother and Father."

"Why didn't you put our names in the dedication?" he immediately asked.

An electric shock passed through my body. I was stunned. Again, the old pattern: I did something special, but my accomplishment was not good enough. I hadn't expected this disappointment. Not this time. The end approached. I thought we had left these issues behind.

He wants to be remembered, I told myself—not just as "my father" but as himself, Sam Kann. It was my mistake. I thought of them as "Mom" and "Dad," not Ann and Sam. I knew how easy it would have been to include their real names in my dedication. But now it was too late. There was nothing I could do about it.

I agonized over how and why I made this mistake, but Dad rallied and let it go. I was relieved to see him proudly showing the book to our few visitors.

I updated Mom and Dad on the other big development in my life: Stephanie. I told them that Stephanie might return to live in San Francisco after graduation. That was our path to a future together.

I felt good giving Mom and Dad these happy reports. I had a steady girlfriend and a published book. I thought, *Remove me from your worries.*

Dad was determined to end his life with ALS. He had made up his mind by our discussions at the end of my October visit. Nothing changed when I returned in December with the means to do it. Dad had long described himself as a realist. He had concluded that ALS would kill him. He refused to tolerate his tortuous, diminished life, suffering and waiting until ALS finished him.

There are other ways to die with ALS. I have read everything I can find about people who lived and died with ALS. There are many variations.

Shirley Knight, in a memoir of her husband Bill's life with ALS, describes an incident a few years before his diagnosis when they watched a documentary on Dr. Kevorkian assisting a man with advanced ALS. The man injected himself with a lethal substance. "I would rather be dead than live like that," Bill said. "If I had an awful disease like ALS, I would kill myself" (Knight 2011, 136-137).

Several years later, Bill was in that position with ALS. Shirley describes him at the end as miserable, with confused sleepless nights, unable to find a comfortable sitting position by day, almost completely paralyzed, drooling, and struggling to breathe. His independence was entirely lost. Shirley tells us she never asked Bill if, with ALS, he wanted to commit suicide. Bill told her he wished he would die quickly, but she relates no attempt to kill himself nor any wish for it by Bill. He waited. Bill died peacefully one morning while sitting in his recliner in their den (Knight 2011, 245-246).

Dad refused to wait for ALS to kill him. For months, he was focused on how to end his life immediately.

Others struggle ferociously to live on with ALS. In an article on her Chinese-born mother with ALS, writer Jiayang Fan describes her and her mother's epic struggle through the 2020 coronavirus pandemic to retain the private aides who sustained her mother in a long-term acute-care hospital. This story is set against the background of her mother's years-long unrelenting struggle to make a life for herself and her daughter as American immigrants. Fan's mother, an ALS survivor for over ten years, was entirely paralyzed, on a ventilator for breathing, and able to communicate only through an alphabet chart and blinks. Fan describes her extraordinary internet campaign to save her mother by obtaining permission for their private aides to remain inside the hospital despite a pandemic lockdown that excluded visitors. This public campaign for help brought Fan and her mother blistering criticism from Chinese countrymen for their loss of face (e.g., loss of respect and social standing by seeking public help). In the end, remarkably, Fan and her mother prevailed—one aide was allowed despite the pandemic. After this successful battle for her life, Fan's mother had the final say, in English: "I am survive" (Fan 2020).

I admired the will and fight of Fan's mother to live on with ALS. I recognized Dad had the same determination but in the opposite direction—to end his life with ALS.

During my December visit, Dad and I did not discuss whether he should end his life. Dad had thought about it for months. We had discussed it in October. He told me in December that nothing had changed except that the ALS was worse. Dad was physically feeble, but he was willful and unequivocal. He wanted to stop living.

Our only discussion was the procedure for doing it. Dad selected the night. It would be a week after I arrived.

I would take over from the aide for a couple of nights, which was not unusual. On an evening of his choosing, when settled in bed for the night, I would give him two tablespoons of the stuff. He would fall asleep as usual. No pain. No discomfort. But he would not wake up again. He would die peacefully in his sleep. He would be dead by the morning.

No "suicide note." It never occurred to Dad or me. ALS seemed like a self-evident explanation for ending his life.

Dad did not worry about it. He never had been a worrier, and he did not start then, at the end. He had confidence in me, the substance I brought, and our plan.

I am a worrier. I worried. Would this actually be as simple as it seemed? I wasn't certain. Would this stuff work? Could we do this without Mom or the aide discovering us? How will they react to Dad's body at a hospital or morgue? What other problems might we encounter?

I was scared. The plan could go wrong. "Wrong" meant failure through a botched attempt, with Dad wakening to discover he had been left alive with ALS. What then? It would leave Mom with Dad, his ALS, and a failed suicide after her letter pleading with me not to do it. And what would happen to me? I could end up facing the police, arrest, and prosecution. And prison? It could go wrong for everyone in our family. "Wrong" was unimaginable.

Do what you have to do, I told myself again. *It will not go wrong.*

This was the real thing. I thought we were ready, as ready as we could be. I would just have to solve any unexpected problems when they appeared.

At Dad's request, the evening before was a practice evening, Monday, December 15. Dad did two of his favorite things that evening. He watched a professional football game with me. And he listened to an opera record with Mom and me, his favorite, Pavarotti singing arias.

Why practice? I didn't know. I didn't ask. I waited until he thought the time was right.

I told the aide that I would cover the night shift that night and the next day. Gratefully, she accepted my offer of precious nights off.

We began the bedtime routine at 9. Come 9:30, he was sitting up in bed and ready.

I did not give him the tablespoons. Our plan was to do that the next evening.

I repeated what I had already told him: I would sleep in the living room, right by his bedroom. He could call me when he needed assistance.

I helped him settle in bed. I kissed him goodnight. The next evening, it would be good night and goodbye.

Then, he surprised me. He wanted me to bring Mom. I fetched her from the back bedroom.

I stood outside his bedroom door. I was not going far from him until we were through this. I heard part of their exchange.

I heard, "I love you, Ann. I've always loved you."

Even from outside the bedroom, I could tell Mom was surprised by this sudden show of affection. Me too. Entirely focused on the job, I had forgotten about Mom. But Dad remembered.

She gathered herself. Then I heard her response. "I love you, Sammy."

She kissed him. And she returned to her bedroom.

I settled onto the living room couch for the night ahead, and off to sleep I went. I relaxed right through the night because this was just the rehearsal.

Come morning, around 7 a.m., I awoke. I bolted up, startled. I had always heard when he called at night. Two or three times, or more. He had not called me through the entire night.

I rushed to his bedroom. His chest barely moved. I tried to wake him. First, I spoke with him. Then, I gently touched him. Then, I jostled him by the shoulders. No response.

The aide and Mom would soon wake. I knew I had to act, or events would quickly spiral out of my control.

I went into Mom's bedroom and woke her as gently as I could.

"Tell me," she said, startled. It was never good news when she was awakened.

I did not want her to be surprised by learning about our suicide plan from someone else. I told her the truth, what Dad and I had planned. I did not know what would happen next. Dad could survive, and he could talk about the suicide plan. She would be ready. She would know.

I explained that the previous night was a rehearsal. I said I thought he was almost gone this morning.

"You didn't? You were going to do it? And this happened first?" She said it with amazement. And, I thought, with admiration. Not censure.

I was sitting on the edge of her bed, face-to-face. I saw her big eyes. Her open mouth. Dad and I had really planned to do it. And instead, ALS intervened.

I was astonished. I felt vast relief, but there was more to do. I was strangely calm.

I needed to reach Dr. Vick. I asked Mom to dress and wait for me to speak with him.

I called Dr. Vick's answering service with an emergency message. For the first time, he called back immediately.

I explained that I found Dad barely breathing and unresponsive. He was peaceful.

We talked. I said that Dad would not want to wake up from this sleep. Dr. Vick knew Dad's condition and state of mind only too well.

"Call an ambulance," he said. "Have him brought to Evanston Hospital."

And then he gave me some genuine help. "They will try to waken him. Don't let them do that. Tell them the doctor said so."

Thank you, Dr. Vick. I was ready as I was going to be.

I warned Mom, "I'm calling an ambulance. Things will start happening fast."

I called 911. I threw on clothes. I woke the aide and told her about Dad not waking and the ambulance. She said she had to call her supervisor. That was the last time I saw her.

Suddenly, our house was filled with men in uniforms.

We were in Dad's bedroom: me with a couple of paramedics, the police, some firemen. And there was my father, almost lifeless in the bed. He was faintly breathing.

I wore a jacket. I was ready to go to the hospital.

One of the paramedics, at the head of the bed closest to Dad, opened his bag and withdrew some equipment. He was about to start working on Dad. Resuscitation.

I was to his immediate left. I gently placed my hand on his and firmly said, "No."

He stopped and looked at me, puzzled. We stared at each other for a moment.

I said, "The doctor told me we should bring him right to the hospital. He said not to do anything." He stared at me.

I needed more. I tried to explain—ALS, paralysis, suffering, he would not want to wake up. I wondered, *Am I making any sense? Could an outsider understand this?*

Quiet. A bedroom full of big men in uniforms circling my father's bed. We stood there in frozen silence. It was difficult for these helpers not to do something to save the life before them.

I explained Dad's ALS to the lead paramedic.

The police officer to my left asked my name. I looked over to him. I noticed only the uniform, a big wall of blue.

I gave my name. He wrote it down.

"Who are you?"

I was surprised. I thought that was obvious. But, of course, it was not at all apparent.

"His son."

The paramedic, God bless him, said, "Let's go."

Someone pulled away the blankets. And there was my father, Dad, in bed, without protective cover. His body was scrawny. Emaciated.

Muscles wasted away by ALS. Helpless. I had an impulse to get into the bed with him, keep him company, protect him.

As we headed out of the house, Dad on a stretcher, I was startled to see a convention of the vehicles that belonged with these men: fire engines, police cars, the ambulance. At our house. Vehicles like this were always at someone else's house.

I was in the ambulance with Dad, holding his hand. We were speeding to Evanston Hospital. I heard a siren. It was us, I realized.

We were in the hospital. The emergency department. We were in a partitioned area. Dad was on a bed, not moving. I was still holding his hand. Our area suddenly filled with people. Now, it was medical uniforms. Then, there was Dr. Vick, who said I needed to leave for now.

I was directed to Mom, who was waiting nearby. I had completely forgotten about her.

A few minutes later, Dr. Vick came back to us. "Sam has died," he told us softly.

He offered us time to be with him. Mom and I went back to Dad and sat with him. We talked about him. We spoke about his courage.

We met with Dr. Vick. He was warm and comforting. He praised Dad's struggle with ALS. Almost talking to himself, he said he was surprised that ALS had run its course with Dad so quickly, less than a year and a half. He understood our relief that it was over.

Dr. Vick asked that we consider an autopsy. "It will help us better understand ALS. It could be helpful for other families."

"*No!*" I insisted . . . almost shouted.

What is he thinking? I wondered. I did not want to mess around with the peaceful death of my father. I thought, *It's over. No more.*

Dr. Vick beckoned me toward my mother. Mom's decision. I shut up and looked.

Mom didn't hesitate. "No. I just would not feel right with an autopsy. I want to bury him as he is."

Mom thanked Dr. Vick. I thanked Dr. Vick. We shook hands.

As Mom and I walked to the emergency department exit, the

ambulance paramedic came over to me and said, "I'm sorry. I didn't understand."

Someone had explained ALS to him. This patient did not want to wake.

Bless him, I thought again.

"You were doing your job. Thank you."

We shook hands.

That was the end. Still dazed, Mom and I walked out of the hospital holding hands.

We went home and began making calls.

The funeral was small and plain. It was as Mom had described wanting the year before at my December 1979 visit soon after the diagnosis. Just a few people: Mom, me, my brothers, and Dad's sister's family. A simple ceremony with the rabbi presiding at the gravesite.

It was an icy gray day with piercing rain. We held umbrellas as Rabbi Stern spoke. We watched the plain pine coffin lowered into the ground. It was a terse ceremony in the bitter, damp cold. He had died too young. He had died with so much suffering. It was a bitter death for those of us who lived on, for me.

We sat shiva, the Jewish mourning period, for several evenings. We opened our house to family and friends, who brought trays of food. Everyone came: the relatives, the friends from the days of the old West Side, the Skokie neighbors, Rabbi Stern, and some colleagues too, those wonderful engineers from Dad's company.

It wasn't bitter. I spoke with many people from the span of my life. I heard high praises of Dad: he was smart, he was generous, he was responsible, he was proud of his family, he was courageous. There were warm reminiscences and even some funny stories. There was a huge collective relief, unspoken, that the ALS ordeal was over.

I felt satisfied. I had helped Dad reach this end, as he wanted. I had given him all that I could. I had been ready to do more. We had said and done everything that needed to be said and done. I thought Dad understood.

EPILOGUE
After Dad

1981 TO THE PRESENT

Half a year later, for the stone marker at Dad's grave, Mom wrote the inscription

Sam Kann—What A Man!

June 12, 1915–December 16, 1980

Loving Husband and Father

Always in Our Hearts

I liked Mom's choice of words: loving, admiring, and sly too. The "What A Man!" made me happy. It was a warm, paradoxical allusion to Dad's life and death with ALS, where he had been courageous and heroic, exasperating and infuriating. Mom remembered Dad with affection and appreciation, as he was, her life partner, a proud and difficult man who had faced a terrible final crisis.

After Dad's death, I resumed my life in California: unattached part-time itinerant teacher and freelance historian. But returning to normal was impossible.

I had taken stock when Dad was sick. My life seemed marginal. Living on the fringes had become intolerable. I wanted different. I wanted more. I wanted better.

Through our ALS crisis, I had seen Dad's life anew, with nothing marginal about it. Now I understood Dad's job as a chemist: his satisfaction with the work, his devoted colleagues, an employer that appreciated him, the compensation that supported our family in Skokie, and the savings and benefits that helped us through the ALS ordeal. I also rediscovered the family and friends around Mom and Dad, the relationships that supported them through the crisis, and the shared history that gave them depth and stability as they faced the irrepressible flux of ALS.

Seeing Dad's life during ALS and helping him bring it to a close brought me a gift: an urgent need to change my life. *I did well through our family ordeal*, I thought. I had met many challenges, some that frightened me. But I knew I had not been ready for this catastrophic illness. I had not been prepared for my father to die and to stand on my own.

And now there was Stephanie. I wanted a long relationship. I knew I had to bring more to our future together than my PhD, books on chicken ranchers, and part-time teaching. At twenty-three, she thought that was plenty. She was not dissatisfied, but I was.

Change began with my work. Now I wanted a real career that would pay well, support a family in comfort, and prepare me for the unexpected and unfathomable, like ALS. I wanted a job where I'd be mixing in the world, a world that would recognize and reward my skills. It would be a profession where I'd eat lunch in a restaurant, and everyone at the table would be over twenty-two. I was through with being an itinerant teacher of undergraduates and a freelance historian—my employment takeaways from the sixties student rebellion. I wanted an adult career.

For the next two years, I searched for that new vocation. I quickly discovered there would be no return to an academic career, where a surplus of PhDs from my own generation were competing for scarce professor jobs. I floundered trying to transfer my academic skills to careers with foundations, museums, education programs, and business communications.

Exploring those vocations, I met many people from my generation who, after the sixties rebellion, had been successful. They held prominent jobs. They had strong work commitments and good compensation. They were well-dressed, with professional polish and confidence. These were high achievers who whetted the appetite I had developed with Dad's illness. They showed me what was possible.

I held one more option in my back pocket, not my first choice but awaiting the right time if nothing else panned out. It was my sensible high school plan from the 1950s: become a lawyer, known then as a good profession that could bring many possibilities.

At age thirty-eight in 1982, after years of complaining that my best students were going to law school rather than graduate study in history, I entered the line with my own applications to law schools. I enrolled full-time at San Francisco's Hastings College of the Law in August 1983 while I continued teaching part-time at UC Berkeley. I started over as if I had just graduated from college.

Law still offered opportunities in the 1980s. New lawyers were finding jobs. I thought I still had the energy and determination to train for law practice and establish myself as an attorney.

After helping Dad with his business affairs, I thought I would do well as an attorney. I had the example of my young cousin Neil, who I had visited at his downtown law office, high above Chicago Loop, to discuss the trust agreement he had prepared for my parents. Neil was a fine attorney, successful, and generous with his professional help to Mom and Dad. Why couldn't I do that?

I had a taste of law practice soon after Dad died when I battled with his health insurance company to pay for the cost of the home aides we had hired. When the company resisted reimbursement, I marshaled arguments showing coverage, and I mobilized support from Dad's company. I won that insurance dispute, a satisfying victory that told me I had the skills to become an attorney.

I marched through law school for three years, fearless of the new world I had entered. I had seen the worst with ALS. Walking into my first class in civil procedure, I thought, *It's just law school.*

This was my second chance. As an older law student, it was strange taking notes in morning classes and then spending afternoons teaching UC Berkeley undergraduates who scribbled notes as I lectured. It was odd taking tests again and being graded alongside ambitious young law students. I competed for summer law jobs. I took it one day at a time, step after step toward a new life. In 1986, six years after Dad's death, I became a lawyer.

Academic friends warned that I'd never find a job as a new attorney at forty-one. But I landed that first job in a small general practice firm in Sausalito. I was back on the road not taken when, instead of enrolling in law school, I drove across the country to Berkeley for graduate study in history, the student movement, and the counterculture.

Within seven more years, I was a seasoned litigator at a downtown San Francisco law firm, fighting high-stakes legal battles for large institutional clients who wanted my representation. Along with the compensation and prestige came unrelenting pressures, with lunches mostly gobbled down at my desk. But I was intoxicated as I discovered I had the brains, skills, and drive to succeed in the ferocious world of litigation.

Just as I had been told as a high school student in the 1950s, law practice did open another career door. After fifteen years as a litigator, in 2001, I took a job with the state agency that administers the huge California state court system: court procedures, budgets, technology, buildings, and personnel. I believed in our mission to foster an impartial and accessible California justice system. Our purpose was to create good government, a comfortable fit with my social justice values from the 1960s.

I flourished at that agency, where I discovered my own surprising leadership and political skills, along with a huge ambition to succeed. Turned out, I was a problem-solver like Dad, not for chemical plating problems but for making public policy in a large state bureaucracy. And thank you, Mom, maintainer of flawless bookkeeping systems, for my strong organizational skills. I rose quickly in the agency. When I retired in 2011, I was in top management, one of the directors.

Dad would have understood my law careers as a litigator and a court system administrator. These were real jobs where my abilities were recognized, my achievements were honored, and I was paid well. I worked in elegant downtown skyscrapers and huge government buildings, with corner offices and floor-to-ceiling windows sporting sweeping views. I led teams of superb attorneys, paralegals, and secretaries. I wore a suit and tie to work every day. I think Dad would have admired these jobs.

I did not give up as a historian. I continued working on the story of the Petaluma Jewish chicken ranching community, a second book, one that would follow my published book on the labor organizer Joe Rapoport. This was my book-in-progress that Dad had boasted about to his work colleagues, whom I had met in December 1979 when Dad took me on that first workplace visit following the ALS diagnosis.

I shelved that project when I entered law school. After several years of finding my way as a new attorney, I worked evenings and weekends to complete the book and find a publisher. It was a labor of love and willpower while practicing law.

I published it in 1993. The book received attention and praise. It was a satisfying conclusion to my long-distance run with those chicken ranchers.

I wished Dad had lived long enough to see that achievement too. He would have been fascinated by this colorful story of Jewish immigration and assimilation over three generations in a little California community, like the story of our own family's American experience in Chicago. I think Dad would have been proud of me.

Stephanie laughed about my bait and switch with her. At twenty-two, she thought she was taking up with a writer when we began seeing each other in 1979. But she was fooled. Me too. She ended up with a hard-driving attorney.

As I encountered my family's ALS crisis in 1980 and Stephanie completed her undergraduate work, she and I became closer through summer weeks together, an avalanche of letters between Oakland and Northampton, telephone calls, and visits. Stephanie understood what I encountered with ALS.

After she graduated from Smith College in January 1981, Stephanie returned home to San Francisco to find out what would happen in "this tangle with you." I was amazed. I felt like I had won the big prize, my chance for a future with this beautiful and accomplished young woman.

We moved in together in 1983 when I began law school. Our romance made me feel like I received a special opportunity to relive my twenties with this young woman actually in her twenties. It was passionate, playful, and exciting. I was remaking my life on a new blank slate, the different life I had wanted when Dad was dying. I was no longer alone. Anything seemed possible.

Stephanie and I married in 1985 when I was completing law school. The wedding was at my ranch in Sonoma County, Chamokome, the place where Dad tried to apologize for not teaching me to use tools. We married under a stand of oak trees amid summer golden grasses, not far from the toolshed where I had placed the tools Dad gave me.

Mom was there for my wedding. She stood under the *chuppah* with my brothers and Stephanie's family. She looked wonderful in a stunning red and blue silk dress. I could feel her joy seeing me with Stephanie, making this lifetime commitment to each other.

Family and friends who had been with us through the ALS ordeal were there, coming across the country for this happy event. My Chicago and Skokie history was at our wedding.

Stephanie, every bit as brainy and ambitious as I had believed from the start, embarked on her own long march for a PhD in psychology.

She became a well-known clinician who treats young children with baffling neurological and developmental problems—and a writer too.

Mom liked Stephanie's young beauty, keen intelligence, and warmth. Mom was in San Francisco to celebrate with Stephanie and me when I passed the bar exam. She came to help after Julia was born. She swapped recipes with Stephanie while accurately suspecting that her delicious Swedish meatballs, with a secret Skokie ingredient (Welch's grape jam), would not fly with a young generation.

Over forty years after Dad's death, Stephanie and I have a lovely San Francisco house near the ocean and Golden Gate Park, another accomplishment checked off my to-do list from when Dad was dying: BUY HOUSE. Stephanie and I work hard and live in comfort. Our age disparity of thirteen years, placing us on both ends of the baby boomers, once daring and adventurous, has become insignificant as we've lived together for decades.

My life seems so sure and predictable that I feel prepared for anything. Except for one unusual but familiar malady out there: ALS. The summer after Dad's death, I once stumbled and quickly decided it was the dreaded dropped foot. I made an emergency visit with my physician. She gave me a rudimentary leg strength test and pronounced me fit. I laughed at myself but felt like I had dodged a bullet. To this day, over forty years later, I monitor myself for dropped foot, fasciculations, inexplicable body weakness, or any other first sign of ALS. Those letters, ALS, still give me the chills. That scary, scary disease. Now I know: I could never be ready for ALS.

When he met Stephanie in October 1980, Dad wondered what would happen with us. He might have been surprised by the similarity of my current life to his: the solid family, steady devotion to purposeful careers, enormous support for our daughter Julia's happiness and success, careful investments and accumulated resources, and dense web of family and friends around us.

It turned out it was the life I wanted when Dad was dying: a conventional, middle-class life. This surprised me after the student rebellion of the 1960s and 1970s when I thought I had traveled far from Skokie with no desire or route to return. This familiar middle-class life made me just as happy and satisfied as I expected in 1980 when Dad was dying and I wanted change.

We have one child, Julia, the splendid granddaughter Dad never met. Julia grew up close to my mother, a.k.a. "Granny Annie." She and I traveled together to see Granny Annie every year. Mom visited us in San Francisco. She loved Julia and was a part of Julia's life.

I didn't see Dad in Julia until high school. Julia has a mechanical aptitude, a curiosity about how devices work, and a keen interest in mathematics. Her idea of fun was designing and building a toaster for her physics course. I thought, *There's Dad.*

When Julia enrolled in physics and math courses in high school and then signed up for math in college, I thought she might become our family's aerospace engineer, the work that eluded my father in 1951 when he had a Southern California aerospace job opportunity. Julia passed on that career option, but she remains the only member of our extended family to have worked in a hardware store and to own a power drill for home repairs, surely generation-skipping proclivities from my father.

When Julia immersed herself in her college drama department, I became certain she'd become a stage manager on Broadway. Julia, a problem-solver like Dad and me, has fantastic organizational skills, excellent people skills, a technical grasp of staging, lighting, props, and costumes, and always her tool kit at hand. *Perfect*, I thought, *light-years from anything Stephanie or I do or anything our parents have done, except Dad and tools*. Each generation finds its own calling. But then, near graduation, Julia informed me that theater people were too self-absorbed. All her career options were open again.

As a father, I was humbled by my ignorance watching my daughter's mysterious path to her career. Perhaps this is what Dad experienced when I became a history graduate student on track to become a professor and then a freelance historian, neither of which were on his career radar screen for me. If I was as puzzled by my child as my father was by me, I hope it was with more curiosity and confidence that, in the end, she would solve her career quandary.

Today, at thirty-six, Julia does "food justice" work. She currently develops food distribution programs for young people at a large community college. She has created food education programs, done commercial farming, held restaurant and bakery jobs, managed a farmers' market, and developed her own catering business and food blog. Her preferred food is vegetarian, organic, local, and prepared with flair, popular with her millennial generation, far from those knishes, blintzes, and pastrami sandwiches consumed by her ancestors in Chicago's West Side and Skokie.

Julia is creating her own original vocation, no profession I recognize. Her work is generations and decades removed from my grandparents' neighborhood stores in early twentieth-century immigrant Chicago, from Dad's science and technology work in mid-twentieth-century industrial Chicago, and Mom's suburban bookkeeping work. She is just as distant from my career as an attorney and Stephanie's as a psychologist in 2000s San Francisco. Nonetheless, we were determined to show Julia our pride in her work achievements and for her to know her value.

Julia assumes a world of limited possibilities with vocation and income. It's not the Depression that Mom and Dad faced in the 1930s, but neither is it the near-limitless career opportunities Stephanie and I have enjoyed as baby boomers since the 1950s. Julia, principled, entrepreneurial, and realistic about her world, is creating her own millennial generation career path.

Julia and her husband, Pete, have given me a glimpse of receiving help as I age. Several years ago, they joined us for a weekend hiking in the high country at Yosemite National Park. Then, in my early seventies, still a backpacker and cyclist, I took pride in my hiking prowess. On one of those Yosemite days, we hiked to North Dome, about ten miles round trip, with some steep sections on the trail. In the afternoon, on the return, I noticed Julia and Pete lingering at those steeper, more precarious points on the trail, ready to give me a hand and see that I didn't end up on my butt or worse. I was alarmed. Ready for help or not, like it or not, they were concerned, and they were there for me. It was one of my possible futures, right before me on the trail at Yosemite: help from my adult child.

I didn't much like it. I am my father's son. I'd rather help others than be helped by my kid. Or, as a ninety-two-year-old friend explained, "It's a burden to be a burden for others."

Dad, with ALS, was nearly impossible for me to help, whether it was morning grooming or adjusting his wheelchair. It was how he had been with his home improvement projects when he preferred to do it himself rather than make room for me as a kid. I thought his extraordinary loss of control with ALS required that he use help from others at the end of his life, which was good for me but also among the causes for him to seek an end to his life. *Be grateful*, I told myself on the Yosemite trail as I accepted the helping hands of my daughter and son-in-law.

When Dad had been suffering, I admired how the relatives, neighbors, and old friends came to our house to be with Mom and Dad. This was the social world of my parents, dating back to Chicago's West Side immigrant neighborhoods of the 1920s and 1930s, people I had known all my life and took for granted. For many months, they arrived in numbers to help however they could or just to be there with Dad and Mom.

I remembered how all of Dad's business ventures in the 1940s and 1950s were with his family or close friends. I remembered Dad's enduring anger at that betrayal by Cousin Irving Tarnople when he refused to return Dad the $20,000 deposit for the fifth year on the bowling alley lease. Dad had a powerful immigrant ethic of loyalty, of helping your own people and relying on your own people, starting with your own family.

He passed on to me a value that propelled me throughout Dad's ALS: take care of your own. Do what you have to do to help. I see that ethic in my daughter Julia. I admire it.

My time of need has not yet come. I don't know if I will need help. But I know the helpers are around me: Stephanie, Julia, our family, and friends, particularly the longtime comrades from my ranch community. I believe they will be there for me.

When Dad was dying in 1980, I questioned whether my generation would be able to care for our own as we age. Now, over forty years later, I can see the world that my slice of baby boomers has created: our own families, friendships, and communities can sustain us in old age. I've become more optimistic for myself and my generation.

Approaching eighty, I feel healthy and energetic, with more to do. I still do not believe I will need help. But Dad had that same belief in his own invulnerability at sixty-four, so near retirement, until the arrival of those strange symptoms that emerged from hell: shoulder weakness, fasciculations, dropped foot. He never understood why he was knocked down by ALS. "Why me?" he once despaired, like many other ALS patients. I've seen what can happen.

Mom sold the house in 1982, two years after Dad's death. She told me she had good memories of her life with Dad and our family in Skokie. But with Dad gone, living alone, she was eager to move on with a new life.

The sale of that house ended an era for me. It was my prolonged adolescence. That was the home I held in mind after I left Skokie for Berkeley in 1966. I felt stricken in 1979 when Dad wanted to sell that house after the ALS diagnosis. Not until 1982, age thirty-eight, when I began living with Stephanie, did my feeling of home change. My first San Francisco flat with Stephanie became my home. Without regret, I helped Mom sell the Skokie house.

As she had planned when Dad was dying, Mom remained in the Chicago area near family and friends. She bought a condo in a farther western suburban building with many older Jewish couples and widowed women. She decorated it beautifully and made friendships in the building. She lived there happily for many years.

Mom held onto the Boca Raton condo for more years than she wanted because of my urgings and memories of talking about ALS with Dad on the veranda while looking out on the gently swaying yachts anchored along our inlet off the Intracoastal Waterway. Finally, as Mom advanced in her seventies and traveled less, it became difficult for her to maintain a semitropical property from Chicago. I sold it for her.

A year after Dad died, his mother, Grandma, passed away. She had outlived Dad, as he feared, and most of her family too. Mom arranged for Grandma's burial next to Grandpa in the gravesite that had awaited her for many years, not far from Dad and Mom's burial plots.

Mom took up with a male friend in the 1990s, also named Sam, and they were companions for many years. I liked this Sam. He was ten years older than Mom, a successful small businessman still working part-time, kind and engaging, not the predatory gold digger Dad had imagined. They had an active social life, traveled together, and were good company for each other.

But Mom kept to her inclinations when Dad was dying. She liked having a man in her life, but she didn't want to marry again. After her long life with Dad, after the catastrophe with ALS, she did not want to be involved so deeply with another person in older age.

Mom and I spoke a single time about Dad's death. I once asked if she still thought about Dad. Yes, she did, often. We talked about their life together. She thought Dad was rigid and overbearing even before ALS. But he was also devoted to her and our family. She said they had a good life together on the West Side and in Skokie.

Sitting there in her new condo, remembering those months when Dad was sick, it was difficult to recall my fear that Mom would not survive the ALS nightmare. I had known she was strong and determined. I had thought she was wise to live in the present with ALS and not look ahead to the frightening future. I had believed she would make it, but I was never certain. She remembered their months with ALS. But she also recalled her life with Dad, the good years, the happy times. She had perspective.

Then, we recalled the events of that final night and the next morning. She was still astonished that Dad had planned to end his life, and she lowered her voice to a hush as we discussed it. She admired his courage in planning to do it, even though she disagreed. She had wanted him to continue living with ALS but to be more cheerful and easier to help. Her views had not changed since he died.

Those wishes, I thought again, had not been possible. Not with Dad. He was proud and unwilling to accept his ALS miseries and feeble, dependent condition in the final months, even if it meant ending his life early.

Mom told me one other thing about them. Without using the word "sex," she told me that everything had always been "good in that department." I hadn't asked about it. I had been content to accept the existence of me and my brothers as enough indication. But I was glad she told me. Dad's final months were so difficult that I welcomed this reminder of their happy times together. As Dad wished, I did not want my recollections of my parents to be all about ALS.

Dad had left Mom financially comfortable. After she retired from her bookkeeping job, she volunteered at a nearby hospital for years. She did not work with ALS patients, but it was her way to give back to the medical system where we found so much support.

Mom joined a writing group at a nearby community college. She stayed with that group for years, writing poetry and essays, much of it printed in their annual publications. Her writing was wry, touching, and often gently self-deprecating and shrewd. She never did try to tape or write about our family history as Dad had wanted. But here's a serious essay she wrote about our family living with Dad's ALS:

THE WORST OF TIMES

Without a doubt, the worst of times was when Sam, my husband, was diagnosed with ALS, a neurological disease whereby the muscles and nerves in the body progressively deteriorate.

Although coping with the illness was very tough, tender and good things happened along the way. I expected to have the full burden on my shoulders, and instead, my sons immediately formed a team, and someone was always there for me with encouragement and moral support.

We learned about laughing together instead of crying.

We learned to argue if need be instead of pampering.

We learned family values.

We learned that "talking books" were readily available for necessary diversion.

We learned that the telephone company would accommodate to the person without use of his hands.

We learned the usefulness of occupational therapy to maintain as much independence as possible.

We learned that being told the absolute truth is not for everyone.

And above all, we learned to be humble, compassionate, and loving in its purest form.

Mom remained at her condo until 2005, when, at eighty-six, she was on a descent from Alzheimer's disease. It had begun as mild dementia, forgetfulness, hardly noticeable to me from California. For several years, with increasing assistance from Mary Gallagher, a wonderful woman we hired who became her good friend, Mom continued living on her own.

I gradually took over Mom's financial affairs. This was no big deal compared to when I had helped my parents back in 1980, then a fear-filled undertaking for me. Now, in the 2000s, I was an experienced attorney, accustomed to working with financial and legal arrangements. Handling Mom's business affairs from my home office was not a worrisome problem, particularly because she had preserved her savings, but also because I had my own resources to support her if need be. With careful management of her finances, there was enough to see Mom through her lifetime and leave some for her three sons, as she wanted.

In 2005, Rob and I moved Mom into an assisted living facility. She had her own apartment and longtime friends who lived there. It was a good home for her final two years.

During that time, on one of my visits, Mom gave me the diamond pendant Dad had given her a few months after his diagnosis. She always wore it, as she had vowed that day Dad bought it for her. Now she removed it from around her neck. She gave it to me for Julia.

I had already given Julia the diamond wedding rings that my grandfather had given to my grandmother back in 1907. Dad had passed them on to me that final year. At the time, I thought it was an act of his faith that I would have use for those rings in my future.

His faith was well placed, with Stephanie and then Julia coming into my life. Julia is still trying to figure out what to do with this jewelry. The diamonds are large and splashy, perhaps too gaudy for her generation and lifestyle. I told her she could sell them if she wanted. But my preference is that she find a way to wear them occasionally, even if they are old-timey diamonds. She's young, with time to find an answer.

Mom's final six months were awful. She lost her memory, capacity to do anything on her own, and finally, recognition of friends and family. We arranged caretakers for her day and night.

When Dad had been diagnosed almost thirty years earlier, I had felt unprepared. I was not ready with my half-formed life and meager resources. I was not ready with my unfinished relationship with Dad.

Looking back, by my reckoning, it had come out as well as possible, considering that there was no beating ALS. I did everything possible to help Mom and Dad through the ordeal.

But I had also vowed then that I would be prepared for any future crisis, whatever it would be. Here it was, twenty-seven years later: Mom's failing health with Alzheimer's.

This time, the crisis was different. Mom was eighty-eight, at the end of a long, full life. Her disease gradually developed over five years. Her end of life was sad for me and my brothers, but not as tumultuous, bitter, and frightening as Dad's surprise ALS calamity had been at a young sixty-four.

I felt ready to face the decisions for Mom's health treatment, living arrangements, and support. I was established in my own life with family, home, work, and resources. Any issues I had with Mom were long ago resolved or simply forgotten.

This time, my younger brother Rob shared the responsibilities, an enormous help. His wife, Caroline, and Stephanie were in it with us too. I was not alone this time and understood what we had to do for her. I felt none of the terror and confusion that I had with Dad.

In contrast to Dad, Mom's body worked well to the end, but her mind slipped away. Alzheimer's was a terrible thing to witness as pieces of her mind disappeared: loss of her past, lost grasp of her own living arrangements, and lost recognition of those close to her. And, like the deterioration of Dad's body with ALS, there was nothing we could do to stop it.

On my final visit, several months before Mom died, she gave no sign of recognizing me over several days. But as I hugged her goodbye just before I left, a tear came trickling down her cheek. She died peacefully in her sleep in 2007.

Mom, a writer in her later years, wrote her own eulogy in 1997, including the fears Dad had tried to protect her from: "The things she feared most never came to pass." We asked the rabbi to read it at her funeral service:

EULOGY FOR ANN KANN

IN THE NAME OF SEPARATION, ANN ASKS THAT YOU CRY A LITTLE.

AFTER THAT, CARRY ON WITH REMEMBRANCE, KIND THOUGHTS OF SHARED LAUGHTER, SHARED JOYS AND SHARED MOMENTS TOGETHER.

ALTHOUGH ANN HAD AN ANXIOUS NATURE, THE THINGS SHE FEARED MOST NEVER CAME TO PASS. INSTEAD, MANY WONDERFUL AND CHERISHED HAPPENINGS TOOK PLACE. ABOVE ALL, HER MARRIAGE, HER HEALTHY RELATIONSHIP WITH HER THREE GREAT SONS, THREE LOVELY DAUGHTERS-IN-LAW, AND THREE PRECIOUS GRANDCHILDREN. PLUS A LOVING RELATIONSHIP WITH SISTERS, BROTHERS, NIECES, NEPHEWS, AND OUTSTANDING FRIENDS.

FOR ALL OF THIS, SHE IS GRATEFUL. AND IF THIS IS THE TIME TO GO—SO BE IT!!

That funeral service for Mom was not at the gravesites I had purchased in December 1979 during my first visit home after Dad's ALS diagnosis. Mom, true to her word in 1979 when she and I discussed Dad's request that I buy burial plots for them, did not want her body in the ground. "Too dirty," she had explained. A few years after Dad's death, she purchased two resting places, crypts, in a wall at the mausoleum at the same Westlawn Cemetery. She arranged for the coffin with Dad's body to be removed from the gravesite and placed in a crypt. He awaited Mom in his crypt next to hers.

Those are their final resting places, the two crypts alongside each other.

I screeched to a halt in 2011 when I retired from my court administration job. I was sixty-seven, two years older than Dad when he retired.

When I turned sixty-five, I often thought of Dad and that sixty-fifth year he had not survived. Would I outlast him? His mysterious early ALS symptoms, the shocking diagnosis, and the grim fifteen months that followed taught me that anything can happen to us too.

I did survive my sixty-fifth year, and I stopped thinking about it. That is, I stopped thinking about an early death—until my retirement. Retiring at sixty-seven, I thought of that morning I accompanied Dad on his final visit to his workplace, wheeling him around, a dying man saying goodbyes.

My own retirement was a celebration, with my employees organizing a party and staging a "This Is Your Life" show, recounting my various careers. I hugged everyone goodbye. I walked out on my own two feet, one of my goals as an attorney, not headfirst on a stretcher.

I recalled the retirement Dad never reached. He had stopped working at sixty-five, but he had not made it to the Florida leisure he had expected. I remembered him talking about it in a Boca Raton restaurant. We were surrounded by old timers happily enjoying lunch and retired life while Dad was barely able to pick up the food off his plate with his atrophied fingers. My brothers and I had many worried discussions about what Dad could do in retirement with ALS. It never occurred to us that he would die less than five months after retirement.

What was next with my retirement? With baby boomer affluence and good health, I could do whatever I wanted. Or nothing. I could simply enjoy leisure as Dad had imagined.

I can't explain why, but I needed a purposeful retirement. I wanted something to accomplish that held meaning for me. Another gift, or burden, from Dad? No, I think this one, keeping busy and productive, came from Mom.

So, at home in my own basement office, I returned to what I know: writing popular history. This time, my own history.

I started with a collection of essays on my generation and the student upheaval of the 1960s. Several of my favorite essays were about Dad and me and the sixties, when I first veered off course from attorney to historian and then took another detour from history professor to freelance historian, shifts that Dad never understood.

One of my essays was about Dad's gift of his gold when I first returned home after the diagnosis. Dad had long ago dissolved the gold into zinc to hide it in plain sight for security. The story was about my decades-long quest to retrieve Dad's gold from the zinc and sell it for our family. This final mission for my father, after our history of clashes, estrangement, and then ALS, haunted me long past his life, over decades to my retirement.

When I completed those essays on baby boomers in 2019, I decided to find something else to do or perhaps try retirement leisure with nothing to do. And then, in March 2020, came the coronavirus pandemic. The pandemic brought me back to my home office and this story.

Why give my precious retirement to writing history? I had abandoned writing when I finally became an attorney in 1986, seeking the life I had mapped as a teenager in the 1950s: family, income, house, cars, vacations, things, comfort, security, public life, and prestige. But I had enough of these law practice benefits by retirement.

Writing is difficult. Alone in my office, communicating with myself, it's work every day. The words do not appear easily. I don't expect fame, not for the story of Dad and me. Experience has taught me that my writing will not be profitable, a hard-earned nickel for every hour.

But I want Julia to have these stories. She needs to know her family history: immigrant great grandparents, my father and Grannie Annie, Sam's illness and death, and how Stephanie and I fit. And now, her place in this tale. I need to pass on our story, as my father wanted.

And my father, I have to write about him. Saying Kaddish was not enough.

A few days after the funeral, my brothers and I went to a late afternoon service at Skokie's temple, B'nai Emunah, where we each had a bar mitzvah. We joined the minyan of old men praying. I stood with my brothers as we chanted the Kaddish in our broken Hebrew, praising God's greatness despite the loss of our father. I kept a vow I made during my Boca Raton visit when I read to Dad from my manuscript on Joe Rapoport's life, avoiding the story of Joe's father's curse that Joe would not say Kaddish to remember him. I assured myself that I would recite the Kaddish in Dad's memory, and I did it that day.

But I was not satisfied to praise God after our months of inexplicable suffering and this terrible loss. Kaddish was not my way.

Writing history was how I could remember Dad and mourn his loss. Throughout those terrible months of ALS, I had considered myself "just a historian" of no practical use in our crisis, not like the physician or attorney I might have been. But in the end, I knew that history would help me understand his extraordinary illness, the life and death of my father, and my own life through it and after.

Dad told me he did not want to be remembered only with ALS, so compromised at the end of his life. It's been difficult to recall anything other than the monster disease, Dad's courage, his sweetness and infuriating stubbornness with a fatal ailment, our difficulty helping him, the fear and worry, and the suffering. But I've told the story of his entire life as a child of immigrants, an ambitious young man making his way in Chicago and America in the 1930s and 1940s, at work and with family, in postwar West Side neighborhoods and Skokie. I've told the ALS story as part of Dad's life story and part of mine.

This time, I've used Dad's names: Sam Kann and Sammy Kann. I'm not repeating the mistake on the dedication page of my first book where I referred to him only as "Dad." I like to think Dad would have approved of this historical account of him and me.

This book is for me too. I need to tell this story of our family encounter with ALS. I am no longer confident my writing will improve the world, as I believed with my books on the Petaluma chicken ranchers and Joe Rapoport. But writing helps me understand my experience, particularly Dad's and mine. It marks where I came from and who I became. So, I am at it again, this time searching for the right stories and words about Dad, me, and the *terrible disease*.

Dad had a difficult end of life with ALS. It was humiliating and frightening. He was cheated out of his retirement by that rotten hand he was dealt from the bottom of the deck. He fought ALS as best he could, but he could not beat it or live with it.

Dad was courageous. For months, he struggled to continue his life despite ALS, with enormous support from Mom, colleagues, family, and friends. When the disease overwhelmed him, when his life became unimaginably difficult, when living did not make sense to him any longer, he planned to end his life.

As he suffered, Dad gave me a gift. It was a gift he could not have given if he was healthy. With ALS, Dad needed me. He relied on me, first with cleaning out the basement, then with financial decisions and medical decisions. He recruited me to listen to his taped life story, remember, and retell it later. He recruited me to mourn with him over his coming death. Finally, he relied on my help to end his struggle with ALS, to end his life.

When Dad was first diagnosed, when I saw him cry over the coming end of his life, I wondered what I could do to help him. I learned. I could be with him as he fought for his life and encountered his death. I could try to understand. I could help us survive his death. That was what I had to give him, and I gave it. I was there with him through it all.

Dad and I had clashed for years before the ALS diagnosis. The disputes had ranged from his outrage that I had reorganized his basement workshop to bewilderment over my career choice of historian to exasperation over my travel with a raggedy suitcase. The clashes ended as I helped him face ALS and the conclusion of his life.

We never discussed our relationship, past or present, those disputes, or the chasm of anger and silence that separated us. But during the months of ALS in 1979 and 1980, we both said and did everything that needed to be said and done between us.

Dad suffered a prolonged death over fifteen months. It was awful for him. But if he had died abruptly, surprisingly, say a fatal auto accident, I would not have had the opportunity to help him, and he could not have completed the job of being my father.

I like to think that is what he meant by the knowing wink he gave me when I returned home after the diagnosis and our family gathered in the den for that happy, familiar evening playing Scrabble. There was a purpose to Dad's ALS, a purpose he and I created: a final opportunity for him to give me this gift of helping him.

Dad's final gift was the opportunity to grow up at thirty-six. He helped me live my life ahead as a responsible, loving adult with Stephanie and Julia, Mom and my brothers, Mark and Rob, family and friends, work and community. He helped me create a life like his.

Like they say, *the apple does not fall far from the tree.*

ACKNOWLEDGMENTS

John Koehler, president of Koehler Books, my gifted editor Miranda Dillon, my terrific graphic designer Lauren Sheldon, and their talented colleagues have contributed to every part of converting my manuscript into this handsome and attractive volume. The book has benefited enormously from their wide publication experience and superb judgment. Thank you, John, Miranda, Lauren, and Koehler Books colleagues.

Family and friends have helped me with everything from finding a publisher to selecting the title and content of the book. These helpers are Tony Bass, Zelda Bronstein, Rabbi Ted Feldman, Mark Greenside, Mark Gunther, Eleanor Hollander, AJ Kann, Betsy Mayer, Tom Mayer, Bobby Pinzur, Susie Pinzur, Stephen Shapiro, Peter Wiley, and Mary Ann Wittenberg. Thank you, family and friends, for everything.

My brothers, Bob and Mark, were there with me in these real-life events in 1979 and 1980. We lost Mark to multiple myeloma, and I did not have the benefit of his keen intelligence for this story. Along with living it with me, Bob has generously shared his memories, different perspectives, and sound judgment. We have discussed these events and this book many times. Bob has reviewed every chapter, often several times, and he has made countless valuable suggestions, large and small, for accuracy and style. He has offered unflagging encouragement for me to tell this story. Bob, along with being a terrific editor and supporter, has been a terrific brother. I have been lucky.

My splendid daughter Julia came after the events of this book. Along with my marriage to Stephanie, Julia is my greatest legacy from this story. Fortunately, Julia knew my mother, Ann, a.k.a. Grannie Annie. I regret that my father, Sam, never had the opportunity to meet Julia; he would have adored her. Julia has helped with fashioning this story into a book. She has listened to it, read it, made suggestions, and helped me make it available to others. And she has been a terrific daughter too. More good luck for me.

My wife Stephanie has supported this project from my first consideration of writing a book when Dad died in 1980 through publication in 2024. Along with urging me to write this book, she applied her superb writing judgment and editing skills to the manuscript, and she encouraged me throughout. Stephanie even became a character in the book—the wonderful girlfriend who appears at the end, assuring my parents and me, and now my readers too, of happy prospects ahead for me. And so it was.

REFERENCES

Airola, Paavo. 1971. *Are You Confused?* Health Plus Publication.

Bureau of Biologics, National institute of Neurological and Communicative Disorders and Stroke, and Johns Hopkins University, Food and Drug Administration. April 5, 1979. *Workshop on Modified Neurotoxin Treatment of Amyotrophic Lateral Sclerosis.*

Delisa, Joel, Mary Ann Mikulic, Robert Miller, and Rosie Raps Melnick. 1979. "Amyotrophic Lateral Sclerosis: Comprehensive Management." AFP, vol 19, no. 3 (March 1979): 137-142.

Fan, Jiaying. 2020. "How My Mother and I Became Chinese Propaganda." New Yorker, September 10, 2020.

Hanlan, Archie. 1979. *Autobiography of Dying.* New York: Doubleday & Company.

Judt, Tony. 2010. "Night." The New York Review of Books. January 14, 2010.

Knight, Shirley. 2011. *A Journey Through Fire: ALS—Memoir of a Caregiver.* Powell, Tennessee.

Lerner, Gerda. 1978. *A Death Of One's Own.* New York: Simon and Schuster.

Merrill, Jean. 1964. *The Pushcart Wars*. New York: W R Scott.

Meyer, Harry M., Director, Bureau of Biologics, Food and Drug Administration, letter to patients of Dr. Murray Sanders. May 23, 1979.

Neva, Kristin and Todd Neva. 2014. *Heavy, Finding Meaning After A Terminal Diagnosis, A Young Family's First Year After ALS*. Hancock, MI: The Christmas Tree House.

Pendergast, Charles and Christine Pendergast.2020. *Blink Spoken Here, Tales From A Journey* To *Within*. Baltimore, Maryland: Apprentice House Press.

Simonton, Dr. O Carl, Stephanie Simonton, and James Creighton. 1978. Getting Well Again: A Step-By-Step Guide To Overcoming Cancer For Patients And Their Families. New York: Bantam Books.

Sontag, Susan. 1978. *Illness As Metaphor*. New York: Anchor Books, Doubleday.

Tyler, Dr. H. Richard. 1979. "Double-blind study of modified neurotoxin in motor neuron disease." *Neurology, 29 (January 1979):* 77-81.

Virgil. *The Aeneid*. 1981. New York: Vintage Books.

Printed in the USA
CPSIA information can be obtained
at www.ICGtesting.com
LVHW041540270724
786433LV00004B/14